964133

# Development and Crisis in Brazil, 1930–1983

## Also of Interest

†*Authoritarian Capitalism: Brazil's Contemporary Economic and Political Development,* edited by Thomas C. Bruneau and Philippe Faucher

†*Brazil: A Political Analysis,* Peter Flynn

*International Politics and the Sea: The Case of Brazil,* Michael A. Morris

*Brazil in the International System: The Rise of a Middle Power,* edited by Wayne A. Selcher

*The Dilemma of Amazonian Development,* edited by Emilio F. Moran

*Controlling Latin American Conflicts: Ten Approaches,* edited by Michael A. Morris and Victor Millán

†*Latin America and the U.S. National Interest: A Basis for U.S. Foreign Policy,* Margaret Daly Hayes

*Development Strategies and Basic Needs in Latin America,* edited by Claes Brundenius and Mats Lundahl

*Technological Progress in Latin America: The Prospects for Overcoming Dependency,* edited by James H. Street and Dilmus D. James

*FOREIGN POLICY on Latin America,* 1970–1980, edited by the staff of *Foreign Policy*

*The Exclusive Economic Zone: A Latin American Perspective,* edited by Francisco Orrego Vicuña

†*Dependency and Marxism: Toward a Resolution of the Debate,* edited by Ronald H. Chilcote

†*Post-Revolutionary Peru: The Politics of Transformation,* edited by Stephen M. Gorman

*Corporatism and National Development in Latin America,* Howard J. Wiarda

†Available in hardcover and paperback.

# Westview Special Studies on Latin America and the Caribbean

## Development and Crisis in Brazil, 1930–1983
### Luiz Bresser Pereira

In this first English-language edition of a book that has seen thirteen printings in Brazil, Dr. Bresser Pereira analyzes Brazil's economy and politics from 1930, when the Brazilian industrial revolution began, up to July 1983. First addressing the period of strong development in Brazil between 1930 and 1961, he discusses at length the import-substitution model of industrialization; the emergence of new classes—industrialists, industrial workers, and especially the new technobureaucratic middle classes; the conflict between the traditional agrarian ideologies of coffee planters and the nationalistic and industrializing ideologies of the new classes; and the new realities of the 1950s that led to the crisis of the populist alliance between the industrial bourgeoisie and the workers. Next he explores the economic and political crisis of the sixties, centering on the Revolution of 1964, when an industrialized and fully capitalist— but still underdeveloped—Brazil experienced the cyclical movements of capitalism. The final chapters of the book examine the Brazilian "miracle" of 1967–1973, the economic slowdown of the 1970s that culminated in the severe recession of 1981, the dialectics between the process of *abertura* led by the military regime established in 1964 and the rede-mocratization process demanded by civil society, and the "total crisis of 1983."

Dr. Luiz Bresser Pereira is professor of economics at Fundação Getúlio Vargas in São Paulo and president of Banespa (Bank of the State of São Paulo). He has written nine scholarly books and is the editor of *Revista de Economica Política*. For twenty years he was the administrative vice-president of Pão de Açúcar S.A., one of the most important commercial enterprises in Brazil.

# Development and Crisis in Brazil, 1930–1983

Luiz Bresser Pereira
with a Foreword by Thomas C. Bruneau

Translated from the Portuguese
by Marcia Van Dyke

Westview Press / Boulder and London

*Westview Special Studies on Latin America and the Caribbean*

Copyright © 1984 by Westview Press, Inc.

Published in 1984 in the United States of America by
  Westview Press, Inc.
  5500 Central Avenue
  Boulder, Colorado 80301
  Frederick A. Praeger, President and Publisher


Library of Congress Cataloging in Publication Data
Pereira, Luiz Carlos Bresser.
  Development and crisis in Brazil, 1930–1983.
  (Westview special studies on Latin America and the Caribbean)
  Includes bibliographical references and index.
  1. Brazil—Economic conditions—1918-   .
2. Brazil—Economic policy.   3. Industry and state—Brazil—History—20th century.
4. Brazil—Politics and government—20th century.   I. Title.   II. Series.
HC187.P392213   1984          338.981          83-10232
ISBN 0-86531-559-0


Printed and bound in the United States of America

5  4  3  2  1

# Contents

# Tables and Figures

# Foreword

In late March of 1983 four days of extensive rioting took place in the city of São Paulo protesting the high rate of unemployment, sharply increased cost of living, and other current inequities of the socioeconomic crisis confronting Brazil. These were the most serious riots in Brazil since the military took power in 1964 and are particularly important as evidence that the economic crisis of high foreign indebtedness ($85 billion), high inflation (100 percent in 1982), and rapidly increasing unemployment is having its impact on the population. The rioting occurred just two weeks after Franco Montoro of the opposition PMDB [Party of the Brazilian Democratic Movement] was installed as governor of the state of São Paulo. In nine other states, out of a total of twenty-two, opposition governors took office. The elections on 15 November 1982 that empowered these twenty-two governors were the first direct elections for governors since 1965 and as such are considered a key feature of the current transition toward democracy in Brazil. It is important to note that the ten opposition governors assumed office in states with 58 percent of the country's population and 75 percent of the Gross National Product. The riots took place during an economic and social crisis that both encouraged the beginning of the transition and at the same time places limits on its continuation.

There is no better time to publish the first English-language edition of *Development and Crisis in Brazil,* by Luiz Bresser Pereira, and no better book for understanding the crisis and concomitant period of transition. There have been thirteen Portuguese editions of the book since it was first published in 1968, and it has been rewritten and updated periodically as the economy and polity have been transformed in Brazil. Through these revisions Bresser Pereira has engaged in the national debate on the causes and limitations of Brazil's development; thus the reader obtains not only information and analysis on the processes of development, but also an insight into the various positions Brazilian intellectuals have assumed vis-à-vis these processes. The great success of the book in Brazil is undoubtedly due to the fact that Bresser Pereira successfully integrates a great deal of material in offering a synthesis of the economic, political, and social nature of this development and also seeks to analyze it by means of an innovative neo-Marxist perspective. Little of what follows is doctrinaire, however, and one finds as much information on politics and political actors as on the economy and international constraints. Informed by this flexible perspective, the book is in fact comprehensive and insightful.

Luiz Bresser Pereira is in an enviable position for writing a book that seeks nothing less than to explain Brazilian development during the half century since the 1930 Revolution. He is professor of economics at the Fundação Getúlio Vargas (FGV) in São Paulo, author of nine scholarly books, and director of the economics journal *Revista de Economia Política.* He is also a prolific essayist, publishing articles in *Folha de São Paulo* and a number of other periodicals. Further, after twenty years as vice-president of Pão de Açúcar S.A., one of the most important commercial enterprises in Brazil, he became early in 1983 the chairman of Banespa (Bank of the State of São Paulo) as a member of the opposition government of São Paulo. With this combination of roles, and the capacity and energy they evidence, Bresser Pereira is not only deeply involved in the economy and polity at a very high level but is able to dissect and analyze events from an informed and extremely critical perspective. It is this informed perspective on current affairs, coupled with his powerful analytical abilities, that has resulted in a landmark contribution to the understanding of Brazilian development.

Bresser Pereira's focus in this book is describing and analyzing Brazilian development over the last half century. Development here concerns not only industrialization and economic growth but also political dynamics and societal change. In order to explain this development, which the author has termed "industrialized underdevelopment," he considers primarily the international context, the role of the state, and the different alliances of classes. His analysis shows how Brazil, with the fifth largest land mass and the eighth largest population, has come to be the tenth largest economy in the world, how it has in fact developed even while remaining on the periphery of the core economies. In his analysis Bresser Pereira looks in particular to the state in bringing about "dependent development" by means of the "tripod" of an alliance between it, multinational corporations, and domestic capital. He finds that there is now a crisis in this form of development that is due in no small part to the incompetence of the policy makers. Indeed, he shows that even under the authoritarian regime there has been inconsistency in economic policy making. Today this has resulted in stagnation and in extremely high foreign indebtedness.

The author finds a certain necessity in the current process of transition. After fifty years of development and the collapse of an alliance of classes that brought about rapid economic growth in the late 1960s and early 1970s, the transition to a democratic political regime is now possible. This is not the same process probably taking place in the Southern Cone countries of South America, but arises out of the lack of legitimacy of the present regime, which excludes much of the population from the benefits of development on the one hand and in which the state is predominant in a capitalist system on the other. The system lacks legitimacy and must be transformed. However, Bresser Pereira shows that there is a very great difference between the plan of the regime, which he calls an opening, or *abertura,* which signifies continuing control, and democratization, which implies an entry of the people into the political system. He argues that the new bourgeoisie plays a key role in this transition, as that group now holds a democratic plan or project that it previously lacked and was in any case too weak to carry out. About this project he can write with confidence and experience, and indeed the regime has splintered. There is some question, however, whether the new project, which includes democracy, maintenance of capitalism, and a moderate redistribution of income, can continue in the face of the major socioeconomic crisis highlighted by the riots in São Paulo. The author does not claim to know, as nobody does, but the reader of *Development and Crisis in Brazil* will be in a position to understand the causes and consequences of economic and political development in contemporary Brazil.

*Thomas C. Bruneau*

# Introduction

This book is an attempt to analyze the political, economic, and social transformations that Brazil has undergone from 1930 to 1983. It concerns Brazil's transformation from an agrarian, mercantile society into a capitalist, industrial society where underdevelopment has been industrialized and the social formation, aside from being capitalist, also has monopoly and state characteristics. It also takes a look at the industrial revolution in Brazil, which had its start in the last century, but gained decisive impulse after 1930.

Consequently, one of the premises of this book is that the world economic crisis that broke out in 1929 and the Revolution of 1930 play a decisive role in Brazil's history. After the 1964 coup, many authors underestimated the importance of this historical moment, seeking the origins of industrial capitalism in Brazil in prior epochs in order to (a) deny the distinction between the industrial bourgeoisie and the mercantile coffee bourgeoisie, and (b) criticize the populist pact made between the left and the "national bourgeoisie." This book, in contrast, insists upon the importance of 1930 as a watershed in the history of Brazil's social formation. Though I consider the idea of a national bourgeoisie somewhat naive, I understand that after 1930, a breach began to form between the industrial bourgeoisie of immigrant origin and the mercantile coffee *latifundiário* bourgeoisie. This breach was to dominate Brazil's economic and political formation until 1964.

Nevertheless, as we will see in Chapter 4, a series of new historical facts that occurred in the mid-1950s would reunite the mercantile and industrial bourgeoisie, doing away with the populist pact and creating conditions for the establishment of an authoritarian regime in Brazil.

Although Brazil, and especially the São Paulo region, had been industrializing since the end of the nineteenth century, that industrialization was peripheral, subordinate to the existing primary export model. It was limited to the production of nondurable consumer goods—

*1*

textiles, food products, and furniture—with almost no vertical integration. There were no industries producing basic inputs, steel, or capital goods. The nation was dominated by an agrarian-mercantile bourgeoisie oriented to the exportation of primary products, principally coffee.

The primary export model, which had characterized the Brazilian economy from the time Brazil opened its ports in 1808 until 1930, was the means by which Brazil was integrated in a backward fashion into the industrial capitalism that was triumphing in Europe. Rather than entering the capitalist framework through direct industrialization, as did the later industrialized nations of Germany and Japan, Brazil, like the rest of Latin America, had no other alternative but to become an exporter of primary products, given the small scale of its internal market and the insufficient technological and cultural base inherited from the colonial period. As a result, the *latifundiária* bourgeoisie that had dominated during the colonial period remained in power, now taking on more clearly mercantile characteristics. With Brazil's integration into the international market, the accumulation of capital was speeded up, creating a mercantile bourgeoisie and a small urban middle class, but the development of the productive forces continued to be minimal. The mercantile and *latifundiária* bourgeoisie is speculative and depends upon the state. It appropriates surplus through the mechanisms of primitive accumulation—basically the expropriation and exploitation of peasants, squatters, and slaves—rather than through the incorporation of technical progress and the surplus value mechanism. As a consequence of this domination of mercantile capital, of which coffee production and exportation is a prototype, very little development of the productive forces occurred. The techniques of coffee production in 1930 were very similar to those practiced a century earlier.

However, in 1930, two decisive facts changed Brazil's history and marked the advance of industrial capital in relation to mercantile capital. On the one hand, international capitalism, which dominated Brazil, was in crisis. This crisis of imperialism, based on the international division of labor, constituted an opportunity for Brazil's development. On the other hand, the Revolution of 1930 took away some of the agrarian-export bourgeoisie's power and established the basis for a new political pact that was much more favorable to industrialization—the populist pact.

In the first four chapters of this book, we look at the period I call the Brazilian revolution, from 1930 to 1960. It was a period of transition from the domination of mercantile, *latifundiário*, and speculative capital to that of industrial capital, which intrinsically incorporates technological progress. The first chapter serves as an introduction; the second examines import-substitution industrialization. The third chapter analyzes social changes and the emergence of new classes: the industrial bourgeoisie, the urban proletariat, and, mainly, the new salaried middle class, which in later works I have come to call the technobureaucracy. The fourth chapter develops an analysis made in 1963 concerning the populist pact and the new historical facts that were to determine its collapse, provoking the political crisis of the first years of the 1960s and the Revolution of 1964. It is perhaps the most original chapter of the first edition, because rather than merely denying the existence of an alliance between the industrial bourgeoisie and workers, it seeks to explain why the collapse of this fragile alliance led to crisis.

In 1962, industrial Brazil entered its first crisis, which would last until 1966. The Brazilian economy had already reached a sufficient degree of industrial integration to become subject to endogenous economic cycles, created by its own dynamic of capital accumulation. Chapters 5 and 6 examine this crisis in both economic and political terms, and also discuss the alternatives open to Brazil after the political consolidation of industrial capitalism starting with the revolution of 1964.

The first, 1968 edition of this book ended here. We were already coming out of the crisis, but in 1967, when I finished writing, this fact was not yet clear. This is why the second and third editions, published respectively in 1970 and 1972, added another chapter, which in this edition corresponds to Chapter 7. This chapter was written to give a theoretical explanation to the great expansion (the so-called "miracle") that began in 1967, and to the new development model. The discussion of income concentration and the economy's recuperation based on the durable consumer goods industry was written in 1970, before the publication of the 1970 census results that verified this concentration. The definition of the new Brazilian model was written in the following year.

Nine more printings were made of this book with no changes. However, when Westview Press showed an interest in publishing it, I thought it advisable to bring it up to date, because, starting in 1974, the economy had entered a new slowdown and the country was again in political crisis. Chapter 8 analyzes the economic crisis of the 1970s, which is still with us today, and Chapter 9 examines the long process of transition toward democracy, which began in 1974 and is still in progress.

Within this fifty-year period, Brazil had a populist dictatorship from 1930 to 1945, democracy for the next nineteen years, a military dictatorship from 1964 to 1978, and a semiauthoritarian regime dating from 1979, when Institutional Act 5 was annulled. The first thirty years correspond to the import-substitution model in economic terms and the populist pact in political terms. However, after the mid-1950s, a new pattern of accumulation was defined, based on the concentration of income and the production of durable consumer goods by multinational industrial enterprises. This is the model of industrialized underdevelopment. With populism's collapse, almost ten years later, the authoritarian capitalist–technobureaucratic pact of 1964 was established and the bourgeoisie accepted technobureaucratic military tutelage in order to consolidate capitalism in Brazil. Yet in 1974, once the bourgeoisie had become strengthened and reassured, it began to break with this pact, as a result of both support and pressure from popular democratic forces—intellectuals, students, workers, and the Catholic Church. At this point, a peculiar dialectical process of transition to democracy began, while at the same time a new democratic social pact was finally outlined.

Today, Brazil is an industrialized underdeveloped country marked by contradictions and instability. It has a strong industrialized economy, which coexists with a subproletariat marginalized from the fruits of development. The economy, though technologically dependent, is making great strides so that its most modern and developed sectors form a part of the world capitalist center. The social formation is predominantly capitalist, yet increasingly technobureaucratic or state controlled. It is an economy in crisis, in the same way that the international economy is, but this crisis will probably imply a transition to a model of mature industrialized underdevelopment. This means that the continuity of the process of capital accumulation will depend upon Brazil's capacity to export goods that are technologically sophisticated yet labor-intensive, in order to compete directly with the central countries.

*Development and Crisis* attempts to analyze the entire historic process that began in 1930. It is an analysis that seeks to be independent, though not lacking in commitment. It was written in three different stages: 1965–1967 (Chapters 1–6), 1970–1971 (Chapter 7), and 1982 (Chapters 8 and 9). Only the conclusion was written in 1983. The book reflects the development through time of my vision of Brazilian society. This is why, except for a few cuts, the text has been rigorously maintained in its original form. It is a historical analysis, yet it is not a history book. Rather, it is an attempt to understand the fascinating phenomenon of Brazil's economic, social, and political development in an integrated and dynamic way.

# The Concept of Development

## Introduction

Development is a process of economic, political, and social transformation through which the rise in the population's standard of living tends to become automatic and autonomous. It is a total social process in which the economic, political, and social structures of a country undergo continual and profound transformations. It makes no sense to speak of development as only economic, only political, or only social; this type of compartmentalized, segmented development does not really exist except for the purposes of didactic exposition. If economic development does not bring political and social modifications with it, if social and political development are not simultaneously the result and the cause of economic transformations, then in fact they are not development. The changes observed in one of these sectors will have been so superficial, so shallow, that they will leave no lasting traces.

A social system is made up of economic relations as much as social and political ones. And, as the expression "system" itself suggests, these relations are interdependent in such a way that when some relations undergo alterations, the others will necessarily be influenced. In this book the term development will always refer to a determinate social system that will be geographically localized. It will always, however, be a social system, and therefore its parts will be interdependent. When real modifications are made in the economic structure there will be repercussions in the political and social structure and vice versa. If the repercussions are small, if the increase in income, for example, is not accompanied by political and social transformations, this increase is not significant for development and should not be considered as such.

Development, therefore, is a total transformation. Perhaps its most important result, or at least the most direct, is the improvement of the standard of living. This is why the expression "economic development" is generally used as a synonym for "development." In the development process the economic aspect is preponderant. But in specific moments the political sector can become the dynamic focus of development, as has occurred, paradoxically, in the communist countries. These phenomena, however, always appear as exceptions. The general rule is that the dominant characteristic of development is the process of economic transformation, and the major result is an improvement in the standard of living of the people in the place where it has occurred.

The use of the term "standard of living" rather than "per capita income" is intentional. It is a universally accepted objective in modern societies to seek to improve the standard of living, to increase the general welfare. It thus becomes very significant to identify development with raising the standard of living. On the other hand, although per capita income is one indicator for determining the standard of living, it is a very deficient one. Many times an increase in per capita income does not improve the standard of living of the population in general because it is absorbed by a minimal, privileged sector. Being unlikely to stimulate political and social transformations, such growth in income must be regarded as uncertain and unstable, and certainly cannot be called economic development.

In order for a real development to occur, the improvement in the standard of living must move toward becoming automatic, autonomous, and necessary. It becomes automatic in the sense that the process of economic development becomes self-generating. When, for example, a country attains the stage of commercial capitalism, reinvestment stimulated by profit becomes the rule and development becomes automatic. When a more advanced industrial capitalist stage is reached, development tends to become not only automatic but necessary, meaning that continued reinvestment and the growth of businesses become the conditions of their survival. The tendency toward autonomy in the growth of income, which generally characterizes economic development, is due to the fact that, once initiated, development not only tends to be self-generating in the necessary form but also tends to find the necessary dynamic factors within itself, particularly in its domestic market.

This concept of development ought not to be confused with that of W. W. Rostow. He is correct in pointing out that development is an historical process, that it occurs through stages, and that it eventually becomes self-sustaining. However, as the sixth chapter of this book will explain, the self-sustaining character of development must be recognized to have several limitations. It does not occur in a deterministic manner, taking place automatically, without reference to human will, after a country has its industrial revolution.

Nor do I accept Rostow's concept of linear development, according to which all countries pass through approximately the same stages.

Development and underdevelopment as they exist today are interdependent phenomena. When the countries that are today developed had their Industrial Revolution in the past century, the underdeveloped countries were put into a situation of economic dependence in a development model based on the exportation of primary products. The import-substitution process that has occurred in this century has very different characteristics from the Industrial Revolution of the industrialized countries. This book will thus be analyzing an original process of industrialization that does not simply repeat the experience of the large, industrial European countries and the United States.

Using this restricted definition, according to which societal transformations must be simultaneously economic, political, and social, resulting most directly in an increase in the standard of living that becomes automatic, autonomous, and necessary, that is, self-generating, one can define the concept of development historically. All these conditions come together only when, in a specific country or region, the relations and techniques of production have acquired a dominantly capitalist or socialist mark; when the government of society, the administration of production, and the social conventions themselves have been guided by and embody the spirit of rationalism; and, finally, when the basic social wealth is no longer land, as it is in traditional economic systems, or even commodities, as in commercial capitalism, but rather capital invested in buildings and equipment geared to production, as in industrial socialism and capitalism.

In these terms one cannot speak of the development of ancient Greece or the Egypt of the pharaohs. In the same way, the Brazil of the gold or sugarcane eras cannot be referred to in terms of development. There were increases in wealth, but as a rule they benefited only an elite. The accompanying social and political changes did not have major importance, since they did not achieve a change in the social structure or the power system of these regions, and these gains in wealth were not automatic, autonomous, and necessary. Therefore, there was no development in the modern sense of the word, the sense in which it is being used in this book.

Generally speaking, a country's development is marked by a clearly defined beginning. As a historically defined process, development appears only when the economic system in which it occurs becomes dominantly capitalist or socialist. However, in a still essentially traditional society, a growth can occur that provides the basis for development. This is what occurred in Brazil from the middle of the nineteenth century until 1930. Yet real development begins only when the traditional society enters into crisis: when rational criteria begin to replace the traditional ones; when capital begins to have more importance than land; when competence begins to take the place of blood relationships; when law imposes itself on custom; when impersonal and bureaucratic relations begin to replace personal and patrimonial characteristics. Development starts when the dual system of gentlemen and servants begins to give way to a pluralistic society, and when political power ceases to be the privilege of a clearly defined oligarchy and becomes continually more diffuse. Development begins when the economy of a traditional agricultural base starts to give way to a modern and industrial economy; when the basic unit of production is no longer the family but the enterprise, and no longer even the family enterprise but rather the bureaucratic enterprise; when traditional labor methods give way to rational ones, and productivity and efficiency become basic objectives of the productive unit; when economic development becomes the objective of the society; when reinvestment becomes a condition of survival for the enterprise; and finally, when the standard of living begins to improve in an automatic, autonomous, and necessary manner.

In order for this transformation to begin and for economic development to take place in a society, a political revolution is not absolutely necessary, although in the majority of cases that is what has occurred. It is essential, however, that the traditionally dominant class—generally an aristocratic oligarchy—be replaced in the political control of the society by a middle-class group. This substitution will be much more rapid, and will be completed much more radically, if there is a political revolution. Cromwell's revolution in England and the Brazilian Revolution of 1930 were much less radical socially and ideologically than the French Revolution or the Russian Revolution of 1917. Consequently, in the former countries the rise to power of the middle-class groups and the loss of power by the aristocracy were more gradual than in those countries where a complete takeover by force occurred, as, especially, in the case of the Russian Revolution. As an exception, political power may be seized by a faction of the aristocracy rather than a middle-class group, as occurred in Japan.

In the great majority of cases, however, development begins at the moment when political power rests predominantly or exclusively in the hands of a recognized middle-class group, whether bourgeois businessmen, nationalist politicians or military men, or communist politicians or military men. All the industrial countries of the capitalist world fall within the first case, except for the countries that are still in the first stage of development, such as Brazil. In the second group are countries such as India, Egypt, and Mexico. The communist countries constitute the third case. In those countries where development is initiated by nationalist politicians and the military, the economic system tends to be indefinite for a certain period. Private ownership of the means of production is allowed, but the socialized sector of the economy is large. After a certain time, however, the tendencies of the economic system in question begin to align themselves in a predominantly capitalist form, as in Mexico, or a predominantly socialist form, as is occurring in India and Egypt.

When a middle-class group takes power and becomes the dominant class, this takeover (together with a series of other economic factors that will be discussed later) signals the beginning of the development process. This is the phase of the country's history that some have called an industrial revolution, in order to point out the basic identification of development with the process of industrialization. Others call it a national revolution, especially when it occurs in a colonial or semicolonial country, which needs both industrialization and nationalism to weaken its traditional oligarchy and to disengage itself from the system of the imperialist powers in order to begin development. W. W. Rostow has called it the takeoff, to emphasize the break with the chronic stagnation that characterizes traditional societies.

## The National Revolution

The year 1930 marks the beginning of the Brazilian National Revolution. Until then Brazil was a typically semicolonial country. With the industrialization that began at that point, it started on the path to development. For a series of reasons, among which those of an economic order are salient, Brazil's history took a decisive turn. An acceleration of change took place. After many years of continuous and uniform progression, events occurred with such impact that history took one of those typical leaps in a new direction. All areas of the nation's life were affected: the economic, the cultural, the social, and the political. The entire nation underwent a profound change marked by a violent crisis over a decrease in the coffee market and, therefore, in all foreign trade. Old structures, ancient prejudices, rigid class structures, and deep-rooted privileges could be seen to be crumbling.

In the economic sphere the transformations are notable. In the first place there was the rapid appearance of a domestic market. One basic characteristic of a semicolonial economy is a limited domestic market; the great majority of the population, working in the country, is outside the national market, producing for its own consumption, living in miserable conditions in circumstances that make it impossible for a strong domestic market to appear. The change in this situation in Brazil, which received an initial impetus from the installation of coffee cultivation and the abolition of slavery, became more widespread only after 1930. Second, there was a rapid modification in the structure of the foreign market, especially in terms of imports. As a semicolonial country Brazil exported primary products in exchange for manufactured products. The industrial boom that took place after 1930 allowed the rapid development of substitutions for these imports. Thus, today Brazil imports virtually no important manufactured consumer products; they are produced nationally. Concomitantly, the dependence of the economy, and therefore of the national income, on exports has diminished drastically. The basic objective has become not to produce more for export (at extremely low prices in relation to imports) but to produce more for internal consumption.

Developmental transformations are always interdependent; another factor in Brazil's economic transformation was industrial development, which today involves heavy industry and equipment manufacture. Rapid industrialization was actually the dominant cause of the changes during this period, and the domestic market was the fundamental result. Finally, there was both an extraordinary growth and a redistribution of national income. Brazil ceased to be basically an agricultural country. In addition to agriculture and trade, two new sectors began to show an important growth: industry and the state.

The social scene offers another basic transformation to be analyzed. A colonial society is characterized by the simplicity of its social structure, with a primary division of labor. After 1930 the diversification of Brazilian society received a new and decisive impetus. Previously the social structure had represented only two basic classes: the rulers, landed gentlemen intimately involved in the high-level commercial exportation of coffee and importation of manufactured products, and the ruled, an enormous rural subproletariat living in extreme misery. Between the small ruling class, totally alienated by the foreign interests on which they depended, and the immense ruled class, a small middle class could be found living in the cities—a parasitical middle class supported fundamentally in the public employ, in a system where the government functioned as the agent of employment and policing, at the orders of the dominant oligarchy. This was the structure of Brazilian society under the old Republic, a situation whose disappearance some incorrigible wishful thinkers still lament.

After 1930 two new classes began to be clearly discernible: the industrial bourgeoisie and the urban proletariat. These two classes have come to mark national society decisively within recent times. The traditional middle class also expanded rapidly. It still continued in great part to be linked to parasitical public bureaucracy. The state itself, however, dropped its passive attitude as a mere instrument used by the ruling class to maintain the social order, and began to participate actively in national development, eventually becoming the principal element behind development. Thus bureaucracy has for the most part ceased to be parasitical. And the middle class found in industry and in all its related activities an ideal field of work. In the same way that a good proportion of the rural subproletariat rose to the category of rural proletariat, with greatly improved living conditions, a part of the old urban proletariat is already tending to become middle-class or has already achieved this new status. Thus there is a new structure to Brazilian society, and the change is being completed by the fall into decadence—although it still has great power—of the old dominant class, which has begun to fight ever more consciously against the rise of the new classes.

In politics, the transformations have been less notable. Semicolonial Brazil was politically characterized by the dominance of a small oligarchy of landed gentlemen who had in the government and in international capitalism, respectively, their principal instrument and major *raison d'être*. In this simultaneously feudal and capitalist regime, political power was limited, by definition, to land owners. Those who held it, seeking to present a democratic image, made use of the state not only to maintain the established order but also as their basic political instrument. They accomplished this exercise through a system of "client politics" by which the dominant class purchased the votes of the poor for promises of compensation, generally in the form of public employment. The small number of voters and their total dependence on the dominant class made this bargain easy.

In addition, since they generally produced for export to the direct benefit of international capitalism—which received many advantages and gave little in return (although sufficient for a high standard of living for those few in the oligarchy)—the agrarian-commercial aristocracy could count on the support of international capitalism. In other words, the Brazilian system of production and commerce was of direct interest to the industrialized nations, which got all the advantages of trading manufactured products for primary products, and therefore supported the ruling class that offered them these advantages.

With the Revolution of 1930 the oligarchy lost its power and began to decline. The emerging social classes described above developed rapidly, beginning to participate in government together with the classes that, although essentially defeated in 1930, had hastened to join the new order. What, then, was the underlying characteristic of the governments of Getúlio Vargas, Eurico Gaspar Dutra, Vargas again, and Juscelino Kubitschek? They were basically governments of compromise, in which forces antagonistic to each other, although all favorable toward indus-trialization in one form or another, shared power. The old oligarchy, although defeated, still continued to retain enormous economic and political force, since open opposition to it would have been very difficult.

After 1930 the characteristics of these various participants became continually more defined. On the one side, struggling for the return of the old regime, were the large estate coffee-growers, and those involved in coffee exportation and international capitalism, supported by the parasitical middle class linked by economic or social (or even family) ties to the old dominant class. On the other side was the government, joining together the opposition classes that sought power to defend their interests: the industrialist class, the proletarian class, and a new middle class. Obviously, it was indeed a government of compromise, of unstable composition. Getúlio Vargas, despite his many errors, was the talented coordinator and at the same time leader of the truly new currents within this government. I shall not make a profound analysis of the Vargas period, but rather focus on the most fundamental characteristics of this government. Vargas was a typical populist leader. Unlike many other populist leaders, however, he was sufficiently capable to accomplish his true mission. He formed a compromise government, knowing how to concede but not losing sight of his objective, as so many facts confirm, including the economic and social results of his regime.

At the end of the Second World War, there arose from these colliding forces within the first Vargas government the large national political parties that the Revolution of 1964 would later extinguish. These were no longer merely all representatives of the same social class, the dominant oligarchy, as had been true before 1930. In 1945, with the return to democratic order, these parties were soon defined, despite their contradictory and hesitant nature. The UDN [National Democratic Union] represented the forces defeated in 1930, as well as the parasitic middle class aligned with them. Its liberal, agrarian, typically reactionary characteristics soon became visible. On the other hand, the PTB [Brazilian Labor Party] and the PSD [Social Democratic Party] stemmed directly from the Vargas base. The first represented its newest and most popular facet, being an amalgam of genuine and government-manipulated union leaders and the new middle class. Despite its innumerable shortcomings the PTB was defined as the party of the moderate left. The PSD, for its part, was representative of widely contrasting and undefined forces in the Vargas government. Because it is possible to find a tendency toward industrialization and planned economic development in the PSD, it can be considered the archtypical hybrid Brazilian political party, the center party.

The observable transformations in the cultural scene were also profound, but they can be summed up by saying that Brazil became aware of itself. Until then Brazil had not known itself. Just as a child refuses to recognize its own nature, the nation had no notion of its own reality. It then began to confront the basic problem of Brazilian culture, the deep colonialist inferiority complex that had enslaved it. Brazilians had thought of themselves as racial and intellectual inferiors to the industrialized peoples, without the same capacity for work, initiative, and success, deriving this attitude from the three basic alienations of their experience: cultural, institutional, and economic. The first is seen in the inauthentic and transplanted character of traditional Brazilian culture. Brazilians did not see for themselves, but through the eyes of others. Our books were judged in quality and profundity by the number of footnotes they contained. We sought to understand Brazil by using foreign cultural categories, without any more scientific criteria. The institutional alienation was characterized by an insistence on transferring foreign political institutions to Brazil, without considering our economic, social, and national differences. Finally, the economic alienation can be observed in the country's tendency to copy the financial and economic practices of the great industrial countries, together with a lack of faith in the capacity of Brazilian labor, especially in relation to large industries. In the years since 1930 Brazilians have been coming to know themselves better, losing these complexes, and discovering for themselves their own reality.

# 2
# Import-Substitution
# Industrialization

It was in 1930, or more precisely during the 1930s, that Brazil's development actually initiated its industrial revolution. The changes that began then, however, did not appear in a vacuum. Although it was only after 1930 that the stagnation of the Brazilian historical process began to be resolved by means of a great leap that broke the country's ties with its traditional, typically colonial base, there are clearly definable antecedents to this sudden surge of activity.

These antecedents can be found in the development of coffee cultivation in Brazil after the middle of the nineteenth century. The coffee cycle differs from that of sugar or gold. The fundamental difference, aside from the fact that the sugar and gold cycles took place during the more explicitly colonial period, is that the cultivation of coffee initiated the large scale use of wage labor rather than slave labor. The large coffee growers soon discovered that it was more economical to pay for labor, usually by means of a system of tenant farming, than to use slave labor. Thus remunerated labor began to arise outside the urban centers on a large scale, permitting the formation of an incipient domestic market. A break had been made with the traditional semifeudal Brazilian agricultural system, in which the *fazendas*[1] had constituted fairly self-sufficient centers, at least with respect to the consumption of the slaves and other laborers. Domestic commerce now began to develop in Brazil. The basic conditions for the establishment of a national industry oriented toward a domestic market were beginning to develop.

The fundamental importance of the appearance of a domestic market, even one not very well developed, lies in the fact that industrialization is possible only to the extent that this domestic market exists. The concurrent expansions in the cultivation and exportation of coffee and in wage labor constitute the basic cause of the emergence of this market in Brazil.

Massive immigration occurred simultaneously with the spread of coffee cultivation and the necessity for paid labor in the last half of the past century. The immigrants, with their great ambition and technical knowledge (which, even if it was limited, was probably superior to that of the traditional Brazilian population) came to be one of the bases for the takeoff of the Brazilian economy.

Some other economic antecedents of the Brazilian industrial revolution are (*a*) the development of the textile industry after the 1850s; (*b*) the industrial expansion associated with the figure of Mauá; (*c*) the installation of a system of railroad transportation, although it served only export demands rather than national economic integration; (*d*) the general installation of an economic infrastructure (not only railroads but ports, hydroelectric facilities, communications systems, etc.), made possible by the prosperity that came with coffee cultivation; (*e*) the still weak and speculative attempt to create a national industry that occurred right after the proclamation of the Republic with the *Encilhamento,*[2] and, especially; (*f*) the First World War, which made possible an extraordinary development of the emerging national industry.

Among the political and social aspects of the national revolution's antecedents are the emergence of a more active middle class during the last three decades of the nineteenth century; the creation of the national army, starting with the Paraguayan War, as an essentially middle-class organization (in contrast to the navy, with its aristocratic origins); the proclamation of the Republic, which permitted members of the middle class to take power from the Brazilian agrarian-commercial aristocracy for the few years until the election of Prudente de Morais; and the revolutions that rocked the First Republic in the 1920s, demonstrating the dissatisfaction that had spread among large numbers of the Brazilian people and that eventually led to the Revolution of 1930.

**The Beginning of the Industrial Revolution: 1930–1939**

The Brazilian industrial revolution had its beginnings during the 1930s because of the confluence of two major factors: the economic opportunity for industrial investments furnished, paradoxically, by the worldwide economic depression, and the Revolution of 1930.

The fundamental significance of the Revolution of 1930, which gave it such extraordinary importance in Brazil's economic, political, and social history, was that it drove from power the agrarian-commercial oligarchy that had dominated Brazil for four centuries, initially in conjunction with Portuguese colonial interests and, after independence, together with the commercial interests of the industrialized countries, particularly England. As in the case of the proclamation of the Republic in 1889, the Revolution of 1930 was above all a revolution of the middle class. However, in contrast to the first revolution, the one in 1930 had successful historical timing. Afterwards the Brazilian agrarian-commercial oligarchy was never able to count on even a portion of the power it had held for centuries.

The government established after 1930 identified itself with the goals of renovating the Brazilian economic and political situation. Confronted with the fierce opposition of the aristocracy and the traditional Brazilian middle class, it felt obligated (especially after the abortive Revolution of 1932 when these classes tried to regain power) to seek the support of the newly emerging classes: the urban proletariat, to which it appealed with extensive labor legislation; the new middle class, which continued to benefit with public employment; and the emerging class of industrial entrepreneurs, for whom the new government soon adopted a clearly industrializing policy. But because the government hesitated at that time to intervene directly in the economic sphere, this policy did not have very consequential effects. As will be seen later, the governmental actions that most benefited the Brazilian economy and its industrial development were taken by chance. Nevertheless, the simple fact that the government of the Revolution of 1930 favored industrialization, in contrast to the negativeness of previous governments, was highly significant. If one were to sum up all the small measures the government took in favor of industrialization at that time, culminating at the end of the decade with the construction of the great iron and steel works at Volta Redonda, it would be obvious that the Revolution of 1930 was essential to the beginning of the Brazilian national revolution. This statement implies no apologies for the government of Getúlio Vargas in its first phase (1930 to 1945), which was irrevocably tarnished by the dictatorship declared between 1937 and 1945. It is indisputable, however, that the Revolution of 1930 marked a new era in Brazilian history, establishing the necessary political conditions for the Brazilian industrial revolution.

The second fundamental factor underlying the Brazilian economy's takeoff is the unexpected and paradoxical appearance of an immense opportunity for industrial investment due to the worldwide depression of the 1930s. Had this not occurred, the Revolution of 1930 might possibly have been reversed by the agrarian-commercial aristocracy, and Brazil would once again have been dominated by its traditional economic activity. The Revolution of 1930 was characterized by the support of army officers of lower rank (*tenentismo*). This is less important as a revelation of military involvement *per se* than because the connection with the reformist middle class that formed the base of the army indicates a part of the motivation for the very successful industrialization policy whose major beneficiary was the emerging national industrial bourgeoisie.

Such a policy had a chance of success in Brazil in the midst of a world economic depression because of two fundamental factors: First, domestic purchasing power was maintained at a relatively constant level, despite the world depression that reduced Brazilian exports; and second, the prices of imported manufactured items rose radically because of exchange rate devaluation, so that the country's foreign purchasing power was reduced while domestic purchasing power was maintained.

Celso Furtado's description and analysis of how the level of demand remained constant in Brazil during the 1930s has already become classic. He observes that in this period of depression the classical method of defending the economy, regulation of exchange rates, although helpful, was insufficient. With the depression the price of coffee fell and our currency was devalued.

> The abrupt fall of the international price of coffee and the failure of the system of convertibility caused a drop in the external value of currency. This drop obviously was a great relief to the coffee-cultivating sector of the economy. The international price of coffee fell 60 percent. The peak of the exchange rate depreciation reached 40 percent. The majority of losses, however, were absorbed by the community in general through the high prices of imports.[3]

The fall in coffee prices permitted a 25 percent increase in the physical volume of exports. This increase, however, was far from sufficient to absorb the coffee production. Even with lowered prices, the producers continued to grow and harvest coffee until the mere cost of the harvest and subsequent activities was greater than the price of coffee. At this moment Brazil was facing economic chaos. The coffee growers quit harvesting coffee and the equilibrium of supply and demand for the product began to be reestablished. It thus became evident that "the exchange mechanism did not constitute an effective defense of the coffee economy under the exceptionally grave conditions created by the depression."[4]

It was imperative, then, to find another solution for the problem of unsold inventories that, because of the low price-elasticity of demand for the product, forced coffee prices down without a corresponding increase in sales. The solution adopted was that the government purchased and destroyed the coffee surplus. It was the only possible solution in view of the objective of defending the coffee economy by making the continued harvesting of coffee possible. "At first glance it seems absurd to harvest the product in order to destroy it,"[5] observes Furtado. But,

> to guarantee minimum sales prices was in reality to maintain the employment level in the export economy and, indirectly, in the productive

sectors linked to the domestic market. A contraction of great proportions in the monetary income of the export sector was to be avoided, thereby proportionally reducing the effects of increased unemployment in other sectors of the economy. . . . What is important to take into account is that the value of the product destroyed was much less than the amount of income created. We were, in reality, building the famous pyramids Keynes would describe years later.[6]

In other words, Brazil was making an unproductive investment in goods that would later be burned. This, however, was better than doing nothing. The problem was not to make investments to increase production but to make them to maintain the level of employment, and consequently the level of aggregate demand. This type of unproductive investment is essential in times of depression or whenever there is a surplus with no outlet. It is obvious that it would be better if a productive investment could be found that would not only furnish employment but also lead to increased production and/or well-being. But solutions like this are not easily found. A capitalist economy is generally not flexible in this respect. This is why it can be said that such economies have achieved a great victory when they are able (as in fact they have done in the postwar period) to utilize their surplus in the arms race and in space exploration. This provides them with a powerful weapon against depressions and recessions. In Brazil, it was extremely beneficial that the government found so simple and easy a formula for making unproductive investments in an era of depression as to buy up the surplus coffee. It does not matter that in doing so the government did not intend to maintain the level of national aggregate demand but only to give a measure of support to the coffee growing sector, which was threatened with collapse. *The General Theory of Employment, Interest and Money* still had not been written. In this case, nonetheless, the Brazilian government was following Keynesian policy, permitting the level of aggregate demand to be maintained during the economic depression.

This simple maintenance of aggregate demand had a fundamental importance in the growth of an exceptional opportunity for industrial investments at the beginning of the 1930s because it was linked to another factor: The prices of imported manufactured products rose dramatically. In fact, between 1929 and 1934 the price in cruzeiros (or milreis) of a pound sterling went up almost 50 percent, despite the devaluation of the pound sterling in 1933. This devaluation of Brazilian money was directly related to the crisis in coffee, whose U.S. price fell from $.225 per pound in 1929 to $.08 per pound in 1931 because of the depression. In accordance with the low price-elasticity of demand for coffee, its exports grew very little: Between 1921 and 1930 8,371,920 tons were exported, in comparison with 8,801,263 tons during the following decade. The slight growth in the physical volume of exports, however, contrasted with the sharp decline in their value. Although Brazilian exports reached 805.8 million gold pounds during the 1920s, in the following decade they did not attain quite 44 percent of that total—that is, they equaled only 377 million gold pounds.[7]

This steep decline in Brazil's foreign purchasing power, at the same time that domestic purchasing power was being maintained by the policy that defended coffee, could only have resulted in an approximately 50 percent rise in the prices of manufactured products imported into Brazil. This fact is made even more significant because during the same period (1929 to 1934) domestic prices in Brazil generally not only had not risen but actually had fallen about 7 percent. Thus the importation of manufactured consumer goods became economically prohibitive, and a great opportunity opened up for national entrepreneurs to make highly profitable investments in the industrial sector.

This opportunity was taken advantage of. The idle capacity of the national enterprises was rapidly utilized. In March of 1931 the Vargas government, closely tied to the representatives of Brazilian industry at that time, prohibited the importation of machinery for all industries considered in a state of overproduction. This was seen as a protection especially for the textile industry, which was already well established in Brazil at the time. New investments were made in new sectors. Factories often began as workshops. The small capital necessary was in most cases raised within one family. With the reinvestment of profits, however, such factories later expanded. Although at first generally limited to consumer goods industries that required only simple equipment (food, health and beauty aids, perfume, pharmaceuticals, light metallurgy, etc.), the industries in time began to manufacture the equipment itself. In this way, by 1935 Brazilian industrial output had become 27 percent greater than in 1929, and 90 percent greater than in 1925.[8] Between 1920 and 1929 4,697 industrial establishments were created, compared to 12,232 during the succeeding decade.[9] Brazilian industrial development had been launched.

### The Second World War: 1940–1945

After 1940 a new series of stimuli arose to condition Brazilian industrial development. The fundamental factor of the era was the Second World War. The inevitable question is: At what point did it constitute an obstacle or a stimulus to Brazilian industrial development? The most common reply is that the war was a powerful stimulus. This opinion is partly due to the cliché that wars benefit capitalist development. But, as Celso Furtado so well observed, "the policy followed during the war years was essentially identical to that adopted immediately after the depression."[10] Although the balance of payments created a strong pressure for lowering the exchange rate, the Brazilian government maintained it at a fixed level, refusing to allow the cruzeiro to be devalued. Again, this action was intended to protect the coffee sector by allowing it to maintain its cruzeiro income. But it also served to join together the interests of the coffee growers and the industries linked to the domestic market, because maintaining the coffee sector's income also maintained the demand for domestic products. In addition, Brazil's terms of trade improved by 18 percent between 1937 and 1945.[11] While the prices of exported products rose 116 percent during this period, in contrast to an 82 percent increase in the prices of imports, domestic Brazilian prices rose by only 97 percent.[12]

It appears, then, that the conditions of the 1930s were being repeated. Not only was domestic demand maintained by the fixed exchange rate policy of the federal government, but the intrinsic stimuli of the system itself grew. Foreign demand also grew, as is well illustrated by the fact that textile exports amounted to 13 percent of Brazilian exports in 1943. On the other hand, the supply of imported products suffered a severe blow from the total commitment of the industrialized countries' economies to the war effort. Thus again an opportunity arose for the realization of investments, and a new surge of Brazilian industrial development might have been expected.

This is not, however, what happened. The statement that the Second World War stimulated Brazil's industrial development is fundamentally an error. The U.S. economy doubtless received a strong impulse from the war. However, nothing justifies generalizing this statement to Brazil. What actually happened in Brazil during the war was a slowing in the tempo of industrial development. Although in the preceding five years Brazilian industrial output had grown by 43 percent, between 1940 and 1944 it grew only 30 percent. Including 1945, there was a growth of 37 percent during the war years, as against 49 percent in the six preceding years. And if industrial output did not present favorable indices during the war, the same can be said in relation to real product and real product per capita, which between 1940 and 1945 grew only 23 percent and 8 percent, respectively.[13]

This reduction in the developmental pace at a time when increasing domestic demand offered ample opportunity for industrial investments can be explained by a very simple fact: Brazil's industrial development was still almost totally dependent on imported equipment. Its capital goods industry was still only incipient. Faced with the war, the developed countries had been forced to reduce drastically their exports of industrial equipment as well as of manufactured items. Brazilian entrepreneurs were thus trapped by the practical impossibility of increasing their production to the extent that the market warranted. The limit of their expansion was often the full utilization of previously installed capacity. One example of this was the great development of the textile industry during this period. This traditional sector of the Brazilian economy, which had long operated at idle capacity, suddenly began to operate at full steam, producing beyond its normal capacity. Between 1940 and 1943 its capacity increased by 59 percent.[14] In 1945, when fabric exports had already begun to decline, textile factory machinery was being used an average of 14 hours a day.[15] Industrial development was thus possible only through the intensive use of existing equipment. The Brazilian economy still lacked a minimum of autonomy in order to develop without the aid of imported capital goods.

**The Postwar Decade: 1946–1955**

The war, however, left a heritage that facilitated Brazilian economic development in the following years. Great reserves in foreign exchange were saved up during the war because of the drastic reduction in imports. These resources were in great part squandered on the importation of nondurable consumer goods and the purchase of some European-owned public services when these countries, particularly England, refused to make payment in any other way. This irrational use of Brazilian resources reflects the economically liberal and politically conservative tendency of the government at that time. (I use the expression "liberal" in its classic sense and not in the North American one. I place "liberal" in opposition to "interventionist" in the economic sphere and to "authoritarian" in the political sphere, rather than to "conservative" as in the North American meaning.) The end of the war coincided with the fall of Getúlio Vargas. His government, although dictatorial, had given constant support to Brazilian development. The provisional government that followed, finding itself holding many foreign exchange credits, opened the doors to all types of imports.

Despite all the waste, however, the very necessary process of re-equipping national industry was begun. And with this began a period of great development for the Brazilian economy and for private industry. The average rate of growth of the real domestic product, which had been 4.7 percent between 1940 and 1945, went up to 7.3 percent in the following five years and still maintained a high average level of 5.7 percent per year between 1951 and 1955. During this decade the average annual growth was 6.5 percent and the total growth was 130 percent. Despite the high rate of population growth (during this period ap-

TABLE 2.1
Real Domestic Product and Industrial Production
(average annual growth rate by periods)

| Period | Real Domestic Product (%) | Industrial Output (%) |
|---|---|---|
| 1940–1945 | 4.7 | 6.2 |
| 1946–1950 | 7.3 | 8.9 |
| 1951–1955 | 5.7 | 8.1 |
| 1956–1961 | 6.0 | 11.0 |
| 1962–1965* | 1.9 | 2.4 |

*Estimate for the first six months.

Source:   Fundação Getúlio Vargas and CEPAL.

proximately 3 percent per year), the real domestic product per capita also showed great improvement. During the decade 1946–1955 it was 3.5 percent. In keeping with the term "Brazilian industrial revolution" for the period between 1930 and 1960, industrial development also received a great impulse after 1946, reinforcing industry's position as Brazil's dynamic economic sector. The average annual growth of industrial output, which had been 6.2 percent during the Second World War, was 8.9 percent between 1946 and 1950 and still maintained a rate of 8.1 percent in the following five years. The average increase in output between 1946 and 1955 was 8.5 percent per year, 2 percent more than that in the entire domestic product,[16] as Table 2.1 summarizes.

The decade immediately after the war was thus an era of economic prosperity. In addition to the foreign exchange credits that stimulated Brazilian economic development by permitting the importation, at a low price in cruzeiros, of equipment the national industry had so needed during the war, various other factors of major importance influenced the Brazilian economy and help to explain this prosperity.

In the first place, Brazil's terms of trade improved during this period. Between 1946 and 1955 there was an improvement of 151 percent. Considering the terms of trade in 1946 as an index of 100, in 1955 Brazil had an index of 251. I have not chosen these years especially to show these changes, but rather because they are the limits of the period being analyzed in this section. If we take the year of the lowest terms of trade in this decade, 1948, and compare it with that of the highest, 1954, there was an improvement of 204 percent.[17] A large increase in coffee prices was basically responsible for the change. In 1946 the average

price of a sack of coffee was $22.41; in 1955 it was $61.62.[18] This
improvement in the terms of trade is very important in explaining the
acceleration of Brazilian industrialization, as it brought in foreign
exchange credits that were necessary for development at a time when
the country still had not reached a minimum level of autonomy with
respect to the domestic production of equipment.

The importance of this improvement in the terms of trade becomes
even stronger if considered in relation to the government's exchange
policy at that time. In 1945 the Superintendency of Money and Credit
(SUMOC), the forerunner of the Brazilian Central Bank, was created.
After the fall of the Vargas government the new provisional government
and later the Dutra government adopted a liberal exchange policy with
ruinous consequences for the country. The official exchange market had
already been abolished by Instruction 17 of the SUMOC. The open
door policy then adopted resulted in the rapid exhaustion of commercial
surplus abroad. In 1947, after a new failure of liberalism in the exchange
policy, the government adopted a rigid system of import controls,
including both a priority system and a fixed exchange rate.

This quota policy was of vital importance to Brazilian industrial
development, despite the corruption of its administrative body, the
Import-Export Department of the Bank of Brazil (CEXIM). For one
thing, with the establishment of a priority system favoring the importation
of machinery and raw materials, the importation of consumer goods
became extremely difficult. Thus the domestic market for consumer
goods was again reserved for national producers, who, in addition, were
able to import machinery and raw materials at unrealistic exchange
rates that overvalued the cruzeiro, making the price of imported equipment and raw materials ridiculously low. Instruction 70 of SUMOC
modified this system, establishing a more flexible system of foreign
exchange auctioning with various importation categories. This system,
which would prevail with modifications until the end of the 1950s,
maintained an exchange barrier to the importation of manufactured
consumer goods at the same time as it guaranteed a relatively low
exchange rate for imports necessary to Brazilian industry. Thus, from
1946 to 1955, and especially between 1947 and 1953, the Brazilian
exchange system was transformed into a powerful stimulus to industrialization.

Also, by means of the governmental control of imports and exports,
the improvement in the terms of trade was redistributed principally to
the industrial sector, against the interests of the exporters, particularly
the coffee exporters. This was the so-called exchange confiscation policy[19]
permitting the redistribution of national income in favor of the government and the industrial sector, the modern sector of the economy

in opposition to the traditional export sector. Since then "exchange confiscation," which has continued to prevail regardless of the ideological orientation of the government, has been a basic political issue. In any case, this policy played an important role in Brazilian industrial development.

Thus, industry developed greatly during the decade immediately after the Second World War. Total industrial output grew 122 percent between 1946 and 1955. It is important to note, however, that this growth did not take place equally in all the various industrial sectors. With the development process, the economic structure of the country was transformed. At the end of the war the light consumer industries had become established in Brazil. After this period the development of the more complex consumer goods industries, such as domestic electrical appliances, would begin. More emphasis would also be given to basic industries and to the manufacture of capital goods. Or, from another perspective, if one distinguishes "traditional" from "modern" industries the latter were developing more fully. Between 1948 and 1955, for example, total industrial output grew 87 percent. The output in traditional industrial sectors such as the food and textile industries grew 61 percent and 77 percent, respectively, both below the average, whereas the output of the metallurgical and chemical industries grew 172 percent and 608 percent, respectively.[20]

The great advance in the chemical industry was of course due to the development of the petroleum industry. Petrobrás was finally founded in 1953, after a long political battle in which the forces of the new Brazil and the old Brazil, of nationalism in full expansion and colonialism limited by a national inferiority complex, clashed. This enterprise, which played a fundamental role in Brazil's development, produced three times more during its first 3 years of operation than the total national output during the preceding 14 years and 7 months under the control of the National Petroleum Council.[21]

The development of the capital goods industry can be illustrated by the following data: Between 1947 and 1954 the output of capital goods grew 147 percent. Although imports grew 105 percent between 1947 and 1954 (largely because of improvements in the terms of trade), the share of domestically produced capital goods in relation to total investments was 54.2 percent in 1947 and rose to 72.9 percent in 1954.[22] The lower proportion of capital goods output in 1947 can in part be explained by the ease of importing equipment in the immediate postwar era. Even so, the growth of domestically produced capital goods from 54.2 percent to 72.9 percent at a time when imports more than doubled clearly demonstrates the development of the production goods industry in Brazil during that period.

## The Consolidation of
## Industrial Development: 1956–1961

Thus the decade following the Second World War can be firmly established as a period of great development in Brazil. At the end of this period, however, Brazil found itself faced with three large threats to its development. First, inflation, which from 1939 to 1953 had shown an annual average rate of 11 percent, climbed to 26.2 percent in 1954.[23] Second, the Brazilian terms of trade, which had reached a high point in 1954, went into decline in the following years with the fall of international coffee prices. There was a 25 percent reduction in the terms of trade between 1954 and 1960.[24] Finally, national economic development was threatened by a crisis in the economic infrastructure.

All development up to this point had been accomplished without major planning, in reaction to external stimuli (fundamentally the exchange shortage that made it impossible to import manufactured consumer goods, and the improvement in the terms of trade) that combined with the maintainence and growth of domestic demand. This development had occurred at a very rapid pace. It was to be expected, therefore, that the infrastructural investments that had not accompanied this development would now become real bottlenecks for the economy. The railroad transportation sector was an archaic, debt-ridden system, poorly equipped, excessively bureaucratized, and still oriented toward the transportation of products from the interior to the export ports, without the capacity to attend to the necessities of the domestic market. In navigation the scene was also bleak, dominated by poorly equipped and over-bureaucratized state enterprises that were also in debt. In the energy-producing sector the foreign firms that dominated 80 percent of production were uninterested in making investments, given the low rates imposed by the government. In the iron and steel sector the basis of national production was still the Volta Redonda plant, whose capacity was far short of the country's needs. As if this were not enough, the growth rate of the real domestic product was 1.9 percent in 1956, resulting in a fall in per capita income, because of the reduced coffee harvest in that year.[25]

Nevertheless, the period from 1956 to 1961 was the golden period of national economic development. In this period the first phase of the Brazilian industrial revolution was consolidated, ending the economic takeoff. In support of this statement, Table 2.1 shows that the annual growth rate of the real domestic product reached 6 percent. More impressively, however, industrial output advanced at an average annual rate of 11 percent, almost double the rate of product growth. This extraordinary growth reached its high point in 1961, for afterwards the economy rapidly plunged into crisis, as Chapter 5 will show. Fundamental transformations had occurred in the economy by 1961, not only from the economic point of view but also from the political and social perspective, as Chapter 4 will show.

In the economic sphere, the basic structural transformation concerned the manufacturing industry's growing share in the gross domestic product (GDP). In 1950 that share was 20 percent; in 1955 it had increased to 22.6 percent, showing a 13 percent increase. In the following five years, however, the manufacturing industry's share in the GDP rose to 27.5 percent, an increase of 21 percent.[26]

In this period the fundamental economic phenomenon was the establishment of a powerful automotive industry in Brazil. Starting at practically zero in 1955, in 1960 Brazil produced 133,078 vehicles with a national content of over 90 percent. The importance of this industry is fundamental to the explanation of Brazilian development in this period, not only because of the savings in foreign exchange that it created, but especially because of the external economies the expanding enterprises brought with them. The presence of great automotive factories in Brazil meant not only wages and profits for their employees and stockholders, but also a huge increase in employment and investment opportunities for the auto parts industry, for basic industry, for dealerships, etc. Thus, the fact that profits from these enterprises would go to foreign stockholders was of little significance in comparison with the stimulus to economic development within Brazil.

But why all this development, why this extraordinary expansion at a time when, as has been shown above, conditions appeared to be so unfavorable?

## Government Policy

The basic answer lies in the government of that epoch. The government of Juscelino Kubitschek began on January 31, 1956. During the following five years Brazil's government was transformed, for the first time in its history, into a deliberate and effective instrument of Brazilian industrial development. Before the Revolution of 1930 the governments had been simply representatives of the Brazilian agrarian-commercial oligarchy, whose attitudes toward industrialization ranged from indifference to open hostility. This naturally changed with the Revolution of 1930, particularly during the two terms of Getúlio Vargas. Especially during his second term, a serious attempt was made to plan the advance of Brazilian industrial development. But it was only with the government of Juscelino Kubitschek that the Brazilian government was transformed into a reasonably efficient instrument for the nation's development.

Three factors explain this positive action by the government. First, it was elected by the same political forces that had been in power since 1930. And these forces, though often contradictory, could generally be defined as nationalistic, industrializing, and moderately interventionist. It was to be expected that the new government would be decidedly in favor of Brazilian industrial development and that the political climate would be favorable to this policy.

This reason alone, however, would be insufficient to explain the situation. Juscelino Kubitschek's personality must also be taken into consideration. History is obviously not merely a record of the work of political and military leaders, but it cannot be disputed that leaders with strong personalities leave their mark on history. This is the case with Kubitschek. He perceived the opportune historical moment through which the country was passing and guided his government along two major lines: forced industrialization at full speed and, more importantly, confidence in the potential of Brazil and its people. His industrialism, the extraordinary support that he gave to Brazilian industrialization, often proceeded despite the industrialists; his unlimited optimism was a direct negation of the colonial inferiority complex, particularly in relation to people of Anglo-Saxon origin, that was then widespread in Brazil.

Finally, the third explanation of the positive role undertaken by the government in regard to Brazilian economic development between 1956 and 1961 is that the new president surrounded himself with a team of technocrats, particularly economists, who appeared in Brazil after the Second World War, in the Getúlio Vargas Foundation, SUMOC, The Bank of Brazil, and the Ministry of the Treasury. This network of technocrats, many of them foreign-educated and under the influence of CEPAL [UN Economic Commission for Latin America], was a new factor in Brazil. The development of the science of economics with even a minimum of autonomy and authenticity was also a new phenomenon in Brazil. During the second half of the 1950s this group of economists, which saw itself as a true bureaucratic class, was in a position to assume increasing control of the national economy and to plan for its development. In addition to the technical capacity of the individual members, the group also had available to it the national accounting system, essential for its planning tasks, that had been developed by the National Income Team of the Getúlio Vargas Foundation after 1947.

In 1955 the president-elect was aware of the existence of this group and its potential. He assigned to it the job of elaborating his *Target Plan* and later gave it many responsibilities in key sectors of the country's economy. It should be pointed out that this group, which was certainly not homogeneous, as the many serious disagreements among its members demonstrated, was characterized above all else by technical competence, and by the dominance of the complex science of economics. This, together with its being a truly bureaucratic group, holding positions within the state and in semipublic enterprises, permitted it to remain in power independent of governments and their political orientations. Under the political direction of the president, to whom its members served as consultants rather than determining a final economic policy, as occurred after the Revolution of 1964, this group constituted a major factor in Brazil's development.

For these reasons the federal government, despite its many limitations, despite the make-work heritage of the semicolonial Brazilian government and the consequent inefficiency of its traditional sectors, was able to take decisive action to promote Brazilian economic development during the second half of the 1950s. The stimulus furnished by industrialization, creating conditions favorable to national and foreign private investment, together with the growth of governmental investments, forms the basic explanation for the extraordinary development that Brazil underwent in this period.

It should be noted that the creation of conditions favorable to private industrial development developed not only from the economic, but also from the political order. Kubitschek's great political ability allowed his government to be one of relative tranquility, despite the conflicting interests of various socioeconomic groups. This tranquility was possible only because of the president's ability to compromise and mediate between these groups, and because he had achieved a high degree of unity among the Brazilian people in support of a particularly fascinating ideology that essentially was created by him and died out (or at least lost vigor) with him—that is, developmentalism.

*Foreign Capital*

A second reason for Brazil's industrial development during this period, although of less importance than the first, was doubtless also influential: the great influx of foreign capital. Actually, this influx was a further result of the government's economic policy during this period. The federal government gave incentives to the entrance of direct foreign investment in Instruction 113 of SUMOC, decreed by the transitional government that succeeded Getúlio Vargas's suicide. This government went so far as to discriminate against national enterprises in favor of foreign ones through major exchange, tariff, fiscal, and credit incentives that the government furnished for the installation of the automotive, shipbuilding, and heavy equipment industries.

It is difficult to see how direct foreign capital investments can constitute an essential condition, much less a basic cause, of a country's development. Indeed, depending on the circumstances, direct foreign investments can become a cause of underdevelopment. It is indisputable that, where certain factors converge, foreign investment can inhibit development. Specifically, direct foreign investments may be involved with minerals, commerce, agriculture, or public services, where the multiplier effects are generally lower. The economy may be so underdeveloped that foreign investment becomes an isolated cyst within a traditional economic sector, in such a way that the multiplier effects of the investments are paralyzed by the nonexistence of national suppliers (of equipment, parts, semifinished products, and even certain primary materials) and of national skilled labor. The government, which at least receives tax income, may be merely representative of a totally agrarian oligarchy, detached from the country's industrial development, which spends its resources on foreign trips and imported consumer goods. The products produced may be intended exclusively for export, given the lack of a reasonably developed domestic market. If these factors converge, as is common in highly underdeveloped economies that still have not begun the industrialization process, then foreign investments will have negative effects on the development of the country.

Even if investments are made in the manufacturing sector, where there are great multiplier effects, unless capital is scarce in the sector involved, foreign investment may be prejudicial to the country because of the future burden of remitting profits. Scarcity of capital is not an absolute given in underdeveloped countries. Especially in sectors where the necessary economic investment is small or even medium-sized, and great amounts of capital are not necessary to organize an efficient enterprise, capital generally is not scarce. On the contrary, it is abundant. For example, the Brazilian pharmaceutical industry was denationalized not because of a scarcity of national capital but because of the technical superiority (defended by patents) of foreign laboratories.

However, if foreign investments are made in a country with a certain degree of development and a reasonable domestic market, in certain large-scale sectors where capital is truly scarce, and if external economies are strong, these investments can become a positive factor in the country's economic development.

This was what occurred in Brazil, especially during the second half of the 1950s. Historically the aim of foreign capital in Brazil, at first English and later North American, was to hinder the industrial development of Brazil in order to preserve it as a market for exported manufactured products. Thus foreign investments in Brazil were especially channeled into public services, transportation (to facilitate the export of primary products), and commerce. After the 1950s, however, and particularly in the period we are analyzing, foreign enterprises exporting

TABLE 2.2
Direct Foreign Capital Movement in Brazil
(millions of dollars)

| Period | Investments | Profit Remittance | Balance |
|---|---|---|---|
| 1947–1953 | 97 | 327 | -230 |
| 1954–1961 | 721 | 269 | 452 |

Source:   SUMOC.

manufactured products to Brazil were forced to change their policy. With the rise of national enterprises and the institution of exchange and tariff barriers to the entry of their products into Brazil, they faced the alternatives of either making large industrial investments in Brazil or losing the Brazilian market. Obviously they have opted for the first solution. Together with the governmental stimuli already mentioned, this choice led to enormous foreign investment in Brazil, as can be seen in Table 2.2. The balance between profits entering and leaving the country, which traditionally had been negative in Brazil, underwent a sudden change. Not only the automotive industry but a number of other industries characterized by scarcity of capital and the strength of the multiplier effect received these investments, which, propagated through the rest of the Brazilian economy, became an undeniable contribution to the economic development of the period.

Thus Brazilian industrial development was consolidated between 1956 and 1961, impelled decisively by the industrializing policy of the government, and seconded by the substantial inflow of foreign capital into the manufacturing sector. The rise of the automotive industry was the dominant economic event of the period, and at the same time furnished the country with a perfect demonstration of the reasons for the rapid industrialization that occurred in this period: The automotive industry was above all the fruit of the government's economic policy, exercised through the Executive Committee for the Automotive Industry (GEIA). But it was also the result of foreign investments that had been stimulated by governmental policy.

It can be definitively stated that Brazilian industrial development was consolidated in that five-year period, because after that extraordinary surge of industrial growth, opposition to industrialization in Brazil, and fundamental doubts about its possibility, disappeared. The belief in

Brazil's agricultural vocation had lost all substance. But, beyond social values, there are other reasons more objective, or at least more quantifiable. The most important of these, aside from the installation of the automotive industry and the average industrial growth rate, which reached 11 percent per year at that time, was the great development of the capital goods industry. Brazil had just attained a degree of overall self-sufficiency; its import coefficient (relation of imports to the gross domestic product) was only 5.7 percent in 1960.[27] It now began to become independent in a very fundamental sector, that of equipment production. According to a CEPAL study,[28] the development of the machine tool industry during this period was extraordinary, reaching a rate of 14.7 percent per year between 1955 and 1961. This development was further illustrated by a 1962 study that found that 55 percent of all units in production were less than ten years old. On the other hand, the proportion of imports in the supply of equipment, which was 52.7 percent in 1949, fell to 32.8 percent in 1958.[29] In other words, in 1958, 67.2 percent (by value in cruzeiros) of equipment for the industrialization of the country was made by Brazilian national industry.

Generally it can be said that this was the period of the development of the automotive industry (the production of the transportation materials industry grew 700 percent between 1956 and 1961), of the chemical industry (106 percent growth), of the machine tool industry (125 percent growth), of the metallurgical industry (78 percent growth), and of some basic industries such as petroleum, aluminum, and lead.[30] At the end of this period Brazil not only was practically self-sufficient in regard to light and heavy consumer goods, but also had made enormous progress in basic industry and industrial equipment.

After a somewhat superficial analysis, it might be claimed that this fact, together with the nation's gradual fall into crisis in 1962, marks 1961 as the year that consolidated Brazil's industrial development but also as the end point of the industrial revolution. Brazilian economic development, although continuously subjected to the crises of neocapitalistic systems, appeared to have already become automatic, necessary, and independent. It can be defined as automatic because a system with a capitalist base (rather than a system with a traditional base) had been consolidated in Brazil, and reinvestment of profits in search of more profits had become institutionalized. It can be considered necessary because capitalist development had taken the form of ample industrial growth (and not merely trade), and reinvestment had become not simply advantageous but necessary to the system itself, a condition of survival for enterprises in an era of competition and technological development. It was independent, or rather, relatively independent, because the necessary equipment for the continuance of industrial development was already for the most part being produced in Brazil.

It will be seen in a later chapter of this book, however, that this analysis is not correct, because it tries to make a simple analogy between the industrial revolution of the countries that are already industrialized today and the industrialization that took place in Brazil between 1930 and 1961. In fact, this was only the first phase of Brazil's industrial revolution.

## Characteristics of the Development Model

Between 1930 and 1961 Brazil's economic, political, and social structures were transformed, setting the stage for a national industrial revolution. Before moving to an analysis of social and political development in the next chapters, we can express this economic development in a model, that is, an abstract schema where only the most fundamental characteristics appear, establishing cause-and-effect relationships but also circular relationships, because many of the phenomena are simultaneously cause and effect and thus occur as circular patterns.

First, it is necessary to present and examine in isolation each of the fundamental characteristics of Brazilian economic development in this period of industrial revolution. Between 1940 and 1961 Brazil's GDP grew 232 percent, more than tripling. More significant, however, is the fact that in this period the gross domestic product per capita grew 86 percent.[31] Therefore there was a full process of economic development. The following sections outline some of its fundamental characteristics.

### *Industrialization*

The dynamic sector of Brazilian economic development was industry. Between 1930 and 1961 Brazilian industrial output grew by 683 percent. Taking the period between 1940 and 1961, the growth of industrial output was 479 percent, while the growth of gross domestic product was only 232 percent.[32] In a period of 22 years Brazilian industrial output grew almost six times, and the developmental tempo of this sector was almost double that of the economy as a whole.

### *Import Substitution*

Fundamentally, all of the Brazilian industrial development during this period occurred through import substitution. It was, as a matter of fact, the only alternative for Brazil, given our limited possibilities to increase exports. During its industrial revolution Brazil focused on its own needs. Industrialization benefited from the existing domestic market for imported industrial products that could be replaced by nationally produced goods. Thus there was a drastic reduction in the import coefficient, which fell from 12.6 percent in 1950–54 to 8.6 percent in 1955–61.[33] This shows that, as income grew, imports grew proportionally less, as they were being replaced by national production. The industrial entrepreneurs of this time had little difficulty deciding in which sector to invest, which products to import. The necessary market research was available, so that one could easily decide where to invest on the basis of previous importation.

## Limitation of Import Capacity

Brazil's industrialization occurred basically through import substitution because its import capacity was limited. This limitation resulted in turn from diverse factors. During the 1930s the basic causes were the worldwide economic depression, the decline in Brazilian exports, and particularly the deterioration of the terms of trade brought about by the low international price of coffee. In the first half of the 1940s the war limited import possibilities. For the 16 years following the end of the Second World War the inability to expand exports was the principal limit on import capacity. Using 1953 prices as a constant, in 1947 Brazil exported $1,961,000 and in 1961, $1,976,000.[34] While the gross domestic product during this period was growing 126 percent, the level of exports remained the same. It therefore was necessary to turn to the domestic market, producing in Brazil what could not be imported, and thus replacing imports. It is true that, because of a general improvement in the terms of trade (which from a low level in 1947 rose 186 percent until 1954 and thereafter fell 25 percent until 1961) and the growth of foreign debt, the limitation of import capacity was not as strong as was the stagnation of exports. But the pressure on import capacity was sufficient to become one of the basic factors creating industrial investment opportunities in Brazil after 1947.

## Rise of an Industrial Entrepreneur Class

A powerful class or group of industrial entrepreneurs arose in Brazil during these three decades of industrial revolution. An industrial revolution along capitalist lines can take place only when a group of men with entrepreneurial spirit arises, with innovative abilities, the possibility of commanding the investment process, and a willingness to take risks. In the twentieth century Brazil was one of the few countries where a class of industrial capitalist entrepreneurs emerged, promoting the sudden takeoff of development at this time.

In a previously published study,[35] I found that Brazilian entrepreneurs, or rather, São Paulo entrepreneurs, were generally immigrants themselves (50 percent), or the children or grandchildren of immigrants. Only 16 percent of these entrepreneurs were of Brazilian origin, meaning that their parents or grandparents were Brazilian. The great majority of them were also of middle-class origin. The study established several criteria for grouping entrepreneurs by social class, taking the childhood or adolescent years and considering the father's occupation, the family economic situation, the connection or lack thereof with large oldtime *fazenda* owners and exporters, the father's education, the entrepreneur's education, the family's ethnic background, and the entrepreneur's age of first employment. According to these criteria, 57.8 percent of the São Paulo industrial entrepreneurs were from the middle class (upper, middle, or lower), 21.6 percent from the lower upper class of wealthy but not traditional families, 16.7 percent from the lower class, and only 3.9 percent from the upper upper class, the Brazilian aristocracy. The Brazilian industrial revolution was therefore carried out mainly by immigrant entrepreneurs, or children and grandchildren of immigrants, of middle-class origin. An understanding of this fact is basic to understanding their economic, social, and political behavior, and the country's development process.

## High Marginal Capital-Output Ratio

The high marginal capital-output ratio, or the high productivity of investments made in Brazil, facilitated the economic development of the country extraordinarily. According to data from the Fundação Getúlio Vargas for the 1947–1961 period, there was a relatively modest average annual rate of gross capital formation (16.6 percent of the Gross National Product) and a rate of net investment (excluding depreciation) of only 11.6 percent. Nevertheless, during this period there was an annual average output growth rate of 5.8 percent, which made the marginal relationship of output to capital 0.5 percent.[36] For each additional unit of capital (excluding depreciation, the portion of capital intended to replace worn-out equipment) production grew half a unit. This very favorable marginal relationship of output to capital

could be attributed to the extensive character of agricultural production; the concentration of investments in the manufacturing industry, above all in industrial lines with low capital-output ratios (or high output to capital ratio); the relatively small proportion of investments in housing and certain public service utilities; and, finally, the recording of imported equipment at subsidized exchange rates.[37]

In other words, investment in Brazil was channeled into the sectors offering the highest and most rapid return on investment, sectors in which a relatively small investment allowed a large increase in production, either directly or through the realization of external economies. It is clear, however, that this favorable factor would have to be compensated for in later periods when it would become imperative to allot a major proportion of investment to infrastructure and housing, which involve lower capital-output ratios. (See Chapter 5.)

*Increasing Government Intervention*

Government intervention is a characteristic of Brazilian economic development that is often spoken of in a derogatory way. Pure liberal ideology automatically condemns government intervention in the economy. However, liberalism has been dead and buried as an economic practice for many years. It exists only as an ideology. Yet even as an ideology it does not have the requirements for long-term survival. Increased state control, not necessarily by means of total dominance of the economy or abolition of private ownership of the means of production, but through increasing participation in national investment and production, is part of capitalist development throughout the world. Governments not only play a stronger role in the economy, planning development, setting fiscal and credit incentives and penalties for private investments, and controlling credit, but also are daily furnishing a larger part of necessary investments. In France, for example, more than 50 percent of investments are made by the government and by enterprises under governmental control. In Brazil,

> faced with structural modifications in the economy, rapid urbanization, and growth of heavy industry, it was perfectly natural that investments in infrastructure would increase in relative terms, necessitating stronger governmental action, both in the rendering of services and the creation of capital, and greater participation of the public sector in total expenditures, as has occurred in all countries in the process of rapid industrialization.[38]

The public sector's share in total expenditures in Brazil went from 17.1 percent in 1947 to 23.9 percent in 1956 and 25.9 percent in 1960. After 1956, when the federal government became a deliberate and very successful agent of economic development, the increase in the government's share in the Brazilian economy was due exclusively to increased investments (which rose from 3.3 percent of total expenditures in 1956 to 5.7 percent in 1960) rather than to any increases in public consumption, transfers or governmental subsidies, or others areas of public outlay.[39]

This extraordinary growth in public investments can be better illustrated with the following statistics: In 1956 the public sector, including government enterprises, accounted for only 28.2 percent of total investment, of the gross formation of capital in the country. In 1960 this percentage had reached 48.3.[40] (This percentage continued to grow so that in 1964, 60 percent of investment was made by the public sector.[41]) Thus the public sector was transformed in such a way that it became responsible for a growing portion of the strategic factor in development, that is, investment in the most dynamic sector of the economy. Increasingly the government began not only to define economic policy through economic planning, but also to execute this policy through large investments in basic industry, transportation, energy, regional development, the exploitation of natural resources, and education:

> The growing participation of the government as allocator of the country's disposable resources ought to be understood as a consequence of the very conditions of our present development, based upon structural modifications in the demand for goods and services. The driving force of this development is far from being only the entrepreneur, as in Schumpeter's interpretation of economic development. For the majority of underdeveloped countries, the development process seems in reality to be a social, national, and nationalistic process. To a greater or lesser degree, the government is its most conspicuous and active agent, and in the majority of cases the government is the bearer of intensely felt popular demands. A general desire for higher standards of living can be felt behind these demands.[42]

Moreover, increasing state control is associated with the very process of development. In the United States the share of public expenditures in the Gross National Product was 2.5 percent in 1880 and grew to 19.8 percent in 1957; in France it was 14 percent in 1913 and 32.3 percent in 1957; in England there was an increase from 8.9 percent in 1890 to 36.6 percent in 1955.[43] The same process occurred in Brazil. In Brazil, however, unlike the former countries, the growth in tax income was not sufficient to meet governmental expenditures, creating one of the principal causes of inflation.

### Inflation

Inflation has been one of the constant factors in Brazilian development. Between 1930 and 1960 prices rose 3,195 percent. During the 1940s the annual rate of inflation in Brazil was around 10 percent, in the 1950s around 20 percent, except for 1959 when the cost of living in Guanabara rose by 52 percent. During the 1960s inflation reached an annual average of more than 50 percent.

As long as inflation stayed at reasonable levels, that is, as long as it was limited to about 20 percent per year, it was doubtless a more positive than negative factor in the country's economic development.

Certainly it would have been preferable to have development without inflation, and this theoretically would have been possible. But for Brazil, an underdeveloped country undergoing a very rapid industrialization, inflationary development was virtually the only alternative. The choice was either development with inflation or price stability with stagnation. Inflation was an escape valve for the country's development, making possible the financing of the increased governmental expenditures and investments discussed above.

There are two schools of thinkers seeking to explain the Brazilian inflationary process: the structuralists, who attribute inflation to the inelasticity of supply in certain sectors of the economy, especially agricultural goods for domestic consumption and imports; and the monetarists, who attribute inflation to governmental deficits and their being financed through new issues of money. When inflation is around 10 percent or even 20 percent a year, the structuralist reasoning, especially in regard to lack of import capacity, explains a considerable portion of Brazilian inflation. However, it is not a totally satisfactory explanation even for this situation.

One of the basic points of structuralist theory is that, in the words of the *Three-Year Plan*, "the joint influence of the indicated factors— the intense increase in demand for primary products consequent upon rapid industrialization, and the relative inflexibility of the primary sector—results in a greater rise in prices of agricultural products than in prices of industrial products."[44] In order to back up this thesis the 1960 plan proposed price deflators of 680 and 426.6, respectively, for agricultural products for the domestic market and for industrial products, using 1949 prices as an index of 100. This deflator, however, is not worthy of credit. According to *PAEG* [Government Program of Economic Action], the wholesale price of agricultural products rose from a base of 100 in 1952 to 411 in 1960, in contrast to 520 for the prices of industrial products.[45] Thus there are obvious contradictions between the two indexes, the first derived from the national accounts published by the Fundação Getúlio Vargas and the latter based on indexes 46 and 49 of *Conjuntura Econômica*. This contradiction has been noted by Antônio Delfim Netto, who, after a thorough analysis, concluded that

there is possibly an error in the deflator of industrial income, an error that leads to the underestimation of price increases after 1954 . . . so that until it is shown how these results were obtained, it seems legitimate to question these prices as much as the diagnosis (which we think incorrect) that maintains that "the relation of exchange prices is increasingly favorable to agriculture, all told, throughout this whole period." [Delfim Netto is quoting from the *Three-Year Plan*.][46]

In these terms the limitation of import capacity supports the structuralist theory. But this element alone evidently is insufficient to explain the Brazilian inflationary process. Must one then concur with monetarist theory? This is the first impression one receives from the major Brazilian work to date on inflation, *Aspectos da Inflação Brasileira e suas perspectivas para 1965*.[47] The authors state that "there are four variable explanations of Brazilian inflation: the deficits in the public sector and the method of financing them; cost pressures derived from wage readjustments; cost pressures resulting from exchange devaluations; and the pressures derived from the private sector of the economy."[48] All these causes are interrelated. The inflationary process can begin through any of the four factors, but "once begun it is able to stimulate its own perpetuation and acceleration."[49]

The inflationary process can begin with deficits financed mainly by issuing new currency; with wage increases (cost inflation) higher than the rate of domestic monetary devaluation; with pressures from the private sector, either aiming to obtain more credits or seeking to reduce liquidity and consequently augment the quick profits of price increases for real goods; or, finally, with foreign exchange devaluation. There is a structural component involved only in this last factor, because increases in the foreign exchange rate can be explained by limitations on the growth of exports. Using these four variables as a base, the authors worked out an equation that allowed them to arrive at a determination coefficient of 92.7, i.e., an equation whose variables explained 92.7 percent of the fluctuations in the annual rate of inflation for the period from 1945 to 1963. Beyond this, they were able to use their model with 1963 figures to predict the 1964 inflation rate. They predicted an increase of 82 percent, and the actual rate turned out to be 87 percent.[50] Apparently, monetarist theory prevailed in this study.

However, a more careful reading of the text yields another interpretation. In their analysis of the two theories that explain inflation, the authors very aptly point out that "the major divergence between the two explanations is in the economic implications that arise from the diagnoses. In the structuralist view, inflation is an almost normal phenomenon that occurs with the economic development process . . . according to the monetarist explanation, inflation has nothing to do with development, but has to be eliminated because of the distortions it provokes in the system."[51]

Therefore, although they never arrive at the exaggerated view that considers inflation a necessary condition of development, the authors are far from condemning inflation totally and never naively attribute it to the irresponsibility of those in power, as many proponents of monetarist theory have claimed. They recognize the fundamental role of the government in the creation of forced savings and in the promotion of economic development, not only through its definition of economic policy but also through its investments.

From an examination of conditions inherent in the development of the presently economically backwards nations, it can be seen that it is unlikely that progress could gain momentum by the unilateral action of a class of Schumpeterian entrepreneurs. The conflict between consumption now and more consumption in the future makes the attempt to accumulate much capital result in inflationary pressures sufficiently strong to inhibit the entire process. The impulse for industrialization, in these terms, comes to be one of the ultimate aims of the government. The political decision makers begin, necessarily, to be directly interested in and in great part responsible for the performance of the economic system.[52]

In other words, the government plays a fundamental role in economic development. Institutional barriers of various types notwithstanding, entrepreneurs' pressures for higher profits, workers' pressure for higher wages as a result of the so-called demonstration effect (imitating the consumer standards of the industrialized countries), demographic pressure, the assimilation of production techniques inappropriate to underdeveloped countries, and the aforementioned behavior of international markets—all these factors push the economy toward inflation.[53]

Theoretically, the solution is for the government to increase taxes as a result of its increased responsibilities. This is what developed countries have done. There is a clear correlation between the level of a country's development and its tax burden in relation to gross domestic product. The greater the development, the greater the tax burden. In 1960, taxation as a percentage of national income in selected developed countries was as follows: Norway, 31.4 percent; Sweden, 31.3 percent; Holland, 30.3 percent; Italy, 28.8 percent; Great Britain, 28.2 percent; and the United States, 27.7 percent. In selected underdeveloped countries, the figures were much lower: Honduras, 19.2 percent; Costa Rica, 14.8 percent; Ecuador, 14.5 percent; Colombia, 11.3 percent; and India, 9.1 percent.[54]

In Brazil in 1960 taxation was 22.9 percent of national income, compared with 14.7 percent in 1947. There obviously had been considerable growth in the proportion of national income collected as taxes. This increase, however, did not keep up with the growth of governmental responsibilities, so that after 1956 the deficit in the federal treasury was around 3 percent of the gross domestic product, resulting in a powerful inflationary pressure.

In other words, although it was necessary for the government to assume increased responsibility for promoting national economic development, it was not possible to increase the tax revenue correspondingly because of the obstacles inherent in the system. For this stage of the country's development tax revenues were adequate, yet nevertheless insufficient. They were adequate in the sense that they were proportional to the country's per capita income, but insufficient because the government's responsibilities exceeded the available revenue. And it would be difficult to escape this dead end, since taxes were levied only on the approximately one-fourth of the Brazilian population who regularly participated in the domestic market and paid taxes, especially indirect taxes. Increasing this group's tax burden in order to promote the integration of the other three-quarters of the population into the market by governmental action would have been a dangerous strategy, possibly resulting in lessening stimuli to private investments. There was no other alternative for the economy except inflation, which, in addition to permitting the government to achieve its programmed expenditures, functioned as an instrument to promote forced savings while demand remained high, though artificially high in some respects.

Contrary to the monetarists' expectations, however, inflation, at least to a certain degree, is a process inherent in the development of underdeveloped countries. In Brazil it is a form of indirect taxation that solves the problem of the government's growing responsibilities in relation to the economy. As long as it does not reach the extraordinary levels of the 1960s, it is not only a natural but also a necessary phenomenon in the country's process of development.

## Urbanization

Urbanization has continued constantly during the economic development of Brazil. According to the 1940 census, 31.24 percent of the Brazilian population was urban, and 68.76 percent was rural; in 1960 the urban population accounted for 45.08 percent of the total population; in 1970 it accounted for 55.9 percent. In general, urbanization has three origins: the industrialization process, which constantly demands more workers in the industries and auxiliary services located in the cities; the development of the transportation system, principally trucking, which allows workers to live in small cities in the countryside and work in the fields (this tendency has been intensified by legislation extending workers' benefits to field workers, lessening the desire of the estate owners to maintain colonies on their estates); and finally, not only the demand for workers in the urban sector, but the impossibility of surviving in the rural sector. In São Paulo, the first, and more recently, the second motivations for urbanization have been prevalent. In the Northeast, the third type of urbanization is very common. The first two are directly related to the economic development process and can be considered national. The third is an aberration. Threatened by hunger, the rural worker seeks the large cities where he is barely able to survive through informal and irregular employment, still under miserable conditions.

## Increase in the Rate of Population Growth

Another constant in the process of Brazilian economic development was an increasing rate of population growth up to 1960. As levels of consumption rise, conditions of hygiene are improved, extending the sphere of preventive medicine. Even curative medicine reaches a greater percentage of the population, through institutionalized medicine with state or private health care. The mortality rate falls in keeping with these developments. At the same time, a considerable percentage of the population does not attain middle-class consumer standards, although the child-rearing expenses of the vast majority of the population with children are relatively limited, covering only food and a minimum of clothing (because education and medical assistance are free of charge or simply not provided). When these conditions prevail in a society such as Brazil's the birth rate does not go down. In such cases the stimulus to reduce births in order to maintain one's standard of living remains small, whereas the stimuli to raise large families, including the idea that "the security of the poor man is his son," continue to prevail. Thus, reducing the mortality rate and maintaining the birth rate results in an increase in the population growth rate.

In Brazil the annual rate of population growth, which was approximately 1.5 percent between 1920 and 1940, climbed to 2.4 percent between 1940 and 1950, and to 3.1 percent in the following decade. During the 1960s, however, the rate of population growth decreased to 2.8 percent and in the 1970s it decreased further to 2.4 percent.

Such an extraordinary rate of population growth, although recently decreasing, brings with it a series of problems. It increases the necessity for investments in social assistance and education. The economically inactive proportion of the population increases. The annual percentage increase in the gross domestic product has to be greater, or the product per capita (the rate of growth of the product minus the rate of population growth) will fall. Problems are created in the annual absorption of available labor. In Brazil, for example, it is estimated that with a growth of 3.5 percent per year in active population, 1,100,000 people are added annually to the labor force. During the 1960s, despite the extraordinary industrial development, the manufacturing industry increased its number of employees at an annual rate of only 3 percent, because of the use of capital intensive technology, which economizes labor. This 3 percent growth, when compared with the 3.5 percent growth of the active

42    *Import-Substitution Industrialization*

TABLE 2.3
Regional Distribution of Per Capita Income
(percentage of national average)

| Region and State | 1950 | 1955 | 1956 | 1957 | 1958 | 1959 | 1960 |
|---|---|---|---|---|---|---|---|
| NORTH | 65.1 | 56.7 | 65.6 | 67.7 | 61.6 | 58.8 | 60.7 |
| Amazonas | 76.3 | 62.8 | 75.1 | 78.1 | 72.3 | 66.8 | 68.3 |
| Pará | 58.5 | 53.1 | 59.4 | 61.4 | 55.1 | 53.9 | 56.1 |
| NORTHEAST | 48.5 | 42.9 | 44.7 | 46.6 | 44.7 | 48.4 | 50.6 |
| Maranhão | 34.0 | 29.3 | 28.6 | 30.2 | 31.0 | 33.7 | 34.4 |
| Piauí | 28.7 | 24.9 | 27.1 | 28.2 | 26.5 | 29.0 | 28.8 |
| Ceará | 47.0 | 35.8 | 39.7 | 41.5 | 30.1 | 41.6 | 44.9 |
| R.G. do Norte | 53.0 | 44.6 | 53.8 | 48.6 | 40.4 | 53.0 | 56.7 |
| Paraíba | 48.5 | 41.6 | 43.4 | 42.7 | 38.6 | 46.4 | 53.9 |
| Pernambuco | 61.1 | 53.9 | 56.7 | 61.4 | 61.9 | 61.4 | 60.4 |
| Alagoas | 43.8 | 39.0 | 43.9 | 48.6 | 50.7 | 49.9 | 50.5 |
| Sergipe | 48.9 | 46.3 | 51.7 | 54.1 | 55.9 | 57.1 | 54.7 |
| Bahia | 49.7 | 48.6 | 47.5 | 48.8 | 50.2 | 51.7 | 55.7 |
| CENTRAL-SOUTH | 140.3 | 141.1 | 138.5 | 137.4 | 137.4 | 135.4 | 133.5 |
| Espírito Santo | 78.7 | 77.2 | 72.1 | 77.1 | 67.3 | 65.6 | 65.5 |
| Minas Gerais | 74.5 | 78.9 | 78.8 | 81.4 | 74.2 | 73.9 | 70.9 |
| Rio de Janeiro | 101.8 | 93.5 | 100.7 | 89.4 | 96.9 | 96.6 | 95.0 |
| Guanabara | 304.0 | 308.2 | 326.1 | 312.4 | 326.0 | 316.5 | 291.0 |
| São Paulo | 188.6 | 187.2 | 178.5 | 177.1 | 180.5 | 177.3 | 177.7 |
| Paraná | 117.7 | 116.5 | 89.3 | 96.4 | 103.1 | 107.9 | 110.7 |
| Santa Catarina | 83.9 | 88.9 | 90.2 | 88.0 | 89.5 | 86.5 | 89.6 |
| R.G. do Sul | 111.9 | 127.2 | 132.2 | 126.7 | 118.9 | 117.6 | 120.0 |
| CENTRAL-WEST | 59.9 | 73.6 | 69.2 | 63.8 | 66.8 | 60.9 | 59.3 |
| Mato Grosso | 72.4 | 97.4 | 93.1 | 84.7 | 94.4 | 71.4 | 78.1 |
| Goiás | 54.5 | 62.9 | 58.4 | 54.3 | 54.3 | 56.2 | 51.2 |

Source: Plano Trienal, 1963-1965, p. 86.

population and with the 5.4 percent[55] growth of the urban population, is obviously insufficient.

*Unequal Distribution of Income*

The only data that exists for the regional distribution of income is for the period 1950–1960. The regional inequality then prevailing has been maintained. In order to get a grip on the question, one can consider the per capita income of the different regions of the country as a proportion of the national average in 1960. The income in the Northeast in this year was 50.6 percent of the national average, compared with 133 percent for the Central South and 177.7 percent for São Paulo. The poorest state in the country, Piauí, had a per capita income of only 28.8 percent of the national average. Nevertheless, these regional inequalities did not increase. As is shown in Table 2.3, the Northeast in 1950 had a per capita income of 48.5 percent of the national average, but by 1960 this percentage had risen to 50.6 percent. It is true that in 1955 the percentage had fallen to 42.9 percent. However, the development of Petrobrás, the San Francisco Hydroelectric Company, and the activity of SUDENE [Superintendency of Development of the Northeast] caused the tendency to change. Among the outstanding factors that caused the relative loss of income in the Northeast for the first half of the 1950s was the immediate postwar exchange policy, which, because it penalized exports and favored imports, especially the importation of equipment and raw materials, was prejudicial to the typically exporting regions such as the Northeast.

*Increased Wages*

Between 1947 and 1960 wage earners increased their share of the national income from 56 percent to 65 percent.[56] This fact, however, ought to be viewed with reserve. This growth occurred especially at the expense of professionals, business administrators, and owners of individual enterprises, whose share was reduced from 26 percent to 18 percent, whereas the share of the capitalist group (profits, interests, and rents) grew from 18 percent to 20 percent. This growth in the share of wage workers, particularly at the expense of free professionals, can in part be explained by the fact that many of the latter became salaried. Beyond this, whereas the direct tax burden grew only 21 percent between 1947 and 1960, the indirect tax burden, which affects wage workers more strongly, grew 74 percent,[57] so that in fact "labor's share of national income when measured in terms of market prices increased considerably less than when measured in terms of cost factors."[58]

There was, nevertheless, a growth in real wages, especially between 1945 and 1960, as can be seen in Table 2.4. The growth in per capita income was thus distributed to the population, at least the urban population. Only public functionaries had their real wages reduced. Even this fact, however, could be disputed. This decrease could be attributed either to the choice of an unfavorable moment for the initial survey, or to the fact that the public service wage scale had been modified.

Wage earners thus maintained a relatively stable share of income; their salaries grew with the growth of per capita income. According to the figures of the *Three-Year Plan* the real average wage of a Brazilian worker between 1950 and 1960 grew at an annual rate of 2.7 percent. This increase permitted an average annual growth of 2.5 percent in private consumption between 1947 and 1960. Public consumption during this period, in turn, grew 5.5 percent per year, so that total consumption rose 3 percent per year, or at the same rate as the per capita income

TABLE 2.4
Index of Real Wages
(State of Guanabara)

| Year | Laborer | Skilled Worker | Public Functionary |
|------|---------|----------------|--------------------|
| 1928 | 100 | 100 | 100 |
| 1945 | 69 | 69 | 101 |
| 1960 | 145 | 111 | 74 |

Source: Desenvolvimento e Conjuntura, July 1961, p. 75.

during the period. These figures show that development had been attained without the necessity of augmenting the rate of savings,[59] which during the entire period was around 16 percent of the gross domestic product.[60]

## A Model for the Development Process

Having completed this analysis of the fundamental characteristics of Brazilian economic development—industrialization, the import-substitution process, limitations on import capacity, increased government intervention, high marginal capital-output ratio, inflation, urbanization, the increased rate of population growth, regional disequilibria, and the growth of real wages and consumption—we can now outline a model for the Brazilian development process. Figure 2.1 shows a graphic schematization of the model. Necessarily, it will deal only with the fundamental elements of this model and the basic relationships between these elements.

The Brazilian industrial revolution had two major fundamental agents: industrial entrepreneurs and the government. During the first two decades the initiative rested primarily with the former. The government's role was basically to create stimuli to industrialization, a role possible because of the Revolution of 1930, which shifted power from the old anti-industrial agrarian-commercial aristocracy. The resulting predominance of the entrepreneurs led the country to develop along capitalist lines. It was only during the 1950s, especially in the second half of the decade, that the government took a more active and direct part in making investments necessary for the country's development. This greater governmental participation carried with it the onus of an accelerated rate of inflation, inasmuch as the government did not have the political

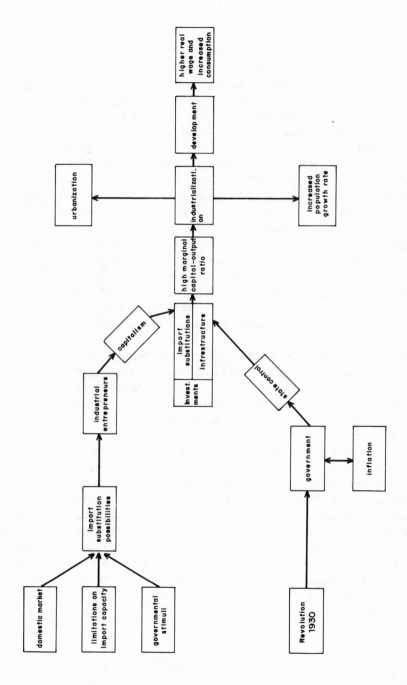

Figure 2.1.  Model of Brazilian Development, 1930–1961

conditions to levy, nor did enterprises have the economic conditions to pay, increased taxes.

The investment opportunities that permitted the rise of a class of industrial entrepreneurs in Brazil fundamentally stemmed from three factors: (1) the existence of a still incipient domestic market; (2) the limitations on import capacity to which the Brazilian economy was subjected after the 1930s, which provoked the rise of prices for imported products, especially manufactured consumer goods, and thereby promoted their domestic production; and (3) governmental stimuli, either through the maintainence of domestic demand, as occurred during the 1930s with the purchase of coffee surpluses, or through subsidies for the importation of equipment, as occurred in the postwar period, or through transfers of income from agriculture to industry, as occurred through the exchange policy, or through the protection of national industry from the encroachments of foreigners, as was accomplished through the exchange policy and taxation. These three factors led to the possibility of import substitutions, and it was fundamentally through this process that Brazilian industrialization was accomplished. Private sector investments were basically geared toward replacing imported manufactured articles. Government investments were focused on infrastructure, petroleum, transportation and communications, energy, and the iron and steel industry, thus creating conditions for private investment.

Investments by the private and public sectors, however, never reached the extraordinary levels that would have forced a very high proportion of savings from the population. A relatively high rate of output growth without great efforts at savings and investment was possible because of the high marginal capital-output ratio, that is, the high productivity of the investments made.

As a result, Brazil went through a full industrialization process, developing its own industry of both nondurable and durable consumer goods, and made extraordinary progress in the sector of basic industries and equipment. Industrialization brought with it urbanization and an increase in the rate of population growth. Above all else, however, industrialization signified economic develement, expressed not only by the increase in per capita income but also by the growth of real wages and levels of consumption. Beyond this, industrialization and economic growth were accompanied by structural transformations in the social and political order. The next two chapters will deal with these transformations.

# 3
# Social Development and
# the Emergence of New Classes

The great economic transformations that took place in Brazil between 1930 and 1961 were accompanied by profound social transformations. Without attaching any value-laden connotations to the term "social development," but defining it simply as a process of social transformation and pluralization, one can say without hesitation that Brazil underwent an extensive social development during this period. There are innumerable signs of transformation, and not just in the physical panorama of the country—the skyscrapers, the asphalt highways, the great dams, the factories. One could also, for example, examine an edition of the newspaper *O Estado de São Paulo*. A reading of the advertisements of jobs available leaves a strong impression concerning the enormous opportunities for engineers, salesmen, accountants, managers, technocrats, skilled workers, advertising personnel, stenographers, personnel workers, purchasing agents—all at the middle level of business. Or one could visit Mappin, one of the most important department stores in São Paulo. In the last thirty years, it has not only grown physically but also experienced major changes in the type of customer it serves. Certainly there are still some customers of the old type, representatives of the old traditional upper middle and upper classes. But today the great majority of customers are of a completely different type, members of the same constantly growing new middle class being solicited in the "Help Wanted" ads.

In fact, many things have happened in Brazil. Vichy water is no longer served in the restaurants. *Fazendeiros* and cattle breeders no

This chapter is based on an article by the author published in the *Journal of Inter-American Studies*, 4, no. 3 (July 1962), entitled "The Rise of the Middle Class and Middle Management in Brazil" and later included in *Revolution in Brazil*, ed. Irving Louis Horowitz (New York, E. P. Dutton, 1964).

longer import butter. Although it seems absurd, this was not uncommon thirty or forty years ago. At that time, Brazil was a rural agricultural country, basically colonial and underdeveloped. Today Brazil is an industrialized country in an intermediate stage of development.

This profound transformation has had immediate consequences in the social structure of the country. The social stratification system has been modified. New classes have arisen. Among them are the new middle class, defined by an intellectual of the old aristocracy, in conversation with friends, in a very curious and significant manner. Someone asked him what type of person would attend a new play being performed in São Paulo, whose poor taste was obvious. The reply came immediately, with an uncontrollable touch of disdain: "Well, the *nouveaux riches* would pay to see such a show. . . ."

It is these "*nouveaux riches,*" this new middle class, and a representative part of the same, the middle managers, who are one of the foci of this chapter. In the developed capitalist countries one thing appears indisputable: If the entrepreneurs, the commanders of industry, were the dominant economic figures in the last century, this century is characterized by the ascension of the professional administrator, generally arising from the middle class. This chapter will attempt to describe the first steps of Brazilian society on its way to pluralization, to the diversification of its social classes, giving special emphasis to the process that gave rise to a class of middle managers.

This task confronts many difficulties. In the first place, there is not much data available concerning this subject. Research regarding class structure and social mobility in Brazil, as well as the development of Brazilian administrators, has not yet begun. In view of this lack one is frequently obliged to depend on personal experience and observation and the general categories of macrosociology, instead of specific research data.

More significant are the personal and social limitations of an author. One always seeks to be objective. Nevertheless, "the vain hope of discovering the truth in a form independent of a group of socially and historically determined meanings ought to be abandoned once and for all."[1] In other words, it is improbable that one can be objective in doing research and seeking to translate the social reality that surrounds one. People are conditioned by the feelings and values of the groups and social classes to which they belong, which in turn can be understood only when placed in a specific historical context. Beyond this, subconscious motivations and all the conflicts of the human personality inhibit perfect control over one's perceptions of reality and one's own values.

Nevertheless, there is no doubt that one can be more or less objective. The degree of objectivity will depend on the precision of the research instruments used, on the author's capacity for self-analysis, and on honesty. In any hypothesis, however, it is important for the reader to be aware of the author's perspectives and preconceived ideas, which should be acknowledged by both parties.

The social development that took place in Brazil in the three or four decades after 1930 arose from the deep economic transformations studied in the preceding chapter. It was a decisive period in Brazilian history. Development, which had proceeded uncertainly, at the mercy of the fortunes of international commerce, began to be both automatic and necessary. The semifeudal forces that had dominated Brazil through a tacit agreement with the great industrial powers began to see their strength rapidly reduced. In this period Brazil changed from object to subject of its history and began to become master of its own destiny. Until then Brazil could be considered a nation only in the legal sense of the word. Its economy was oriented toward Europe and the United States, which considered it to be no more than a complementary unit. Its role was to export agricultural products in exchange for manufactured goods to be consumed by a small rich minority of the population. The domestic economy was a subsistence one; whatever was not produced for export was intended mainly for consumption by the producer. The domestic market, essential for economic development, began to reach significant proportions only after 1930.

The industrialization that occurred between 1930 and 1961 transformed this situation strikingly. The first phase of the Brazilian national revolution took place during this period. This does not mean that Brazil became a developed country, with cultural, political, and economic independence. However, great progress was made in this direction. It was a tortuous and sometimes contradictory process, full of compromises, concessions, successful and unsuccessful endeavors, advances as well as retreats. Nevertheless, it cannot be disputed that great general transformations in economic and social development took place in Brazil. Economically, although it still remained an underdeveloped country, it developed a powerful industrial sector and regions in which the standard of living was raised. Politically, although it was still a dependent country, it established its own international personality. The nation also underwent deep social transformations, as the following discussion will show.

**The Traditional Social Structure**

To the extent that Brazil was a peripheral, agricultural, and entirely underdeveloped country, its social structure was very simple before 1930. The Declaration of Independence did not transform Brazil into a truly independent nation; nor did the Imperial Constitution of 1824 or the Republican Constitution of 1891 transform the country into a democracy. Elections were controlled. During the First Republic, for example, one political party always won the elections, although the opposition party was always guaranteed exactly one-third of the seats in Congress. As a semicolonial society with almost feudal characteristics, whose economy was based on the cultivation of land held by a small group of owners, Brazil was dominated by a small and powerful oligarchy. The masters of the land, the *fazendeiros*, who looked upon themselves as aristocrats, were traditionally allied with the great commercial interests dedicated to foreign trade, and after the Declaration of Independence continued to ally themselves to foreign capitalism, initially British and later, in the twentieth century, American. These oligarchs dominated not only the economy but also politics with considerable influence and stability, mainly because there were no social groups with the minimum of consciousness and the political force needed to oppose them.

In addition to this aristocratic oligarchy, which could be called the upper class, there was the lower class, which included the vast majority of the population. This class was essentially composed of agricultural workers. Some were descendants of slaves. Others were descendants of the first Portuguese immigrants, mostly now having black or Indian blood as well. A third group was made up of Italian, German, and other immigrants, who began to arrive in Brazil in great numbers after the middle of the last century, often to work on the coffee *fazendas*. All these groups suffered from miserable living conditions, poverty, illiteracy, and low productivity, in the midst of a highly underdeveloped, subsistence economy.

Between the agrarian-commercial oligarchy and the great mass of workers was the middle class—of little significance but growing. It first appeared with some slight importance in Brazil after the Declaration of Independence. With the exit of the Portuguese it was necessary to organize the state, to exercise legislative, executive, and judicial functions, to establish the bases of an administrative order. It was to be the middle class, generally linked by family relationships to the upper class, that would carry out these functions. The first law schools were created to prepare these people. A little later, with the abolition of slave traffic and the concomitant prosperity brought about by coffee in the mid-nineteenth century, a market of free workers arose. This change permitted the formation of an incipient domestic market and the development of coastal or neighboring cities where domestic trade was carried on. The first textile industries also arose in the cities. It was within this urban milieu that the middle class developed. As Nelson Werneck Sodré observed, "the middle class occupied a considerably broader space: the most varied urban activities, small business, new emerging professions, the army, the priesthood, and public employment."[2]

The growth of the middle class, however, was greater than that of the opportunities Brazilian economic development offered it. Originally made up in great part of distant relatives linked to the wealthy families, by simple biological multiplication this middle class became larger than the country's productive system could support. Accordingly, Hélio Jaguaribe observed with great clarity that the Brazilian middle classes "were formed and expanded within the framework of Brazil's underdevelopment, as a subproduct of urbanization in a country that remained an agricultural nation and did not offer them conditions to enter into the productive process; the inevitable marginalism that resulted led them to direct parasitism on the state."[3] This fact helps us to understand the precarious nature of public services in Brazil, especially those services that originated in the colonial and semicolonial periods, when one of the most important functions of the government was to furnish employment to this parasitical middle class. The detachment of the middle class from the productive process becomes even more understandable because this class "originated in great part from the dominant class, maintaining through the years the morality, the standards of conduct, the rules of behavior of the dominant class, and acquired characteristics of its own little by little only because of the pressure of necessity."[4]

Finally, the parasitical nature of the traditional Brazilian middle class also explains its reduced political expressiveness during the Empire and the First Republic. It is certain that the middle class had an important role in the military movement that resulted in the proclamation of the Republic, and afterwards remained in power for some time. However, the agrarian-commercial class returned to power with the election of Prudente de Morais. The middle classes returned to the political scene only in the 1920s, participating in a series of unsuccessful revolutions that ended with the Revolution of 1930, the "lieutenants' revolution," as it has been called, in which the middle class, represented by civilians as well as military, was to be dominant.

Generally speaking, then, this was the traditional Brazilian social structure: on the one hand an agrarian-commercial aristocracy whose power was based on land ownership and the production and export of agricultural products, and whose interests were intertwined with those of the international capitalism that exported manufactured consumer goods; on the other hand, a great number of peasants and some urban workers living in extreme poverty; and somewhere in between, a small but growing middle class.

**New Classes: Entrepreneurs and Industrial Workers**

The national and economic revolution produced profound modifications in this scene. Industrialization modified standards of behavior, interrupted and transformed traditional economic relations, and provided a base for deep social changes. New classes arose; Brazil developed and left many of its feudal characteristics behind.

In the upper class the industrial entrepreneurs arose to take their place alongside the great *fazenda* owners, merchants, and bankers. Mostly descendants of the middle class—particularly immigrants from Italy, Germany, Portugal and Lebanon (in that order of importance),[5] they gained power and prestige rapidly with the process of industrialization. Today, although without corresponding political power, they can be considered the dominant economic group in the country. Their rise, however, was not easy. The political and ideological battle they waged against the agrarian-commercial oligarchy that represented the traditional, antiprogressive sector lasted for years.

In the lower class, the transformations are also clear. In the same way that industrial entrepreneurs constituted an entirely new sector of the new upper class, in the lower class industrial laborers and urban workers in general became sufficiently numerous and significant to constitute a definable new group. A majority of laborers came from the countryside. They were peasants or the children of peasants who left their homes attracted by higher wages in industry. In agriculture hidden unemployment was (and still is in many areas) the dominant condition, and consequently wages were extremely low. This situation led to a rural exodus and urbanization. More importantly, the rapidly developing industrial sector could count on an abundant and relatively cheap supply of labor, which greatly hastened industrialization.

This new sector of the lower class, made up basically of industrial laborers, differed in two important ways from the traditional, rural lower class. First, it benefited from an improved standard of living in better food, health, and education. Second, it brought about a fundamental political change. Rural workers had never participated actively in politics, being completely dominated and controlled by the *coronéis*[5] of the interior, autocratic rulers of the *fazendas*, whose absolute power and intermittent wars are reminiscent of those of feudal lords. Industrial workers gradually developed into a relatively organized group, active and with reasonable power to make demands.

In addition to urbanization and the formation of a new class of industrial workers, there were also significant social changes among rural workers. The most important of these are related to the regional differences within Brazil. The north and the central west continue to be practically a desert—a human desert. The industrialization of the central-south region has already been completed, whereas the densely populated northeast has only recently begun to benefit from the consequences of the industrial revolution. In 1960 the per capita income of the northeast was only 28.5 percent of that of São Paulo.[6] The central south, particularly São Paulo, was introducing capitalist methods of production—modernizing and mechanizing agriculture, with labor relations little by little losing their feudal dependency and coming to be ruled by more rational criteria, and the typical figures of the settler, the sharecropper, and the tenant farmer giving way to salaried rural workers. In the northeast, however, agriculture and labor relations continued to be ruled by basically traditional criteria. Thus, while the peasants of the south saw their standard of living rise and had access to education and political life, the rural workers in the northeast, unless they migrated to the south, continued in miserable conditions, in the hopeless situation of a disadvantaged caste within a relatively open society.

## Changes in the Middle Class

The transformations in the middle class during the industrial revolution in Brazil were also crucial. It may not be appropriate to speak of the rise of an entirely new and different group within the middle class, as was the case with the industrial entrepreneurs in the upper class and the laborers in the lower class. But a new element did appear within the middle class, coming to coexist and, in many cases, to merge with the traditional middle class.

The new middle class can be distinguished from the traditional because whereas the latter was separate from the productive process, the former is integrally involved in it. Whereas the old was made up in great part of public functionaries and independent professionals, plus a few store and office employees, the new middle class is made up of a great range of professionals, including business administrators, technocrats, office workers, employees of the service occupations auxiliary to business and industry, salesmen, skilled workers, and members of countless other occupations, as well as public officials and independent professionals. Actually, the clearest distinction between the traditional and the new middle classes is not the occupation of their members but the simple fact that the members of the traditional middle class belonged to it before 1930, that is, before the Brazilian industrial revolution, while the members of the new middle class rose into it during the process of the industrial revolution; a distinctive characteristic of the members of the new middle class is that the great majority are immigrants or descendants of immigrants.

These observations are made with one reservation: There is no single middle class, but rather many middle classes, many social groups that consider themselves in between the upper class of rich and/or aristocratic families and the lower class of the poor or relatively poor, the manual laborers and semiskilled workers of both the city and the countryside. Between these two groups are the diverse groups that together constitute the middle class. They can be classified in many ways: as the traditional and the new middle class; as the upper and lower middle class; as the small proprietors and their employees, etc. The classification of new versus traditional middle class has been chosen as most appropriate for this context. The reader should be warned, however, that the generalizations being made here should be considered in light of the heterogeneity that characterizes the middle class. Therefore only the most salient generalizations are being made. Other than the rise of the new element described above, three fundamental tendencies characterize the development of the middle class during Brazil's national revolution: progressive integration into the productive process, rapid growth, and diversification.

*Integration*

The middle class used to be, above all, a marginal social group composed mainly of public functionaries who could not be expected to work very hard because they did not have much to do. Now the middle class participates effectively in productive activities. The industrial sector demands a great number of middle-level employees. The services that develop along with industrialization and the formation of a domestic market—retailing, banking, transportation, public services, advertising, real estate, stock brokerage, independent professions, legal and fiscal auditing—also offer employment opportunities to the growing middle class.

The state has also been involved in these transformations. During the semicolonial period the state had four functions: to maintain order, administer justice, defend the country against enemies, and offer employment to the traditional middle class. Along with these functions, during the colonial period it also defended the fiscal interests of the crown, and in both periods it served the interests of the agrarian-commercial oligarchy. In contrast, the Brazilian government after the 1930s, and especially after the Second World War, has been an active participant in the development process, despite all the restrictions that have been placed on it. Innumerable businesses have been created by the federal and state governments, such as the Companhia Siderúrgica Nacional (iron and steel), Petrobrás (petroleum), Campanhia Vale do Rio Doce (mining), Electrobrás (electricity), and various state electric companies. Both the necessity of and the efforts toward efficiency in these concerns are obvious. Even in public governmental offices, a growing comprehension of the urgent need for better organization and greater productivity can be seen. Competitive admission exams for public functionaries are becoming the rule, at least for less important positions. Commissions of inquiry to oversee the ethics of public service are increasingly common. Public functionaries and the middle class with which they have been becoming integrated since the industrial revolution are slowly losing their marginal character within Brazilian society.

*Growth*

Integration into the productive processes necessarily results in growth, and the middle class has become a numerically significant sector within the Brazilian social structure.

> It is basically the growth of the middle classes that makes the new Brazil different from the old, which had no place for such classes. The descendants of ambitious immigrants, the excessively numerous sons of the aristocratic families (which still do not use methods of birth control), all are directed toward the free professions, public bureaucracy, commerce, the army, industry, forming an individualistic society. . . .[7]

The growth of the middle class in the large cities, especially São Paulo and Rio de Janeiro, is an obvious fact, but even in the small cities in the central-south countryside a middle class has emerged to the extent that a capitalist system has taken over the traditional agrarian system.

There are no statistics regarding this growth. Social research still has not been begun in Brazil. Despite its lack of precision, however, Tobias Barreto's testimony in his "Discourse in Shirt Sleeves," given in 1877 in Escada, near Recife, is very clear with respect to the Brazilian social structure during the semicolonial period before the national revolution:

> To the twenty thousand heads of the population of the district, this city contributes three thousand, more or less. In relation to these three thousand souls, or, to put it a better way, in relation to these three thousand bellies, the following calculation is probable:
> 90 percent are needy, almost indigent;
> 8 percent live tolerably;
> 1.5 percent live well;
> 0.5 percent are relatively rich.[8]

In this estimate, which the author claims may "err by an excess of rosiness,"[9] the insignificance of the middle class, the 1.5 percent who

TABLE 3.1
Division of Labor by Occupation*

| Occupation | Thousands |
|---|---|
| I    – Domestic employees | 795 |
| II   – Laborers | 10,692 |
| III  – Lower rank military, etc. | 151 |
| IV  – Unskilled white collar workers | 792 |
| V   – Skilled workers in industry and commerce, etc. | 2,194 |
| VI  – Middle level managers and military, supervisors, rural and urban craftsmen | 665 |
| VII – Professionals, independent intellectuals, and military officers | 276 |
| VIII – Directors and top management of business | 152 |
| IX  – Owners of businesses | 779 |
| TOTAL | 16,496 |

*Excluding occupations of less than 5,000.

Source: Desenvolvimento e Conjuntura, October 1958, p. 99.

"live well," is shocking in contrast to the lower lower class (90 percent) and the upper lower class (8 percent).

Today the picture is completely different. The magazine *Desenvolvimento e Conjuntura* made a study of the distribution of the Brazilian population, based on the 1950 census. The study divided the Brazilian population into five classes (lower class, lower middle class, middle class, upper middle class, and upper class) and classified the work force into these categories, using occupation as its only criterion. (See Table 3.1.) On the basis of this table, a classification of the approximate distribution of Brazilian population by social class can be made. (See Table 3.2.)

The imprecision of the division into social classes presented in Table 3.2 is obvious. Although occupation certainly is one criterion for measuring social structure, it certainly is not the only one. Income, social prestige, type of residence, family customs, social relations, and neighborhood are some other fundamental criteria. In addition to this, the classification by occupations in Table 3.1 is a rough one, excluding

TABLE 3.2
Social Classes in Brazil
(approximate)

| Social Class | Thousands | % |
|---|---|---|
| Lower (groups I–III) | 11,638 | 70 |
| Lower Middle (groups IV & V) | 2,986 | 18 |
| Middle (group VI) | 665 | 4 |
| Upper Middle (groups VII & VIII) | 428 | 2 |
| Upper (group IX) | 779* | 6* |

*Not significant because includes small and middle
entrepreneurs.

Source: Desenvolvimento e Conjuntura, October 1958,
p. 99.

occupations with less than 5,000 people and, necessarily, the inactive population.

There is another reservation concerning these tables. Group IX does not truly represent the upper or highest class. The owners of businesses ought actually to be considered members of the upper middle or middle class, as their businesses are frequently very small. Eighty percent of Brazilian industrial firms employ fewer than ten people.[10] Probably less than one percent of the population should be considered as truly upper class.

Nevertheless, especially since no other classification is available, the table presents a reasonable division of the Brazilian population by social class and helps in understanding Brazilian social structure. The upper class, made up fundamentally of rich people and members of the old agrarian-commercial aristocracy who have not yet fallen into decadence, constitutes approximately one per cent of the population. In the upper middle class are found the independent professionals, those with higher education in general, and the professional business managers. This class usually imitates the consumer patterns of the upper class, although it does not have as many resources. Two percent appears to be a perfectly acceptable number for this group. The middle middle class, well defined under Group VI as the military, middle level employees such as supervisors or directors, and craftsmen, includes 6 percent of the population. The lower middle class, made up of office and commercial employees and skilled workers, constitutes 18 percent of the population. Most members of this group belonged to the lower class before Brazil's industrial revolution. With industrialization they were offered employ-

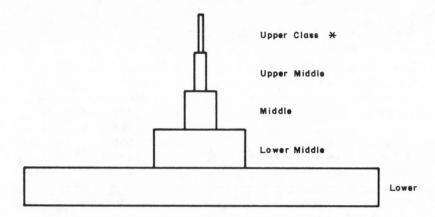

Figure 3.1. The Brazilian Social Pyramid

ment in offices, commercial firms, and factories. They raised their living standards and now make up the majority of what has here been called the new middle class. Finally there is the lower class, with seventy percent of the population. Thus the three middle classes together make up approximately one-fourth of the Brazilian population. Its growth, then, has been confirmed.

Industrialization and the concurrent capitalist development in Brazil (contrary to Marx's predictions, and reproducing what occurred in the more industrialized nations) nourished and benefited the middle class instead of extinguishing it. This is not to say that industrialization did not have unfavorable effects on certain groups within the middle class. Representatives of the traditional middle class—many of whom had fixed incomes, often from rents—were greatly harmed by the development process, with its combination of a highly inflationary climate and a freeze on rents. In more general terms, these people were forced to adapt to a very different life-style than that to which they were accustomed. For them as for many representatives of the upper class—the old agrarian-commercial aristocracy, the "Paulistas of 400 years"[11]—this adaptation was always painful and often unsuccessful.

The growth of the middle class, however, was not sufficiently large to "plump up" the Brazilian social pyramid. As can be seen in Figure 3.1, Brazil still has the flattened social pyramid, with a very wide base and very small top, that is typical of underdeveloped countries.

*Diversification*

The third tendency to be observed in the Brazilian middle class is diversification. Social pluralism, even in economically developed societies, implies the diversification of social groups in general and of the middle class in particular. Specialization and the division of labor are much more developed in industrial societies than in agrarian ones. New occupations, new types of activities appear, offering opportunity especially to the middle class (and those in the lower class who want to rise to middle-class positions). In a modern enterprise, for example, a great number of new middle-level functions are created between top administration and labor. The holders of these jobs, particularly line managers, supervisors, and accountants, whose numbers grew greatly in Brazil, make up the most representative part of the new middle class that arose with Brazil's industrial revolution. This affirmation becomes clearer when one analyzes the so-called second industrial revolution, during which the middle class, and particularly the middle management level, had its great opportunity to develop as a result of the formation of large-scale bureaucratic organizations.

## The Second Industrial Revolution

The first Industrial Revolution, which took place in Europe in the nineteenth century, marked the transition from commercial capitalism to industrial capitalism, initiated the era of mechanized production, made production more efficient, opened the way for a process of full development without parallel in mankind's history, and represented a definitive blow to the feudal system. The feudal system and commercial capitalism, which had coexisted for some centuries, were replaced by liberal capitalism, also called the Manchester school of capitalism. In economic terms this capitalism, fruit of the first Industrial Revolution, was marked by low productivity, by current standards. Socially its principal characteristics were urbanization, the proletarianization of peasant families, and the rise of a class of industrial entrepreneurs. Politically, it was defined by liberal ideology, social tensions, the beginnings of labor union organizing, and an individualistic ideology. "This type of capitalism, which was what Marx was familiar with and which continued . . . to be the abstract model upon which the criticisms of socialism rested, underwent deep transformation after the end of the nineteenth century, and particularly after the Second World War."[12] What occurred then was a second industrial revolution centered not only in England but also in the United States.

If the analysis of the first Industrial Revolution furnishes the basic facts for understanding the beginnings and the first consequences of Brazilian industrialization, the second industrial revolution helps in comprehending the evolution of events in the last part of the 32 years between 1930 and 1961. Actually, the Brazilian industrial revolution that occurred during this period, one hundred and fifty years later than that of England, brought together the characteristics of the two world industrial revolutions. The use of electricity for commercial purposes, the internal combustion engine, electromagnetic waves, the discovery of industrial applications in the field of chemistry, along with mass production techniques and the use of petroleum and its derivatives, marked the beginning of the second industrial revolution in the United States. The development of large enterprises, the rise of the standard of living, the growth of the middle class, and the related increase in social mobility are among the most notable consequences. "The transformation was so great that in retrospect the typical factory of 1910 appears closer to its grandfather, the workshop of the artisan in the days before the discovery of the steam engine, than to its son, the modern mass production factory."[13]

In the social realm, the emergence and the extraordinary growth of the new middle class represent the great social transformation brought by the second industrial revolution. The traditional middle class in the already industrialized countries—made up fundamentally of small businessmen and small rural landowners, as well as independent professionals and the employees of business, public service, and the government—began to lose its importance compared to the new middle group that arose to serve the large corporations, directly or indirectly. "Negatively, the transformation of the middle class is a change from a situation of ownership to a situation of non-ownership; positively, it is a change from a situation of ownership to a new axis of classification: employment."[14]

### Overlapping Phases in the Social Process

Brazil's rapid social development during the 1930s, 1940s, and 1950s was characterized by overlapping phases and consequently by hybridism in structure and social institutions. There are two reasons for this overlapping. First, the sheer speed of social development makes the very necessary delineation of the phases of social progress difficult. Second, the principal dynamic factor in social development—that is, economic and technological development—operated in a derivative nonoriginal way. Contrary to the experience of the United States and England, in Brazil technology did not have to develop slowly. At the beginning of the Brazilian industrial revolution it was possible to import the most advanced production techniques. As a result, the historic phases of economic and capitalist social development through which Brazil should have passed frequently overlapped: the pre-capitalist period, commercial capitalism, Manchesterian industrial capitalism, and the modern mass production capitalism that is rapidly becoming automated. Thus, in the same community, in the heart of the same organization, there can be found vestiges of a preindustrial, semifeudal, slave system side by side with characteristics of Manchesterian capitalism and the modern capitalism that arose after the second industrial revolution. These characteristics, which are always in conflict because they are incompatible and contradictory, can be found in the technological sphere, the social structure, the system of values and beliefs, and the realm of ideologies. The result is a hybrid situation, constantly present in the Brazilian social system, economy, politics, cultural expressions, and bureaucratic organizations.

One of the places where this hybridism can most easily be recognized is in the enterprise—for instance, in the production system. It is common to find the most modern machines and the most obsolete system of administration side by side within the same corporation. A typical contradiction is that of the small or medium-sized family firm, closed, paternalistic, working at a relatively low level of productivity, mainly because of poor administration; yet using modern techniques, furnished with the latest word in equipment produced in the large industrial countries, and dedicated to the production of goods that began to be produced in the large industrialized countries only after the second industrial revolution, such as plastic or rubber products, domestic electrical appliances, electronic equipment, automotive parts, etc.

### Managers and the Middle Class

The middle class, and particularly the technocracy, the technical experts and professional middle-level administrators who have come to be one of the most representative parts of the new middle class, became highly visible in the industrialized countries only with the second industrial revolution, whereas industrial entrepreneurs and laborers emerged on the social scene after the first Industrial Revolution. In Brazil, where these two revolutions overlapped within one period, the result was an accelerated growth of the middle class, and particularly of middle-level administrators and experts.

It can be seen that the growth of the new middle class represents the great social transformation provoked by the second industrial revolution. According to C. Wright Mills, in 1870 the labor force in the United States had three basic components: the traditional middle class, with 33 percent of the work force; the new middle class, with only 6 percent; and wage workers, with 61 percent. In 1940, after the second industrial revolution, this picture had changed radically. The traditional middle class accounted for 20 percent of the work force, the new middle class had come to represent 25 percent, and wage workers had been reduced to 55 percent.[15]

As in the United States originally, during the last few years in Brazil the increase in the middle class and in professional middle-level administrators has resulted fundamentally from mass production techniques, the extraordinary increase of productivity, and the beginnings of automation—all linked to the appearance of enormous, bureaucratic state enterprises and organizations.

With the development of bureaucratic organizations—understood in the Weberian sense as rational social systems, formal and impersonal, administered according to efficiency criteria by professional administrators—the expansion of the middle class became a necessity. It can thus be affirmed that the development of the middle class was due principally to the growth in the number and size of great public and private bureaucratic organizations. This in turn is the most important consequence of the second industrial revolution in social terms. Bureaucratic organizations had existed before. The pharoahs had a complex bureaucratic organization to control the distribution of water from the Nile. But it was only with mass production techniques, with petroleum, the internal combustion engine, plastics, the great petrochemical industry, the automotive industry, electric appliances, all stemming from the second industrial revolution, that the bureaucratic organizations became a dominant phenomenon because they were the only efficient model for ordering and administering such large social systems of production, as the enterprises were now forced to become.

When this happened, the accelerated growth of the middle class became a necessity, not only because by definition bureaucratic organizations are administered by professional managers but, more specifically, because of the greater importance of coordinating activities. Such coordination is the essential function of middle managers, the "organization men" described by William H. Whyte, Jr.[16] They are the line managers and accountants who in large organizations establish a bridge between the top administration and the laborers and lower rank office workers, being directly responsible for production tasks and working in auxiliary sectors such as public relations, production control, quality control, stock control, purchasing, transportation, time and motion studies, product research, tool and product design, maintenance, financial planning, accounting, cost control, etc.

Frederic W. Taylor was their prophet. In 1911, describing the principal characteristics of scientific administration, he wrote: "There is a division almost equal to work and responsibility between the worker and the administrator. . . . Under an administration of 'initiative and incentive' practically the whole problem is under the care of the worker, while under a scientific administration half the problem is under the care of the administration."[17] For each unit of a laborer's work Taylor considered a corresponding unit of administrative work necessary. Thus he established a theoretical base for the rise of middle-level administrators, who in Brazil, as in the United States, were to be the base of the new and continually larger middle class.

Besides middle-level administrators, there is another middle-class group whose appearance was significant in all countries that went through the second industrial revolution. These are the salesmen and other people who perform marketing functions in the large modern corporations. One of the results of the second industrial revolution in capitalist countries was to increase production efficiency much faster than income distribution, so that enterprises and the economy as a whole were confronted with a great problem of excess production. Need continued to exist, for even an immensely rich society such as the North American one was far from having reached a phase of abundance. However, an unequal distribution of income kept all that was or could be produced from being consumed. It was only partially possible to resolve the problem by promising better distribution of income in a slow, very moderate process, because powerful interests were at work. The reforms necessary would be so profound, affecting the social structure so deeply, that they would probably be incompatible with the reigning capitalist system.

Other solutions had to be found. On the part of the state, military expenditures and more recently space exploration constituted an efficacious escape valve. The solution found by the enterprise was a marketing orientation: the growing importance given to sales, advertising, market research, and sales promotions. It is not important to discuss here whether or not these solutions were adequate. It is enough to point out that they have resulted, especially in the case of the enterprises, in new and immense employment opportunities at the middle level, that is, for salespeople, market researchers, advertising specialists, and market analysts as well as the marketing administrators themselves, all seeking to convince the consumer to buy more and thereby permit their businesses to win a greater share of the market.

The second industrial revolution and the consequent rise to dominance of large public and private bureaucratic organizations has resulted in an extraordinary need for middle-level personnel: administrators to carry out coordinating functions, technical experts, and salespeople and related personnel to carry out marketing activities. In a society such as that of the United States, where economic and social development occurred in a more orderly manner, this need was fulfilled more or less naturally. In Brazil, however, where development has been characterized by overlapping phases, the need for middle management personnel, especially technical experts and administrators, increased very abruptly. The result was a great lack of middle-level personnel technically capable of working in the emerging large organizations, as well as a lack of adequate institutions to train such personnel.

In fact, the great majority of middle-level personnel in Brazilian enterprises and government service are self-educated. Only a few of them have had any higher education. Many of those who did studied law, which has little to do with their corporate tasks. The excessive number of law graduates has an historical explanation. Since their founding in the last century, law schools have served to educate the sons of the upper and upper middle classes who had no particular vocation but wished to obtain a higher degree and the title "doctor."[18] Even today such schools continue serving this basic function, so that a large number of law graduates are unable to find opportunities to practice law and instead enter the corporate sector.

This problem is being slowly resolved by the development of schools of engineering, economics, and business administration. At first, the great majority of these colleges educated civil engineers who worked independently. Today the majority of the graduates have degrees in mechanical, electrical, or chemical engineering, and go to work for large enterprises and the government. Schools of economics and accounting are relatively new in Brazil, and were developed to take care of the needs of middle-level personnel in the government. The schools of business administration recently developed under the leadership of the Fundação Getúlio Vargas are the most specific response to the need for competent professional administrators in Brazil.

**The Technocracy**

To the extent that professional administrators and technical experts have assumed power within bureaucratic organizations, they have transformed themselves into a technocracy (or a technostructure, to use John Kenneth Galbraith's term).[19] Brazilian social development after 1930 simultaneously witnessed the formation of powerful public and private bureaucratic organizations and the rise of a technocratic group within the new middle class.

Brazil was unlike the majority, if not all the rest, of the capitalist countries, in that its public sector technocrats and professional administrators became a true technocracy—that is, they assumed a considerable part of the decision-making power—well ahead of their counterparts in the private sector. Actually, as I have shown elsewhere,[20] the power of the professional administrators in Brazilian businesses is still very small, although growing. Virtually all Brazilian businesses are still under the almost total control of their owners.

In contrast, the public sector technocracy has developed greatly. In addition to professional administrators of varied backgrounds, groups of technocrats, particularly economists, have growing power—especially in the Bank of Brazil, the Ministry of the Treasury, the Fundação Getúlio Vargas, and the universities—as the government leaves behind its classical liberal characteristics and, for better or worse, assumes new functions in planning and promoting economic development, redistributing income and guaranteeing a minimum of social justice, educating for and promoting scientific development, and protecting children, women, and the elderly. At the moment when the government expanded its function beyond policing in order to intervene directly in all sectors of society, it became necessary to form large public or semipublic bureaucratic organizations. And within these organizations power continues to increase in the hands of the technocrats who have come to share governmental control over Brazilian society with the military since the Revolution of 1964.

# 4
# Political Development and the Crisis of the Populist Alliance

Various approaches can be used in the effort to understand the general lines of Brazilian politics, to find an explanation for the Brazilian political process. A personalist approach attempts to explain political events through an analysis of the personalities of the principal leaders. A structuralist approach searches for an explanation in terms of the country's economic and social structure. This book focuses on the interests and ideologies of diverse socioeconomic groups, broadening and transforming the structuralist approach into an historical-structuralist approach, which seeks the basic causes of Brazil's political structure in its social and economic structure, viewed dynamically as an historical process in which each moment can be understood in terms of previous historical developments.

This does not mean, however, that the personalist approach will be ignored here. Especially in a short-term political analysis it is absolutely essential. And even in long-term analyses, when exceptional individuals arise who leave a personal mark on history, the personalist approach is essential to complete the historical-structural one.

## Ideological Struggles

The Brazilian industrial revolution—the radical but peaceful process of economic, social, political, and cultural transformation through which Brazil passed between 1930 and 1961—sets the scene for an understanding of Brazil's social and political processes in the 1960s.

Three fundamental ideological struggles marked the Brazilian national revolution, and continued until the end of the 1950s: industrialism versus agriculturalism; nationalism versus cosmopolitanism; and state interventionism versus economic liberalism.

## Industrialism Versus Agriculturalism

The first ideological struggle, that of industrialism versus agriculturalism, had already begun in the nineteenth century. For example, a debate was waged over the protectionist tariff proposed by Alves Branco, but it never attained great significance because the defenders of industrialism lacked sufficient strength. The rural aristocracy dominated the country; it was during this period that the production and exportation of coffee became the dominant phenomenon in the Brazilian economy, strengthening the position of the great *fazenda* owners and the ideology of agriculturalism. It was only after the 1930s, with the crisis in coffee exports, and principally after the Second World War, with significant industrial development in Brazil, that the arguments favoring industrialism gained force and the struggle became important within the Brazilian political scene.

Agriculturalism was based in the belief that Brazil not only had been but should remain for a long time, if not indefinitely, an essentially agricultural country, because it did not have the necessary conditions for industry. Any industrialism would be artificial, producing goods at high cost, and would survive only through government protection. Besides, what advantage was there in industrializing the country? Nothing prevented agricultural productivity from being as great as or greater than that of industry. In fact, it would be through agriculture rather than industry that Brazil would become ripe for rapid economic development. And at this point in the debate the supporters of agriculturalism offered the argument they intended as the definitive scientific proof: the law of comparative advantage in international trade.

The supporters of industrialism defended the opposite argument. Brazil not only could but must become an industrial country. Perhaps in abstract theoretical terms it was possible to imagine Brazil as a highly developed country without industrialization, but in practical terms it was impossible. In the short run, the production costs of a national industry would be high, requiring government protection, but in the long term the problem would be resolved. At any rate, even if production costs in certain industries remained permanently higher than those abroad, it would still be wise to protect these industries. When Brazil was on an equal footing with the industrialized, developed countries, then it could be guided by the law of comparative advantage. Ricardo's famous law could not be applied between industrialized and agricultural countries. The dispute between industrialism and agriculturalism continued in these terms, becoming an interminable debate between conflicting interests until it finally reached its conclusion at the end of the 1950s.

## Nationalism Versus Cosmopolitanism

The second ideological struggle, that of nationalism versus cosmopolitanism,[1] also has origins in the last century. At that time, however, nationalism was confused with nativism or with patriotism. It was only after the beginning of the Brazilian industrial revolution, and particularly after the 1950s, when Brazilian industrialization was transformed from a project into a reality, that the industrial entrepreneurs became a strong enough group to sustain an ideology that could arouse the entire nation. Only then did the struggle between nationalism and cosmopolitanism erupt.

The advocates of nationalism proclaimed it as a total ideology, subsuming industrialism and interventionism. Their central thesis was that Brazil, which until 1930 had been a semicolonial country entirely dominated by a local aristocracy servilely allied to international capitalism, had now attained the necessary conditions to become an independent country, a true nation.

What were these conditions? The fundamental one was the industrialization that had already occurred and that ought now to be accelerated. As a result of industrialization, Brazil would no longer be a mere exporter of primary products. It would not only develop economically, but also give rise to a new middle class from among the industrial entrepreneurs and eventually from among the industrial workers. These would form new elements capable of administering the country in acccordance with the interests of the Brazilian people. In Celso Furtado's words, industrialization would "transfer the centers of decision making"[2] from outside to within the country. Industrialization would also allow the development of an authentic national culture and diversify the social structure, definitively excluding the rural aristocracy from governmental control. Nationalism thus encompassed industrialism, with one qualification: industrialization had to be carried out by a national bourgeoisie. The supporters of nationalism considered industrial development through foreign investment impossible. But even if it were possible it still would not be of interest for political reasons. If international capitalism controlled national industry then it would continue to dominate the country politically, and Brazil would remain a semicolonial country. The only difference would be that this dominance would be exercised directly, rather than through a rural import-export aristocracy.

Thus nationalism's fundamental project was to transform a semicolonial country into a truly independent nation. (The neutrality of many of the nationalists originated from this orientation.) Industrialization was the key to bringing about this transformation, and the nation's attention should focus on the best way to promote this industrialization. Its defenders claimed that Brazil could and ought to industrialize. Developmental interventionism would protect national industry, promoting its development.

The supporters of cosmopolitanism denied, formally or implicitly, all the nationalist theses, beginning with the thesis that Brazil was a semicolonial country. A typically defensive ideology, complemented by agriculturalism and economic liberalism, cosmopolitanism never succeeded in organizing its ideas completely. Only on one point did the cosmopolitan ideology have a strong and coherent argument: its defense of foreign capital. Whereas the weakest point of the most radical form of nationalism was its total rejection of foreign capital, cosmopolitanism, at the other extreme, was marked by a complete lack of confidence in Brazil's potential. Either directly or indirectly, it affirmed that Brazil's climatic and racial characteristics would not permit it to develop as a great civilization—a typical example of the colonial inferiority complex.

Accordingly, the advocates of cosmopolitanism denied any possibility of economic development for Brazil without direct foreign investment. And, in relation to this point, just as with the law of comparative advantage in international trade, orthodox economic theory gave more support to cosmopolitanism than to nationalism in general and to the most extreme nationalists in particular. It is natural, therefore, that the advocates of cosmopolitanism wanted to concentrate their discussion on this point, strategically omitting most of the nationalists' other theses.

## State Interventionism Versus Economic Liberalism

The third major ideological struggle during the first phase of the Brazilian national revolution was that of state interventionism against economic liberalism. State interventionism should not be confused with socialism or communism. As it was presented and debated in Brazil, state interventionism is a moderate ideology that complements industrialism and nationalism. It is an attempt to determine means by which to promote Brazilian industrialization. The fundamental thesis of its proponents is that state intervention in the economy is necessary for rapid economic development. Without such intervention—leaving the economy to the mercy of market laws, as the liberal ideology proposes—the economy would either remain stagnant or develop very slowly.

It is true that some countries, such as England and the United States, have developed without major state intervention, but these countries are the exception, having benefited from an extremely fortunate convergence of natural and human resources along with particularly favorable conditions in the domestic and international markets. Other capitalist countries, such as France, Germany, and Japan, have attained development only as a result of significant state intervention. In Brazil in the mid-twentieth century such a favorable convergence of factors does not exist. On the other hand, planning and rational economic administration have been greatly improved by the development of economic theory as well as national accounting methods. Thus the state should play a fundamental role in the promotion of the country's economic development, devoting its efforts to the protection and stimulation of national industry.

State intervention should be put into practice through two complementary means: economic planning and direct investment by the state. Economic planning, using fiscal, monetary, credit, and exchange policies (the last being the most controversial) would make the process of public and private investment more rational, by means of a well balanced system of stimuli to those investments considered to be in the interests of development. Through direct investments, the state could control certain basic sectors of the economy, such as public services, transportation, and the petroleum, steel, and petrochemical industries, either as monopolies or in competition with private initiative. According to the proponents of developmental interventionism, such direct investments are necessary not only because of the private sector's inability to invest enough in these areas, but also because without state control of them, economic planning would become practically impossible.

It is not necessary at this point to review the fundamental theses of economic liberalism, which developed in Europe as a rationalization for the bourgeoisie's emergence as the dominant class. But there is one curious aspect of the transplantation of this ideology to Brazil: Whereas in Europe liberalism was an essentially bourgeois ideology, that is, an instrument of the commercial and industrial businessmen in their fight against the privileges accorded to the rurally based aristocracy, in Brazil just the opposite occurred, and economic liberalism was transformed into the ideological arm of the Brazilian rural aristocracy. Such a fact appears paradoxical, but in fact it is perfectly understandable. Although typically bourgeois, liberalism was not necessarily useful only to the bourgeoisie. In its purely economic aspect, liberalism affirmed the superiority of the market economy, regulated by the price system, as opposed to any system of state intervention in the economy. According to liberals no special protectionist measures should be taken. The task of controlling the economic system should be left to the natural processes of competition, excluding those who are less efficient.

Economic liberalism thus becomes an arm of those economic groups that are more efficient in the short run and are able to compete in the domestic as well as the foreign market. Whereas in Europe the most efficient, most competitive group was made up of the industrialists and the bourgeois businessmen who arose with them, in Brazil in the short term only the tropical and semitropical agricultural crops were able to compete under the terms proposed by liberalism. Liberalism thus became the ideological tool of the great *fazendeiros* and of the Brazilian importers and exporters: an ideology that would in practice oppose the emergence of an industrial entrepreneur class in Brazil. Thus, since the beginning of the past century, when D. João VI proposed to give moderate protection and stimulation to Brazil's industrial development, the liberal creed has inspired bitter criticisms of government interventions in the economy.

### Socioeconomic Groups and Ideological Struggle

It is not difficult to discover which socioeconomic groups were on which side in these struggles. Industrialism, nationalism, and interventionism were clearly the political expression of the newly emerging social groups. To the extent that the Brazilian national revolution emphasized industrialization, however, these ideologies were above all representative of the interests of the emerging class of industrial entrepreneurs. This is especially true of industrialism, which directly served the needs of Brazilian industrial entrepreneurs.

In the same way, nationalism, which had its major expression during the 1950s, could be characterized as an essentially bourgeois ideology. In particular, the nationalism of the industrialists was restrained, with more restricted objectives than the more fanatical nationalism of certain leftist groups. In many respects this nationalism could almost be identified with industrialism. The industrialists were nationalists to the extent that they wanted to protect their businesses against the competition of imported products, even those manufactured in Brazil by foreign enterprises. It has already been noted that the central thesis of nationalism was that Brazil could overcome its semicolonial phase only through the creation of a national industry. The majority of Brazilian industrial entrepreneurs agreed with this thesis. Thus in matters concerning exchange or tariff protection for national industry, or special exceptions for the importation of equipment, or the transfer of income from agricultural exports to industry, or the creation of barriers to certain foreign enterprises interested in entering the country, the industrial entrepreneurs identified with nationalism. Nationalism then served their interests directly. They were less interested, however, when the subject was control of profit remission, royalties, or the nationalization of foreign enterprises already installed in the country.

The industrial entrepreneurs' support for developmental interventionism follows naturally from what has just been said. All protective measures lauded by nationalism could be carried out only through state intervention. The industrialists also felt that for the development of their own industries, it was necessary that the state invest directly in some sectors of the economy, such as steel, for example.

Defense of the three contrary ideologies—agriculturalism, cosmo-politanism, and economic liberalism—naturally fell to the traditional middle class and, more particularly, the rural aristocracy and the major exporters and importers, whose interests were threatened by industrial development. Such development would call into question the dominion that had been exercised peacefully by the rural and commercial aristocracy since independence, in perfect consonance with the interests of the industrialized nations and under the protection of economic liberalism. It was in these nations' interest to keep Brazil agriculturally based, as a complement to their own economies. This objective was shared by the old Brazilian aristocrats, who saw industrialization as a threat to their position. Certainly industrialization might benefit agriculture, but the benefits would arise out of the production of agricultural goods for the domestic market, whereas the traditional Brazilian dominant class was strongly tied to production and sales for export. The export market would not be significantly strengthened by industrialization, whose principal objective was import substitution. In addition, the old Brazilian aristocracy, which suffered a rude jolt with the Revolution of 1930, understood that industrial development could occur in Brazil only under government protection. Any type of protection would immediately result in a transfer of income to the benefit of industry and probably to the detriment of export-oriented agriculture. This was the case, for example, in the policy of "exchange confiscation."

It can thus be seen that the rural aristocracy and the exporters of agricultural products and importers of manufactured products had a series of reasons to defend agriculturalism, cosmopolitanism, and economic liberalism: Their political and social position was threatened by the emergence of a new socioeconomic group, the industrial entrepreneurs; industrialization would not increase their market for export products; the importation of manufactured products from their traditional trading partners would be halted or gradually reduced; and governmental protection of industry would put traditional export agriculture at a disadvantage.

### The Role of the Left

The major interested parties in the political battles that occurred from 1930 through the presidential term of Juscelino Kubitschek were on the one side the class of industrial entrepreneurs, and on the other, the old dominant class made up of the large *fazendeiros* and those involved in foreign trade. The struggle was thus between two groups within the upper class. What, then, was the role of the other socioeconomic groups in this political debate? More particularly, what was the role of the left groups? The struggle was taking place between two socioeconomic groups both of which generally belong to the forces of the center or the right in any political process. Could it be that the members of the left— the most politically aware workers, students, intellectuals, and members of the military—were alienated from the great political battles of the Brazilian national revolution?

Before answering this question one must first define the left. In this book, the left means those political groups that want to institute any type of socialist regime in Brazil, through reform or revolution, gradually or radically, desiring at least that in the basic sectors of the economy a system of collective or state ownership of property should replace private ownership.

Second, one must determine at what point the left, so defined, could begin to be considered a significant political reality in Brazil. This began to occur only after the beginning of the Brazilian national revolution, and particularly after the Second World War. Leftists had existed in Brazil before this; there already were socialist, communist, and workers' organizations—left groups ranging from the most moderate to the most radical. But they were not significant political groups. They were generally restricted to a small group of intellectuals and some leaders who had no real impact on a considerable portion of the Brazilian people. In 1935, for example, the Brazilian Communist Party tried to gain power through a coup, rather than through a revolution with genuine popular participation. Predictably, the attempt failed, revealing the lack of political representativeness in this radical left current.

After the Second World War, however, a more authentic left began to emerge, more representative of the aspirations of certain sectors of the population. Communism continued to be a completely alien ideology in Brazil. Inconsistent and with a foreign orientation, it never succeeded in becoming a strong political force within the country. However, in all the parties, and especially the Brazilian Labor Party (PTB), leftist groups did arise. In Congress they joined together to form the National Parliamentary Front. A great number of student organizations and labor unions came to be controlled by the left. Finally, by the 1950s a left with meaningful political significance could be found in Brazil.

But what were the political objectives and the ideologies of the left during this period? Did the leftists aim to transform Brazil into a socialist country within the short term? No. This objective was put aside as impractical by the great majority. Socialism or even social reformism were not, therefore, the typical or most important ideologies of the left groups in Brazil. They did exist, but only in a latent form. Then what were the real left ideologies in Brazil? Simply put, they were nationalism, industrialism, and developmental interventionism. In summary, the left ideologies were the same as those defended by the most representative elements of the emerging socioeconomic group of industrial entrepreneurs.

There is no question but that the nationalism of the left was more radical than that of the industrial entrepreneurs. Some left groups went so far as to deny the advantages of any and all foreign investment in Brazil, and to recommend the nationalization of almost all the already established foreign enterprises. Such ideas were not shared by the industrialists, nor by the less radical nationalists. Developmental interventionism, which was moderate among the industrialists, was also more radical among certain left sectors. Only in relation to industrialism was there a clear indentity of objectives between the left and the industrial bourgeoisie.

Although differences did exist between the industrial entrepreneurs and the most representative left elements, they were only minor ones. Much more important was the identity of points of view in the common struggle against cosmopolitanism, agriculturalism, and liberalism. And thus it is not surprising that a group of left intellectuals such as the so-called Itatiaia group, who published *Cadernos de Nosso Tempo* from 1953 to 1956 and afterwards met in the Advanced Institute for Brazilian Studies (ISEB), came to be the ideological spokesmen of the Brazilian industrial bourgeoisie during the Institute's first phase.[3] Nor is it surprising that the PTB, which, for better or worse, was the political manifestation of the left, allied itself with the Social Democratic Party (PSD), where, among others, the interests of a good part of the Brazilian industrial bourgeoisie were represented.

What conclusion can be drawn from this identity of ideologies between the left and the industrial entrepreneurs? It has already been shown that the Brazilian nationalism of the 1950s was essentially a bourgeois ideology. Nationalism, which was the basic ideology, and industrialism and developmental interventionism, which served as means to attain nationalist objectives, were above all else in service to the emerging industrial bourgeoisie. What we are calling the Brazilian national revolution had as its central objective the transformation of Brazil into a truly independent nation. Industrialization, to be carried out by the industrial entrepreneurs with the aid of the state, was by far the best method to reach this goal. The socioeconomic group that benefited most from the Brazilian national revolution was therefore that of the industrial entrepreneurs. The important conclusion to be drawn from this fact is that the role of the left, in the first phase of the Brazilian national revolution, was not to put forward an independent policy but to serve as an auxiliary political force to the industrial bourgeoisie.

## New Historical Facts

This, then, was the political alignment that characterized the Brazilian national revolution: on the one side the old forces that had dominated Brazil since its independence; on the other, the industrial bourgeoisie allied (at times explicitly, at times tacitly) to the left groups that arose as industrialization gained impetus. This alliance was established by Getúlio Vargas in his first term and fully confirmed in the 1955 presidential elections, when the left supported Juscelino Kubitschek, a typical representative of the industrial bourgeoisie. Obviously this is a very simplified description of a much more complex reality. Certainly there were many industrial entrepreneurs who were unaware of the struggle taking place with the old rural aristocracy. In the same way, there were also left elements that did not perceive or did not want to admit their role as auxiliaries to the industrial bourgeoisie. Yet this attempt at a united front was without a doubt the most significant political characteristic of the first phase of the Brazilian national revolution.

After the presidential elections of 1955, however, a series of new historical facts appeared that provoked structural modifications in Brazilian politics.

The first and most important new fact was the consolidation of Brazilian industrialization. During Juscelino Kubitschek's term an extraordinary industrial development took place in Brazil. Using Rostow's model, Hélio Jaguaribe states that the takeoff of Brazilian development took place at this time.[4] I do not agree with this analysis. The takeoff, or to use a more traditional term, the onset of the Brazilian industrial revolution—the accelerated transformation of the country into an industrial economy—occurred during the 1930s and particularly the 1940s. It was during the earlier period that Brazil developed a consumer goods industry and established its industrial base, for example, with the iron and steel mill at Volta Redonda. As we saw in Chapter 2, however, it was during the Kubitschek government that the heavy industrial sector was definitively set up in Brazil, with the establishment of the automobile industry, the industrial equipment industry, and the naval industry at the same time that basic industry gained a new impetus through the installation of the petrochemical industry, the construction of new iron and steel mills, etc. In other words, this was the time not of industrial development's takeoff, but rather of its consolidation.

The most direct consequence of industrialization was the victory, and the subsequent loss of importance, of industrialism as an ideology. After the great industrial investments made in the 1950s, especially during the second half of the decade, it no longer made sense to discuss whether or not Brazil ought to become an industrial country. São Paulo was already an industrial state. Reality had refuted the thesis that Brazil could not industrialize, that its natural and ethnic conditions would not allow it to breed a powerful industrial sector like that of other developed countries. Indeed, reality continued making clearer, more indisputable, the truth of the theory that economic development was not possible without industrialization, that agriculture could attain high levels of productivity only if the country were industrialized. Economists, sociologists, and almost all social scientists interested in economic development were forced to reach the same conclusion. These two factors, especially the consolidation of Brazilian industrial development, turned agriculturalism into an anachronism. This change completed the victory of industrialism, which ceased to be the ideology of this or that socioeconomic group of the left or the right and became a generally accepted idea.

A second new fact was the crisis of overproduction of coffee. This crisis was a serious blow to the old rural aristocracy's power, another setback in the chain of defeats suffered after 1930 by those interested in agriculture for export, particularly coffee. The power of the industrial entrepreneurs grew with the coffee crisis, at the same time as the *fazendeiros'* power was being reduced. The focus of the *fazendeiros'* battle was the "exchange confiscation" policy through which the government transferred income from export-oriented agriculture to various other sectors of the economy, particularly the industrial sector. With the coffee crisis, this battle ceased to have the same importance. Exchange confiscation continued but was for the most part compensated by government purchase of surplus, under the policy that supported coffee prices. The groups involved with coffee continued to protest against the confiscation, but had lost their energy and vehemence.

The convergence of these two facts resulted in a consequence of major importance. With the industrial entrepreneurs strengthened by their consolidated position and the rural aristocrats and importers and exporters weakened, there was no more reason for the two parties to engage in direct struggle. The industrial entrepreneurs finally became accepted as members of the capitalist class, and immediately assumed leadership positions, especially in the more industrialized areas such as São Paulo. Up until this point, the industrial bourgeoisie had been a class on the rise, making use of its progressive ideologies to facilitate its social mobility. Now, having reached the top, it began to abandon the ideologies that supported a continual transformation in the social process. The industrial bourgeoisie's new interest was to maintain the advantages it had achieved. In other words, the industrial entrepreneurs, whose industrialism had never been of an advanced, progressive stamp, began to move to the right, breaking their alliance with the weak left.

Another consequence of the consolidation of industrial development and the coffee crisis was the fact that nationalism began to lose its importance on the Brazilian political scene. In the case of nationalism something similar to the metathesis of industrialism occurred: In becoming a victorious policy it began to lose its force as a political instrument. The difference is that whereas industrialism's victory was practically a total one, this was not the case with nationalism, which continued to be an ideology of struggle. With the consolidation of Brazilian industry, which was the main aim of nationalism, the latter began to weaken. There was still much to be accomplished, but the primary thrust had already been made and industry was a definitive fact in Brazil.

The collapse of nationalism was accentuated by the passage in 1958 of the new tariff law, the third new fact in Brazilian politics. Before the tariff law, national industry was protected by means of administrative measures, with a system of import licenses and exchange measures such as the exchange auctions established in Brazil by Instruction 70 of SUMOC. These protectionist measures were unstable, under constant threat of repeal by a simple administrative decree. Therefore they were under continued attack from the adversaries of protectionism. With the approval of the tariff law, however, nationalism achieved a great victory. The protection of national industry would no longer be contingent, provisory, and unstable. Now Brazilian industrial development was safeguarded by a law rather than a mere administrative decree. To the extent that this victory was accomplished, however, and the industrial entrepreneurs became more secure in their positions, they lost the *raison d'être* for their nationalism, or at least nationalism as they understood it.

A fourth new fact further diluted the industrialists' interest in nationalism. Unlike the first three, however, it did not weaken the nationalism of the various left groups; in fact, it strengthened their nationalism. This new fact was SUMOC's Instruction 113, which gave foreign enterprises an advantage over national ones with respect to the entrance of industrial equipment. Initially this instruction provoked a negative reaction from various national enterprises. When their complaints received no response, many of them opted for the easiest solution: They allied with foreign enterprises that could bring equipment into the country without the exchange charge. Concomitantly, because of the protective system organized for Brazilian industry, foreign businesses were no longer able to export to Brazil. The only way to avoid losing the market was direct investment in the country. National enterprises' interests in associating themselves with foreigners thus dovetailed with the interest of the foreign enterprises in investing in Brazil. As a result a great number of joint investments were made by national and foreign firms.

Obviously, this development would also tend to merge the interests of the two groups. Thus the industrial entrepreneurs' support for nationalism lost vigor. A new nationalism with different characteristics, and without ties to the interests of the industrial bourgeoisie, began to arise as a tool of the left. This new nationalism did not have the same general impact as the first. Its major focus had shifted away from the protection of national industry to a struggle against foreign enterprises installed or about to be installed in Brazil: that is, from support for industrialization by Brazilian entrepreneurs to the desire to nationalize foreign enterprises and control profit remissions, with the most radical nationalism seeking to freeze all remissions.

Another significant new fact was that during the 1950s labor unions gained power. In 1953 the first seamen's strike took place. It was also during the 1950s that Brazil's first important interunion agreement was made—the Pact of Union Unity (pacto de Unidade Sindical). This agreement was followed by many others. During this period the unions began to organize, abandoning the governmental patronage that had been established in the 1930s; the co-opted *pelegos*[5] lost force and more authentic leaders, although still representing only a small portion of the working class, assumed control of the unions, either legally or illegally.

There were two basic consequences of this increased union power, which was controlled mostly by leaders with basically left positions, including a few communists. First, by strengthening the claims to power of workers' movements, it moved the position of the industrial entrepreneurs to the right in reaction. Second, it strengthened the position of the left, which found in the union movement one of its major sources of support.

Finally, during the 1950s there was increased popular participation in Brazilian politics. Guerreiro Ramos said of the times, "The cardinal political factor in Brazilian life today is the existence of the people . . . as the outstanding actors in the political process."[6] During the entire previous history of Brazil it had been meaningless to speak of the "people" in relation to the political process, because the preponderant portion of the Brazilian population was minimally involved in politics. In early times, before independence and for many years afterward, political control remained the task of a small dominant class of landed gentlemen in alliance with Portugal and later England. At the end of the last century, with the development of an incipient domestic market, and with the growing importance of the army after the Paraguayan war, the middle class began to emerge as a political force. It assumed power with the proclamation of the Republic, lost it soon after with the election of Prudente de Morais, and regained it only with the revolution of 1930. The old dominant class, except for the coffee planters, maintained a substantial part of its power, but a new upper class, the industrial entrepreneurs, emerged from the middle class, and after 1930 the participation of the middle class in the Brazilian political process was assured. The rest of the population, however—rural workers, laborers, and even large portions of the lower middle class—remained completely marginalized from the political process, as it had been during the Empire and the First Republic.

With the Brazilian industrial revolution, however, the situation changed. The growing importance of industrial workers as a socioeconomic group, the spread of mass communications, particularly radio, and various other factors provoked among the population at large a growing interest in the country's political destiny. The populist leaders who arose, particularly in the postwar period, took advantage of this interest to get elected. Populism, despite its demagogic character, represented progress in relation to the previous style of client politics in which *coronéis* manipulated the elections. At least now it was necessary to try to convince the electorate. And in the 1960 elections, as had occurred to a lesser extent in the two previous presidential elections, there was a clear manifestation of popular will. After these elections one could say that the Brazilian people had come to exist. At least in the elections for executive offices, and particularly for the presidency of the Republic, the population truly participated in the political process.

### The Collapse of the Alliance Between the Left and the Industrial Entrepreneurs

The union of the industrial bourgeoisie with the rest of the capitalist sectors and the relative strengthening of the left are basic to Brazil's political evolution immediately after 1960. On the one hand, as Brazilian industrialization became an accomplished fact, the industrial entrepreneurs were slowly abandoning the progressive ideologies that had been appropriate to an upwardly mobile socioeconomic group in need of new ideologies and new value systems to support its climb to power. On the other hand, the left was gaining strength as the country was moving from clientele politics to populist politics and then to ideological politics. No expert wisdom is required to conclude what would be the principal result of these two occurrences. The old political alliance between the industrial entrepreneurs and the left was broken. The left would no longer serve an auxiliary political force for the industrial bourgeoisie. It became autonomous. For the first time in Brazilian history one could actually speak of the existence of an autonomous left with reasonable political significance.

Obviously, neither all the industrial entrepreneurs nor all the left elements desired this split. In particular, the most progressive industrialists, those who understood that the Brazilian national revolution as a process of economic, social, political, and cultural development was still incomplete, together with the moderate left, felt that the break was unnecessary and premature. But the process of political radicalization through which Brazil passed, especially after Jânio Quadros's resignation in 1961, weakened the position of these elements.

### Reformism Versus Conservatism

With the consolidation of industrial development, the victory of industrialism, the dilution and transformation of nationalism, the breaking of the alliance between the industrial entrepreneurs and the left, and the latter's concomitant achievement of autonomy, the first phase of the Brazilian industrial revolution came to an end. In this phase the larger goals of the struggle waged by new emerging groups had been subordinated to the goal of industrialization. Now a new phase in Brazil's development began, in which there emerged a demand for the reform of social and economic structures, with the objective being not only to facilitate development but also to improve the distribution of income. The term "basic reforms" came into vogue. The more popular reforms began to be discussed throughout the country—agrarian reform, fiscal reform, bank reform, etc. Actually a new ideological struggle had begun that would characterize this period in Brazilian history: the battle between reformism and conservatism.

Reformism surged forward with great vigor after the 1960 presidential elections. It was an ideology of the left, both of the left's moderate sectors and of a good part of those sectors today considered extreme. The fundamental thesis of reformism was that the Brazilian juridical structures, which regulated economic, social, and political relations in Brazil, were archaic; for the most part they corresponded to the semicolonial and semifeudal phase of Brazil. According to reformism, these structures, especially ownership of agricultural land (it should be noted that the old rural aristocracy continued to be the principal target of the left), represented the institutionalization of privilege and were an obstacle to the economic and social progress of Brazil. It was therefore necessary to reform these structures, eliminate privilege, and improve in the short term the lowest living standards in Brazil, not only by means of economic development and the resulting general increase in income, but also through more even distribution of the presently available income. These reforms were to be made peacefully.

The reformist ideology thus encompassed nationalism as a subsidiary component. International capitalism continued to be regarded by the left as an enemy, an exploiter in search of easy profits, but not as the principal enemy. The latter was to be found within Brazil itself, in the most reactionary semifeudal and capitalist groups, now strengthened by the adhesion of the industrialists.

Conservatism denied the necessity for reforms, or at least reforms of the depth called for by the reformists. The majority of reforms desired by the reformists were not really radical. They did not aim to change Brazil's social structure overnight—for example, to abolish private ownership of the means of production and institute a socialist regime. Nevertheless, in the long run, they represented a tendency in this direction. The conservatives did not see any necessity for these constitutional reforms. According to them, what Brazil really needed was more education, more moral leadership, greater economic development. Social justice would follow naturally from the development process and some appropriate legislative measures that would arise out of it.

This was the political picture that began to emerge after the 1960 presidential elections. These two conflicting ideologies resulted in the break in the alliance between the left and the industrial bourgeoisie and the realignment that had been taking place since the mid-50s. It is curious, however, to see how slow the political groups themselves were in perceiving these changes. The presidential elections of 1960 serve to illustrate this. In an article published some weeks before the elections, the *New York Times* stated that in Brazil the candidate with a personal position leaning toward the right was supported by the forces of the left, while the candidate with leftist tendencies was supported by the right. The statement is paradoxical but was not very far from the truth. This paradox was a result of the great political confusion brought about by the series of new facts described above. The leftists continued to think in terms of the ideologies of the 1950s. For them a candidate would have to be a nationalist and a supporter of industrialism. General Henrique Teixeira Lott was both of these, although personally he was a man of the right, a conservative. And Jânio Quadros, despite all his personal contradictions, was a reformist. Yet because he never particularly defined himself in nationalist terms and never allied himself with the political groups that had remained in power during the first phase of the Brazilian revolution, he was in a position to win the support of the right.

### Alarmism and Radicalism

There is a simple explanation of why it was reformism that predominated in the struggle against conservatism, rather than a more radical ideology such as communism or socialism. Many of the left groups had not yet come to see socialism as a short term goal for Brazil. And those who did clearly saw that in Brazil at that time conditions did not exist for a socialist revolution, given the relative success of capitalism, which through industrialization was raising the standard of living at the same time as it allowed the development of an entrepreneurial group and a powerful middle class.

Thus it was logical that the dominant ideological struggle, at least for some years, would be between reformism and conservatism. However, after the resignation of Jânio Quadros, and even more so after 1963 when João Goulart proposed some basic reforms, a process of political radicalization and polarization began in Brazil. Between reformism and conservatism a dialogue had still been possible; an atmosphere had still existed that was favorable to compromise, to a bargaining process through which the various socioeconomic groups could resolve their conflicts by means of mutual concessions. As the positions polarized, however, such dialogue became increasingly difficult. Many of the reformists became revolutionaries, uninterested in transforming society by peaceful means; many of the conservatives became rigid, determined not to give in on any point, reasoning that any compromise would be a defeat and would encourage the left to call for more changes. Conservatives who, before the 1963 National Democratic Union party convention in Curitiba, had accepted the idea of agrarian reform by constitutional amendment no longer considered the idea. On the other hand, reformists who had been willing to settle for moderate agrarian reform now began to demand a more radical program.

What explains this polarization? The answer lies in the structural modifications referred to in this chapter. These modifications united the forces of the right and strengthened the left, creating the conditions for the latter's independence. It was to be expected, then, that the extremist elements of the two political wings would not be content with the moderate platforms of reformism and conservatism, but would attempt to test their own strength by the propagation of revolution and immobilism.

The polarization that had reached great extremes by the end of 1963, and finally resulted in the Revolution of 1964, thus had roots in the structural transformations that had just taken place in Brazil. The left, despite its relative weakness in the Brazilian political scene (its political ideology was only beginning to take shape), became autonomous, stronger than it had previously been. The most extreme groups, because of the relative growth of their power among the labor unions, student groups, lesser army officers, and rural workers linked to the peasants, began to believe that they possessed great political strength in Brazil. The path to the radicalization of the left was obviously open.

On the other hand, the right began to see that for the first time in the history of Brazil, left groups with a certain degree of political significance were trying to gain power. Formerly the battle could be carried on between subgroups within the dominant class. At the most there were conflicts between the upwardly mobile middle class and the old rural aristocracy. Now, however, left groups existed whose objective, at least in the long run, was to do away with the capitalist system. Such groups were indeed entering the political arena to contend for power. Thus the door was opened to alarmism, and the radicalism of the right had a favorable environment in which to develop.

Alarmism, then, was the major instrument of radicalization for the leaders of the far right. (It was also of service to the radicals of the left, but with less efficiency.) First, rightist leaders spread apparently defeatist statements such as "communist revolution is knocking at our door"; "I don't think a year will pass before there is a communist revolution in Brazil"; and "Let's take advantage of the last days of bourgeois comfort. . . ." This last had a humorous tone, but its effect was to create an atmosphere of fright. These statements were slogans without a fundamental base in reality. Communism never had any great political significance in Brazil. And even the noncommunist left was too weak to bring about an armed revolution. But as the left began to emerge as an autonomous political force, the slogans began to resound. They began to be repeated, and the alarmists of the right concluded that if the communists were knocking at the door it was high time to organize a resistance; no compromise should be made with reformism; it was necessary to join forces against the communists. In other words, the times demanded radicalization. And thus many people who until then had not been very radical, that is, who had had conservative but not immobilist tendencies, underwent a radical shift to the right without realizing that they were victims of political manipulation by certain radical leaders who benefited greatly from this shift.

The radicalization of the right was used by radicals of the left to transform moderate leftists into radicals. "Reformism won't solve our problems," they said. "Brazil needs reforms, but it is impossible to attain them through peaceful means. The right dominates the press and the Congress and is not ready to give in on any point. Only through revolution can we transform the country." And to the extent that these statements appeared to be confirmed by the increasing radicalization of the right, the left radicals also won converts.

Two other causes contributed to this polarization: personal factors and inflation, whose acceleration after 1961 brought major economic and political instability, favoring political extremism. The only personal factors it is necessary to mention here are the frustration of the right and the left respectively provoked by the resignation of Jânio Quadros and the accession of João Goulart to the presidency of the Brazilian republic.

Quadros's resignation was frustrating primarily for the right, which thought it had achieved political victory in 1960. During his short term in office, from January to August 1961, however, Quadros created a series of frustrations for the right, especially as it became aware of his political independence. The medal given to Ché Guevara during his brief visit to Brazil is an example of the strange and independent behavior of the president. As if this were not enough, Quadros resigned, handing over power to João Goulart, an historical enemy of the right in Brazil. Obviously such a frustration would arouse an aggressive, radical reaction.

The presidency of Goulart was particularly frustrating for the left, which believed that with his ascension to power Brazil finally had a president who would carry out its programs. However, because of his personal characteristics and, more importantly, because of the weak left's inability to provide the support to keep him in power, Goulart did not fulfill these hopes. The frustration of the left was profound. Yet the right also felt frustrated. Goulart could not have carried out a rightist program. If he had done so he would have found himself in an intolerable political situation, having lost the left's support without having gained the confidence of the right.

This frustration of both the right and the left, together with inflation (increasing at an extremely high rate) and, principally, the structural modifications that resulted in the realignment of political forces and the transformation of the ideological struggle in Brazil, brought about an ever increasing polarization, a total suspension of political dialogue that resulted in the absolute refusal of both the radical right and the radical left to participate in a bargaining process in order to negotiate mutual concessions. It was an impasse, with some factions promoting revolution and others promoting immobilism, neither of these solutions being in the best interest of Brazil. The result was the Revolution of 1964, which marked the predictable victory of the right over an immature left, and represented the consolidation of the capitalist system in Brazil.

# 5
# The Crisis of the 1960s

Until the beginning of the 1960s few people thought in terms of crisis. They spoke of the "industrial revolution," of the great economic, social, and political transformations through which the country was passing in the "Brazilian revolution." Of course, problems that arose during the process of economic and social development were pointed out and discussed. Yet the dominant attitude in Brazil was optimistic and positive. Since the end of the Second World War the country had been dominated by a sense of optimism that was transformed during the 1950s into a feeling of euphoria. Brazil was not merely "the country of the future": It was rapidly becoming this country in the present.

After 1961, however, the situation changed. Optimism (not to mention euphoria) gave way to doubt and later to a decided pessimism. Little by little the country was entering into a crisis in which the emerging difficulties outpaced the available solutions. Brazil was entering a historical phase that will be termed here the Brazilian crisis.

## The Crisis Defined

The Brazilian crisis assumed a fundamentally economic and political character, although it also had social and even cultural aspects. The economic aspect was most salient. The rate of growth in per capita income, which had been about 3 percent until 1961, was negative in 1964, with a reduction of 6.1 percent. This data corresponds to a 3 percent decrease in aggregate income. The principal factor that explains this phenomenon was the 4.5 percent decrease in agricultural production, but industrial output also dropped 0.4 percent. This fact is particularly serious when we remember that postwar Brazil, of all the Latin American countries, showed the largest growth in industrial output. In the period from 1945–1950 to 1956–1961, the average growth of manufacturing had reached a high rate of 9.4 percent.

However, according to the figures of the National Income Team of the Getúlio Vargas Foundation, the entire drop in industrial activity in 1964 occurred during the first half of the year, whereas the second six months marked a recuperation that almost canceled out the initial reduction.[1] From this it might have been concluded that after the second half of 1964 the economy had already begun its recuperative process, so that one could no longer speak of crisis.

Unfortunately, however, this optimistic vision was not verified by the reality. The decrease in industrial output in early 1964 was due partly to the rationing of electric power, which continued until April or May, and partly to the political crisis Brazil went through at that time. With these two most immediate causes of the problem eliminated, one might have hoped that the economy would be vigorously reactivated. This did not occur, and recuperation was slow and weak. Starting in 1965 new short-range causes, particularly the government's anti-inflationary policies, began to result in economic recession.

In this state of continuing economic uncertainty, sales fell, especially those of durable consumer goods. Without a market for their production, enterprises were forced to cut back. Many resorted to shutting down their plants for collective vacations. Often this became simply a prelude to the more severe measures that soon followed: a reduction in the work day and the firing of employees. The result was that for the first time in Brazil's history there was serious industrial unemployment.

Hidden unemployment had always existed, with people working in rural areas and even in the cities at unproductive activities in which the marginal productivity of their labor was zero. Unfortunately, this is a general evil in underdeveloped countries. But open unemployment of workers already integrated into the country's industrial economy had never occurred on a large scale before 1965. According to figures from careful research done by the Federation of Industries of the State of São Paulo (FIESP), unemployment in metropolitan São Paulo in June 1965 affected more than 13 percent of the industrial work force.[2] In the city of São Paulo alone there were more than 80,000 unemployed, while in the state of São Paulo the total unemployment was around 140,000. These figures, however, are conservative, for three reasons: First, they are based on the hypothesis that there was full employment in São Paulo in December 1964 (the data base used), which is highly unlikely. Second, this does not take into account the young people who reached working age and were unable to find jobs. Third, these figures do not take into account the shortened working days. Unemployment must have been worse than these figures show, and it was not confined only to São Paulo. The same phenomenon was occurring in all the large cities. The situation was especially discouraging in Recife and Belo Horizonte, but was also bad in other cities. In Rio de Janeiro and Porto Alegre the news was basically the same: a reduction in industrial activity and unemployment.

It is not necessary to point out that this type of unemployment is much more serious than hidden unemployment. The latter is a chronic problem brought about by economic underdevelopment, and can even become a positive factor in development to the extent that it can provide a reserve of labor power that makes industrialization possible without endangering agricultural production. But open industrial unemployment is a rude blow to the economy. Beyond its obvious social impact, it forces a segment of the population that had been actively participating in the consumer market to reduce its purchases drastically. This begins a vicious circle in which the situation tends only to worsen.

Crisis thus dominated the Brazilian economic scene in early 1965. Unemployment was its most tangible evidence, but other factors also pointed to crisis. Sensing the weakness of the market, entrepreneurs suspended their investments, and the situation continued to worsen. Foreign investors did the same thing. Industrial leaders in almost every sector related pessimistic news in their reports and interviews. They also urgently recommended that labor legislation be modified to allow enterprises to reduce their working hours so that they would not be forced to fire qualified employees. It is unnecessary to point out how much it costs to train a specialized worker, and how much such workers had been sought after only a short time before. Retail stores selling home appliances began to hold drastic liquidation sales, seeking enough cash to pay off their liabilities. Credit, whose scarcity had originally been one of the short-term causes of the crisis, became very easily obtainable. Whereas previously the entrepreneurs had insistently pressured the banks, the latter now began to offer credit freely, something previously unknown in Brazil. But with their sales reduced the businesses did not have enough bonds based on merchandise to utilize the available credit effectively.

Thus during the first half of 1965 Brazil went through a drastic reduction in economic activity, the most serious crisis the Brazilian industrial economy had ever undergone. After August 1965 a rather partial recovery began. The Brazilian economy ceased to be in acute crisis, but returned to a kind of chronic crisis that had characterized it since 1962. The problem of unemployment was not resolved. The FIESP's employment index, which until February had remained at 100 percent, went down to 97 percent in March, 93 percent in April, 89.6 percent in May, 87.7 percent in June, and 86.5 percent in July. In August it began to climb again, to 88.2 percent, and then reached 90.7 percent in September, 92.6 percent in October, 94.2 percent in November, and 95.5 percent in December. However, this was still an unemployment rate of 4.5 percent, in a month in which economic activity is usually intense, and without considering the young people who reached working age that year. The economic crisis was thus still present, although abated. In 1965 the product grew 2.7 percent. However, this growth was due basically to good agricultural harvests, an improvement over the poor year for agriculture in 1964. Industrial development during this period was negative (a reduction of 3.6 percent in industrial output in 1965), and it was here that the most important characteristic of the economic crisis lay.

There was a certain degree of economic recovery in industrial development in 1966, resulting in a 7.6 percent growth rate, due mostly to the pace of development during the first half of the year. But in the second half of 1966 the economy again showed signs of crisis. Using December 1963 as its base of 100, the FIESP's industrial employment index, after having fallen to a low of 83.5 in July 1965, rose to an extremely modest high of 101 in July of the following year, and then declined again to 94.7 in December of 1966. On the other hand, research carried out by DIEESE [Department of Statistics and Socioeconomic Studies] in São Paulo revealed that between 1963 and 1966 the number of employees in the metallurgical, mechanical, and electrical supplies industries decreased from 242,834 to 195,615, a drop of 19.4 percent. Finally, the help wanted advertisements in São Paulo's major daily newspaper, *O Estado de São Paulo*, indicate that the number of available jobs began decreasing again in mid-1966 and continued falling into 1967, reaching a low point in May that was comparable to employment opportunities in 1958.[3] After June 1967 economic recovery began, starting a new expansive cycle that would continue until 1974.

Actually, there was an economic recession in Brazil between 1962 and 1966, as is shown in Table 5.1, which presents figures on the annual increase in the net domestic product in Brazil after 1962, and compares them with the period from 1956 to 1962. Even if we include 1962, a good year, the average increase in national income was only 2.6 percent per year between 1962 and 1966. As the population was increasing at more than 3 percent, per capita income declined during this period— a clear demonstration of the economic aspect of the Brazilian crisis.

But this crisis was not limited to the economy. It was also political. Without concerning ourselves greatly with the causes at this moment, we will indicate the political elements of the crisis, limiting ourselves to the two most representative ones, which include the other factors. They are the lack of political representation and military interventionism.

One of the fundamental objectives of any democratic system is to be representative. There is no democracy without representation, nor is

TABLE 5.1
Net Domestic Product by Types of Activity
(annual growth rates for given periods, in percentages)

| Activity | 1956-62 | 1962-66 | 1961-62 | 1962-63 | 1963-64 | 1964-65 | 1963-66* |
|---|---|---|---|---|---|---|---|
| Agriculture | 5.7 | 2.4 | 5.5 | 1.0 | 1.3 | 13.8 | -5.7 |
| Industry | 10.7 | 2.3 | 8.3 | 0.1 | 5.5 | -3.6 | 7.6 |
| Mining | 10.8 | 19.4 | 1.5 | 18.4 | 22.4 | 21.4 | 14.6 |
| Manufacturing | 10.8 | 1.8 | 8.1 | -0.3 | 5.1 | -4.7 | 7.5 |
| Electricity | 9.8 | 5.3 | 11.3 | 2.6 | 7.2 | 4.1 | 7.3 |
| Construction | 5.4 | -4.4 | 0.6 | 1.3 | 2.2 | -24.0 | 6.4 |
| Transportation | 8.4 | 3.7 | 6.7 | 6.2 | 3.6 | 0.8 | 4.4 |
| Other Services | 4.5 | 3.1 | 3.2 | 2.3 | 3.0 | 3.7 | 3.6 |
| TOTAL | 6.7 | 2.6 | 5.3 | 1.6 | 3.1 | 3.8 | 1.9 |

*Preliminary estimates. Cf. "A Evolução Recente da Economia Brasileira,"
Desenvolvimento e Conjuntura, April 1967, p. 25.

Source: 1956-65 based on unpublished materials by the Fundação Getúlio Vargas.
1966: estimate made by the CEPAL/BNDE Center based on various sources as well
as its own studies.

there liberty without participation in major decisions. One cannot speak of government by the people unless all groups and social classes, all political and ideological currents, have a voice in government.

Lack of representation is at the heart of many of Brazil's political problems. One illustration is the simple fact that more than half of the adult population in Brazil does not have the right to vote. Recently this problem has become more serious, and the lack of representation has moved to center stage, to the extent that the gulf widens between the governing and the governed.

This situation does not originate merely from the fact that after 1964 the Brazilian government was the result of an armed movement rather than of a popular election. No doubt this fact is relevant, but it is not necessarily the most important one. Nor is it sufficient to point out that this movement was more of a coup than a revolution: It did not involve all the people, nor represent structural modifications in the country's economic and social systems, nor result from armed conflict. The Congress, which had never been representative, served only to rubber-stamp government proposals after 1964. On the other hand, the executive assumed a stronger, more active role, legislating by decree. It represented only a very small segment of the broad socioeconomic spectrum. The result was a government with practically no representation, from which entire social groups are absent, conspicuously the working classes, students, the left (from the most moderate—nonradical labor groups—to the most radical), and the industrial entrepreneurs.

The other major facet of the political crisis is the emergence of dominating militarism. A professional national army arose as a powerful and organized force only after the Paraguayan War in 1865, when it took the place of the national militia. In contrast to the latter, which was no more than an unstable assemblage of military groups organized on a semifeudal basis under the control of local *coronéis,* the army has from its beginning been an organized and stable force, recruited primarily from the middle class.

Its first large-scale political action resulted in the creation of the Republic in 1889. Since then, the army has played a very important role in Brazilian political life. After Prudente de Morais's presidency (1894–1898), the army assumed a special role in Brazil, expressed by a form of military tutelage. Originally the army and the Catholic Church were the two great organized forces in the country. This fact guaranteed the army great strength, but it could also count on the force of arms, concentrating its power immensely. Naturally army officers were aware of their position, and in consequence adopted a militarist attitude. Yet for various reasons that it is inappropriate to discuss here, this militarism did not take on domineering or interventionist characteristics, but was always moderate and tutelary in its action. The members of the military considered themselves the guardians of the country. Governing the country was the responsibility of the politicians, linked to the interests of the *fazendeiros*, big exporters and importers, bankers, and industrialists. But the military remained vigilant, arbitrating conflicts, moderating disputes, exercising its guardianship. This was the role conferred upon it by the power it represented and the position it occupied as relatively remote from immediate political and economic interests. This type of military tutelage, which tended to transform military officers into the guardians of the constitution, democracy, and public morality, did not bring particularly negative consequences to the country. The military's ideology, often characterized by a moderate nationalism, was usually exercised in favor of the progressive forces in the country. And after completing an act of more direct guardianship the army always withdrew.

This situation underwent radical change after the Revolution of 1964. Militarism as guardianship ceased to be the dominant concept, and the military not only intervened in conformity with its traditional role as guardian, but also resolved to remain in power. This was a decisive change, one that called into further question the already weak democratic system and helped to define the political crisis through which Brazil was passing.

## Medium-Range Causes of the Economic Crisis

It would be naive to think that the Brazilian crisis had only recent causes or that its origins lay entirely in the government of Castello Branco. Any study would at least have to consider the medium-range causes and should also deal with the long-range causes. The latter include the developments already reviewed in the preceding chapters: the Brazilian industrial revolution, the emergence of new social classes, changes in the equilibrium of the political forces and the resulting conflicts, the emergence of political ideology, the emergence of the left as an autonomous though still weak force, the dominance of the international scene by autarchic powers such as the United States, etc. This section therefore focuses on the medium range, on those causes that date back not more than five or ten years from the period we are studying.

### Personal Causes

Two factors that can be termed personal are generally pointed out as causes of the crisis: the inflationary actions of the Kubitschek government and the political insecurity and administrative incapacity of the Goulart government. The first of these can be accepted only with many reservations. In the first place, the Brazilian economic crisis, which has already been defined as basically a recession, should not be confused with inflation. Doubtless inflation increased at a more rapid pace in the period under study, constituted a serious economic problem for the country, and was one of the causes of the reduction in the rate of Brazil's economic development. But it was not the principal cause of that reduction and was even less the cause of the recession of 1962–1966.

Second, it is only a half-truth to attribute to the Kubitschek government responsibility for this inflationary process. In 1956, 1957, and 1958 the inflation rate remained the same as in previous years. According to the cost of living index for Guanabara (Rio de Janeiro) published by the Getúlio Vargas Foundation, the rate of price increase from December to December had been 26.2 percent in 1954, and in 1956, 1957, and 1958, respectively, 21.2 percent, 13.4 percent, and 17.3 percent. In 1959, however, inflation received a sudden impulse and prices rose 52 percent. This would appear to confirm that the Kubitschek government was responsible for the inflationary surge. However, in the following year the inflation rate dropped radically, to 23.8 percent. It was only after the end of Kubitschek's term that inflation began to rise again. It is thus apparent that the Kubitschek government's role in the acceleration of inflation, while real, especially in 1959, was not so great as is often claimed. On the other hand, it was during this period that Brazil experienced its greatest period of accelerated economic growth, and that Brazilian industrial development was consolidated. Thus, it does not seem that this period is particularly relevant to the causes of the Brazilian economic crisis.

However, the same cannot be said of the Goulart government. This was truly a period of political insecurity, and it is hardly necessary to point out that in such a situation capitalists withdraw and reduce their investments. It was also a period of administrative inefficiency, of plans initiated and left unfinished, of a total prevalence of politics over administration and economics. There is no doubt that the crisis stemmed from this period to some extent.

Nevertheless, if the origins of the Brazilian crisis had been only in the Goulart government, then a recovery should have been evident when that government was toppled, or soon after. However, that is not what occurred. True, there were vague outlines of a recovery, but they were very weak. Soon the crisis returned, in dramatic proportions in early 1965, and more moderately throughout the year. What does this indicate? The personal causes help to round out an understanding of the situation but are far from explaining it fully. As will be seen below, the fulcrum of the crisis lay in structural factors.

Three medium-range causes related to Brazil's economic structure basically explain the economic crisis: the diminution of investment opportunities, limitation of export (and therefore import) capacities, and inflation.

## Diminution of Investment Opportunities

The decrease in investment opportunities was the most important medium-range structural cause of the Brazilian crisis. As long as investment opportunities were limited, as long as there were no prospects for high profits with full possibilities for expansion, private investment was insufficient. National entrepreneurs and foreign investors either stopped investing or drastically reduced their investments, and without investment there is no development. The clear reduction of investment opportunities in Brazil after 1962 could be illustrated with precision if statistics were available for corporations' average real profit rates. As such figures do not exist, the fact that a reduction of investment opportunities really did occur can be established only by means of reading company balance sheets and reports and newspaper interviews with industrialists, as well as from personal experience.

The facts can be verified in Table 5.2, which shows that the percentage of gross capital formation (gross investments) fell from around 16.5 percent of the national income at the beginning of the decade to 10.7 percent and 12.8 percent, respectively, in 1965 and 1966. The responsibility for this drop, as the table shows, lies completely with the private sector. Whereas the government maintained its level of investments, the private sector, which at the beginning of the decade had invested between 11 percent and 12 percent of national income (gross domestic product), reduced its share to 5.5 percent and 7.8 percent in 1965 and 1966. Three interrelated factors directly contributed to this reduction in investment: the reduction of import-substitution possibilities, the lack of domestic markets, and idle capacity.

*Reduction of Import-Substitution Possibilities.* The reduction in the number of import-substitution possibilities is probably the most serious problem that Brazilian industrial development has had to confront in recent years. From its beginnings until its consolidation in the 1950s, Brazil's industrial development was carried out basically through import substitution. The new industrial enterprises began their activities with a captive market that had been opened up by the importation of manufactured goods now barred from the country because of tariff and/ or exchange policies. Only after having saturated the traditional market did these enterprises endeavor to expand the domestic market by seeking out sectors that had not previously been reached by imported products. It was this policy of import substitution that allowed Brazil to continue

TABLE 5.2
Macroeconomic Relations

|  | 1959 | 1960 | 1961 | 1962 | 1963 | 1964 | 1965 | 1966 |
|---|---|---|---|---|---|---|---|---|
| Government Consumption/Y* | 13.8 | 15.3 | 15.5 | 15.5 | 16.3 | 15.4 | 13.7 | 13.8 |
| Gross Capital Formation/Y | 15.9 | 16.5 | 17.1 | 16.3 | 16.5 | 14.3 | 10.7 | 12.8 |
| Govt. Capital Formation/Y | 4.7 | 5.2 | 4.4 | 5.7 | 4.6 | 4.8 | 5.2 | 5.0 |
| Private Sector Capital Formation | 11.2 | 11.3 | 12.2 | 10.6 | 11.9 | 9.5 | 5.5 | 7.8 |
| Imports**/Y | 8.5 | 8.4 | 8.6 | 8.1 | 12.6 | 7.8 | 7.5 | 8.2 |
| Exports**/Y | 7.4 | 6.9 | 7.9 | 6.2 | 12.0 | 9.1 | 10.4 | 9.3 |

*Gross Domestic Product
**Includes exports and imports of both goods and services.

Sources: Computed from figures of the Centro de Contas Nacionais da Fundação Getúlio Vargas. Taken from Werner Baer and Andra Maneschi, "Substituição de Importações, Estagnaçao e Mudança Estrutural," Revista Brasileira de Economia, 23, no. 1 (March 1969), p. 74.

to develop, even without increasing its exports proportionally. But after the 1950s a reduction in import-substitution possibilities occurred, much as Celso Furtado observed in *Dialética do Desenvolvimento.*[4]

Until the end of the 1950s it was relatively easy to start a new industrial enterprise in Brazil. All that was necessary was to find some manufactured product that had been imported, acquire the know-how to make it, either by paying royalties or by merely copying it, obtain the necessary initial capital and financing, and begin business. Today the situation is very different. Brazil continues to import a wide range of products for which import substitution is still viable in theory. In practice, however, there is another reality. By examining the list of imports, one can see that the products Brazil continues to import are those it would be difficult to produce efficiently in Brazil or else (and this is the major problem) those that demand huge investments that national entrepreneurs, even the larger ones, are unable to finance. The solution is no longer as simple as merely raising trade barriers. For example, take the case of urea, an important raw material and fertilizer that Brazil imports in great quantity. There would be substantial difficulties in producing urea in Brazil. To begin with, domestic production would necessitate an investment so large that no financial group in Brazil could handle it. Second, in order to be efficient, urea production must be on a large scale, far surpassing the needs of the national economy. This difficulty could be overcome by exporting the surplus, notwithstanding all the difficulties that such an operation would entail. But the financial problem of the large investment necessary for its production is really the essential point, well illustrating the reduction of import-substitution possibilities.

*Lack of Markets and the Fall in Real Wages.* The second and third causes of the diminution of investment opportunities—the lack of a market and idle capacity—are interrelated. Decreased investment opportunities are a function equally of the lack of markets and of idle capacity, which in turn is directly related to the lack of markets.

Obviously, except for what is strictly necessary to replace worn-out equipment, companies will stop investing when they see no prospects for introducing new products or increasing production. This problem arises only after import substitution for a given article has been achieved, after the entire traditional market for what was formerly imported has been satisfied by the national industry. This process generally takes some time, allowing various enterprises to become established in order to supply the market. Until that moment there is no lack of markets. But once the so-called traditional market is satisfied, the question of how to widen the market arises. If the domestic product is cheaper than its imported counterpart because it does not include tariffs or the cost of international transportation, the initial expansion will be easy. But later (barring increased demand brought about by such dynamic factors as changes in style, the introduction of revolutionary technological innovations, advertising, etc.) the demand for the product will tend to grow in proportion to the growth of the population and of its purchasing power, given that the income-elasticity of demand for the product is equal to 1. That is, demand will grow to the extent that per capita income and real average wage increase. If the income-elasticity of demand for industrial products is a little greater than 1 (as in fact was the case in Brazil) then demand will tend to increase a little more quickly than income, but not much more.

Thus, in order for Brazilian industrial enterprises to expand faster than the rate of population growth, real average wages would have to keep up with the growth of the per capita product—or at least, if the income-elasticity of demand is greater than 1, the average real wage would have to increase by at least the same growth rate as per capita income. Otherwise there would be insufficient markets for industrial output.

This was the phenomenon that began to occur after 1958 in Brazil. Whereas the per capita product continued to grow, real wages fell. This fall resulted in a distribution of income less favorable to the consumer class, while output and, more particularly, productive capacity were increasing. Unfortunately the statistics concerning real wages are incomplete. The only satisfactory data concerns the real minimum wage. This shows that the real minimum wage (in terms of prices in March 1964, when the minimum wage was established at 66,000 old cruzeiros), defined as the average of the real minimum wage in June and December, fell from 85,374 old cruzeiros in 1958 to 54,405 old cruzeiros in 1965 and 52,437 old cruzeiros in 1966. Thus there was a 38 percent drop in the real minimum wage between 1958 and 1966.

It is true that this represents the extremes. Table 5.3 presents the real minimum wage deflated by the cost of living in Guanabara for 1956 through 1966. It shows that the drop between 1961 and 1962 was severe and exactly coincided with the year in which economic development began to slow down. It is very unlikely that this correlation was merely coincidental. Despite intensive state intervention in the economy, Brazil is still basically a capitalist country. Thus the dynamic factor in its development is demand, not supply. In terms of aggregate demand, it was consumption rather than investment that created the dynamic forces. Investment could still be carried on for some time after consumption fell, but when reduced consumption persisted, as it did in Brazil because of reduced real wages, investments would also have to be reduced.

TABLE 5.3
Real Minimum Wage in Guanabara
(in relation to March 1965 prices)

| Year | Minimum Real Wage (in old cruzeiros) |
|---|---|
| 1956 | 71,591 |
| 1957 | 72,205 |
| 1958 | 85,374 |
| 1959 | 73,879 |
| 1960 | 80,910 |
| 1961 | 79,906 |
| 1962 | 61,603 |
| 1963 | 55,019 |
| 1964 | 57,753 |
| 1965 | 54,405 |
| 1966 | 52,437 |

Note: The figure for each year is the average
of the real minimum wage in June and
December of that year.

Source: Fundação Getúlio Vargas.

The average real minimum wage from 1956 to 1961 was 77,311 old cruzeiros; for the four following years, it was 57,195 old cruzeiros. The drop is extraordinary, about 26 percent. In other words, from the first period to the second the buying power of workers earning the minimum wage fell by about one-fourth. Aside from the social injustice involved, the effects of such a phenomenon on the economy were highly negative.[5]

This reduction in the real wage did not affect only those earning the minimum wage. The median wage in the manufacturing industry in Guanabara, in 1955 prices, fell from 2,861 and 2,790 old cruzeiros, respectively, in April and November of 1958, to 2,822 and 2,613 old cruzeiros in April and November of 1962. Nor was 1958 the year with the highest real wage for manufacturing industry workers. The decrease in real wages of workers in wholesale commerce in Guanabara was even more abrupt. Using 1955 prices, in April and November of 1958, respectively, real wages averaged 3,761 and 3,708 old cruzeiros, as compared to 2,399 and 3,285 old cruzeiros in 1962.

Thus, there was an effective drop in real salaries after 1962 that was to have negative consequences on consumption. The national product, however, continued to grow, though at a slower pace. Thus enterprises did not have a sufficient market for their output and eventually began to reduce their investments. This problem was soon to be aggravated by the Castello Branco government's wage policy, which sought to reduce wage workers' share in the national income even more.

The backdrop of this wage reduction was the concentration of income provoked by continually more capital-intensive investments, conditioned by technology imported from the developed countries. This technology seeks to economize on labor power, which is precisely the abundant factor in underdeveloped countries. The results of this imported technology are a lower capacity to absorb labor power and, consequently, unemployment, lower wages, reductions in purchasing power, and a lack of markets.

The lack of markets is also related to Brazil's agricultural structure,[6] which is marked by deep disequilibria between very large estates and very small farms. This fact is closely related to low agricultural productivity, poor utilization of land in the large estates, rural unemployment, and even unemployment.

These phenomena are not new to the Brazilian economy. They have always existed, and were even more pronounced in the past. The industrial revolution and the emergence of a strong domestic market created the opportunity (especially in São Paulo and adjacent states) for a rationalization of agriculture through capitalist criteria of production. There was also considerable progress in agricultural methods, as well as in the marketing of agricultural products, although this function still continued to be one of the critical points in Brazilian agriculture, dominated by speculative intermediaries and oligarchically organized industrial purchasers.

Such progress, together with the very vitality of Brazilian agriculture, was an essential factor in Brazil's economic development from 1930 to 1961. During this period agriculture was always relegated to a secondary role. In addition, the economic policy of the governments of this time was based on the transfer of income from the agricultural sector, particularly coffee, to the industrial sector. This was the only viable policy for the industrialization process in which Brazil was involved. It is an established and well-known fact that industrialization generally begins in a given country only through a transfer of income from the traditional agricultural sectors to the modern sectors.

In order for this development to occur, however, agriculture must be resilient enough to survive the transfer of income and also be able to free labor power (through a rural exodus) to be employed in industrial activities and related services. At the same time, agriculture must continue to increase production in order to meet the increased demand for agricultural products brought about by increases in population and income. If agriculture does not have such resilience it will eventually become a serious obstacle to the process of economic development. Aside from the appearance of structural inflation, it will be necessary to import foodstuffs, diverting precious foreign exchange resources away from the importation of machinery and equipment.

Brazilian agriculture has the necessary resiliency to support this double impact—the transfer of income and the loss of labor power. There are indications, however, that the limits of this resiliency are being reached.[7] In addition (this being the most serious aspect of the problem) the import-substitution phase with its captive markets for new investments no longer exists. As a result, agriculture has been called upon to play a new role in the Brazilian economy: that of a market.

This is a role Brazilian agriculture has never played because the extreme inequality of the agrarian structure would not permit it. Agrarian reform, always promised and always hoped for, has never been carried out. During the João Goulart government a frantic and dramatic political battle revolved around this issue. Reform continued to be proclaimed after the Revolution of 1964. Until it is carried out, however, it will be difficult to incorporate the two-thirds of the Brazilian people who are alienated from the national market. Comprehensive agrarian reform and an effective and revolutionary literacy campaign are the two most important conditions for an extraordinary growth in the Brazilian domestic market, which in turn would open new and extraordinary perspectives for the Brazilian economy. Brazil still has a frontier economy. This frontier is not geographical, but consists rather in the limits on the market, which is hindered by the country's archaic agrarian structure.

Obviously there are other problems besides agrarian reform and literacy that must be dealt with in order for agriculture to cease being a stumbling block to Brazilian economic development to the extent that it marginalizes its workers. There are problems related to transportation, rural energy, the development of cultivation techniques, mechanization, the introduction of rational methods of production, and the organization of labor and systems of distribution. All these factors, however, ought to be considered within the perspective of the inadequate and injust agrarian structure that still survives in Brazil. During the 1960s, when the lack of markets for industrial output became a crucial problem for the country, the agrarian structure was the most serious obstacle to the integration of the rural population into the domestic market.

*Idle Capacity.* Idle capacity is related to weak markets. If the market lacks dynamic force, enterprises will reduce their investments and development will lose some of its impulse. The result is idle capacity. It was not created, as might be expected, because the economy entered a recession after a great development. Rather, it occurred because enterprises continued to invest for a while despite the increasing weakness of the market, and the country continued to develop. Inflation, provoking an artificial demand, made the rate of interest generally negative and complicated the calculations of profitability, leading businesses to continue to invest when in fact economic conditions favoring investment no longer existed. Thus idle capacity was created in various sectors, particularly in the consumer goods industry. Obviously, this idle capacity aggravated the lack of investment opportunities. Even though the market began to increase again and demand presented a new impulse, it was first necessary to reduce idle capacity before investors were again disposed to invest.

## Limitations on Import Capacity

After the diminution of investment opportunities, the second medium-range cause of the Brazilian economic crisis was the limitation of export capacity (and, thus, of import capacity). This cause is related to the first in the sense that difficulties in importing raw materials and especially equipment reduce investment opportunities, because of the concomitant rise in the price of foreign exchange. It is true that limitations on the import of equipment create obstacles to investment, rather than directly reducing it, because investment opportunity exists internally. In one way or another, however, one of the fundamental causes of the Brazilian economic crisis was to be found in the realm of international trade.

The limitations of Brazilian import capacity can be illustrated simply. Average annual imports, which were $1,400 million in 1950–1954, fell to $1,360 million in 1955–1961, while the domestic product was increasing by 6.1 percent per year. The result was a reduction in the import coefficient, which went from 12.6 percent in the first period to 8.6 percent in the latter period.[8] The situation did not improve, and in fact worsened. In 1964, Brazilian imports were only $1,263 million. In 1965 and 1966 there was an improvement in Brazil's balance of payments, due in part to increased exports, but principally to the reduction of imports provoked by the crisis.

The 31 percent drop (from 12.6 percent to 8.6 percent) in the import coefficient demonstrates that import substitution was the escape valve that allowed the country to continue to develop despite the drop in import capacity. But when the possibilities of import substitution were drastically reduced it became necessary for import capacity to begin to grow again. However, as can be seen, this did not happen. Import capacity continued to decline, creating an extremely difficult situation for the Brazilian economy. There was an encouraging recovery in 1965, but the general picture was still not very heartening.

The limitation in import capacity was naturally related to a parallel limitation in export capacity. This in turn had classic causes such as the tendency toward a deterioration in underdeveloped countries' terms of trade, the income-elasticity of international demand for agricultural products (among which coffee is an outstanding case), growing international competition as a result of the entrance of new producers into the market (as again is the case with coffee in relation to the African countries), and the introduction of artificial substitutes such as the synthetic fibers that have reduced the international demand for cotton. These general causes were beyond Brazil's control. In addition, because Brazilian economic development was for the most part accomplished through import substitution, the Brazilian government neglected to stimulate exports of manufactured products to its traditional markets and to Latin America, and of primary products as well as manufactured products to new markets in Eastern Europe, Africa, and Asia.

This neglect is why the gap widened between exports and necessary imports, which during the mid-1960s tended to grow proportionally to the increase in national output. There is an important reservation, however, in relation to the effects of the limitation of export capacity. During the worsening of the economic crisis in 1965 and 1966, this limitation ceased to be, in the short range, an obstacle to development. Especially in 1965, Brazilian imports were drastically reduced, not because import capacity was limited but rather because the demand for imports was sharply lowered by the crisis. To the extent that enterprises reduced their output, they also reduced their imports of raw materials. And the increase in idle capacity discouraged the importation of equipment. The result was that during these years limitation in import capacity ceased to be a cause of the crisis. After 1966, however, Brazilian exports began to climb, reaching $1,890 million in 1968. Nevertheless, a limited import capacity continued to be one of the major challenges facing the Brazilian economy.

## Inflation

Finally, inflation figures as one of the medium-range causes of the Brazilian economic crisis. After maintaining for many years an annual rate of about 20 percent, inflation accelerated, starting in 1961, just as the economy was entering its crisis. At this point the discussion between monetarists and structuralists as to the causes of inflation began to become meaningless. As long as inflation was in the range of 20 percent it was still possible to seek its origins in foreign trade (that is, in a rise in the price of the dollar because of the chronic tendency toward disequilibrium between imports, essential to a country in the midst of industrialization, and exports, still based in the traditional agrarian economy); in the insufficient supply of agricultural products for domestic consumption; and in other points of constriction of demand. The issuing of money was then more a consequence than a cause of inflation. In the mid-1960s, however, it became clear that Brazil's inflation had changed its character.

*From Demand-Pull Inflation to Cost-Push Inflation.* During the first phase of the Brazilian industrial revolution, which ended in 1961, one could speak neither of insufficient demand nor of predominantly cost-push inflation. But the beginning of the Brazilian crisis was marked by a change in the causes of inflation from the pull of a dynamic demand to the push of rising costs. Ignácio Rangel, in *A Inflação Brasileira*, was the first to perceive this. This book, despite its many theoretical imprecisions, is doubtless one of the most important Brazilian books on inflation. The author's extraordinary imagination and sharp observation allow him to open up new perspectives on the inflationary phenomenon in Brazil:

> This missing beat in the evaluations of both these theories is idle capacity. Both schools ignore it openly or implicitly. . . .The problem is that . . . both the structuralists and the monetarists . . . place a hypothetical insufficiency of supply at the heart of the problem in relation to a supposedly excess demand, whereas the truth is that it is the level of demand that is insufficient—unable to assure a satisfactory degree of utilization for existing productive potential—precisely because of inflation.[9]

Therefore inflation stems not from demand, but rather from costs. The function of inflation is to stimulate demand, given the existence of idle capacity.

Further on Rangel gives a more precise definition to the function of inflation in the Brazilian economy:

> Once the areas institutionally prepared to absorb new investments are saturated, and before new fields are ready, the profitability of new investments declines, reducing the system's total investments. In other words, a tendency toward economic depression gathers strength that would pass from potential to reality if investment were really allowed to decline. An elevated inflation rate is one of the methods by which the economy resists this tendency, sustaining the system's rate of investments. . . .[10]

Thus inflation "is the economy's defense mechanism against the tendency toward reduction in the rate of investment."[11] Continuing, Rangel shows how inflation has historically acted on the economic system in its role as a defense against economic depression:

(*a*) initially, as an efficient means for the accumulation of resources by
the state, enabling it through its own expenditures to increase total
expenditures during the initial phase of the industrialization process; (*b*)
later, in the end of the consumer goods phase of the import-substitution
process, when exchange rates were frozen, as an efficient tool to raise the
marginal efficiency of capital, by reducing the price of fundamental fixed
cost items (imported equipment) in relation to the principal variable cost
items (labor power and domestic raw materials) and as a result inducing
an increase in private investments; (*c*) in the end of the phase of industrialization linked to the substitution of production goods (after Kubitschek's *Plano de Metas*), as an efficient means to impede the condensation
of surplus value in monetary or "liquid" form—which would imply
economic depression—causing it to invest indiscriminately in either durable
consumer goods or capital goods.[12]

These relatively extensive quotations are taken from Rangel's work
not only because of their intrinsic importance, but also because that
work presents both an inspiration and a parallel to the ideas that I will
begin to develop in this section on inflation, although there are some
basic divergences. For example, although the structure of rural land
ownership is obviously one cause of the insufficient development of the
domestic market in Brazil, I do not consider this as important as does
Rangel in explaining the causes of idle capacity and insufficiency of
demand. As has been shown above, the problem of idle capacity must
also be considered in relation to the narrowing of opportunities for
import substitution and the concentration of income.

*The Causes of Cost-Push Inflation.* The economic crisis was defined
by an increase in idle capacity. The process of import substitution that
marked Brazil's industrial development between 1930 and 1961 allowed
the realization of industrial investments without a concomitant and
proportional growth of the domestic market. Enterprises found already
existing markets that had previously been supplied by imports. But
when these preexisting markets were satisfied, businesses began to depend
on the activities of the domestic market, because the concept of an
international market was beyond the grasp of the majority of the
entrepreneurs.

It has just been shown how the Brazilian domestic market in absolute
terms did not grow in proportion to the country's economic development.
Aside from wage policies that tended to reduce wage workers' buying
power to the benefit of the capitalist classes, after 1955 there was also
an additional process of income concentration caused by the move from
the first phase of the import-substitution process, characterized by the
installation of light consumer industries, to the beginning of the second
phase, characterized by an emphasis on equipment production, durable

consumer goods, and chemical products. The investments necessary for this type of production are much more capital-intensive than in the case of the light consumer goods industry. The technology developed by the industrialized countries seeks to economize on labor as much as possible. The nature of certain products facilitates the attainment of this objective: In the capital goods industry, the durable consumer goods industry, and, especially, the chemical industry, the capital-labor ratio tends to be considerably higher than in the light consumer goods industries typical of the first phase of the import-substitution process. The result was a tendency toward an even greater concentration of income than that already defined by the drop in real wages.

Income concentration and the relative reduction of the consumer market were aggravated to the extent that capital-intensive investments became dominant, the economy becoming increasingly less capable of absorbing the available supply of labor resulting from population growth and the rural exodus. Unemployment thus increased. Between 1950 and 1960, whereas the urban population was growing 5.4% per year, industrial employment increased only 2.6%. At the same time, the industrial sector's share in the GNP rose from 20% to 29%, while the proportion of the population actively employed in industry fell from 14% to 13%. At that time, however, the tertiary sector was still relatively capable of absorbing part of this unemployed labor, and another part adopted the activities and behavior typical of hidden unemployment. Open unemployment was avoided. During the 1960s, however, the problem got worse and open industrial unemployment arose, not only because of the economy's incapacity to absorb the approximately one million new workers who annually appeared on the Brazilian labor market, but also because of the absolute reduction of employment in various industrial sectors.

Given the inherent tendency of the capitalist system to create unemployment at the same time as it concentrates income in periods of prosperity, such as the late 1950s in Brazil, there is nothing strange in the fact that industrial sector after industrial sector found itself with idle capacity to the extent to which possibilities of import-substitution had been exhausted. It was precisely this idle capacity, resulting fundamentally from the concentration of income, that was to become one of the mainstays of Brazilian inflation in the 1960s, and that at least temporarily rendered obsolete the dispute between monetarists and structuralists.

In addition to the concentration of income and idle capacity there is another factor that helps explain the inflationary process: the monopolistic nature of the Brazilian market. We need not dwell on this factor, because it is very obvious. Oligopolies and cartels prevail in

Brazil. The concentration of income is at the same time cause and
result of a permanent process of economic concentration. On the other
hand, the invasion of the national economy's industrial manufacturing
sector by foreign capital during the 1950s gave a large impetus to the
creation of trusts. The result is that many Brazilian industrial sectors,
including those that fill special orders for the government, are organized
in an oligopolistic manner. The marketing and distribution of agricultural
products are also notoriously oligopolistic. And the oligopolists as well
as the oligopsonists (even those less structured and defined as such)
organize easily into cartels, making any true price competition unthink-
able.

Obviously there were other inflationary pressures. The large surplus
in the trade balance in 1965 forced the government to issue a great
quantity of money to pay the national exporters, at the same time as
they were collecting exchange credits abroad. The enormous deficits of
the state railroads and shipping enterprises, in part caused by excessively
low fares and freight rates, also occasioned money issues and were thus
a cause of inflation. After the Revolution of 1964 the situation reversed,
and a drastic increase in rates contributed to cost inflation.

*The Inflationary Process.* With the causes thus defined, it is easy to
understand the inflationary process that affected Brazil after the beginning
of the crisis. Enterprises, operating with idle capacity, saw their costs
rise and their profits diminish. The marginal efficiency of capital was
rapidly decreasing, to the extent that various economic sectors were one
by one finding themselves with idle capacity. In self-defense, businesses
immediately began to (*a*) raise prices, (*b*) pressure the government to
increase its purchases from the private sector, and (*c*) pressure the
government and the banking system to increase credit.

Price increases during an epoch of insufficient demand were possible
only because of the oligopolistic nature of the market. In face of a
demand that was growing inadequately, if at all, as well as an inflationary
process already at full steam, which had until then been based on excess
demand, price increases were the obvious solution. In this way enterprises
defended themselves against already existing inflation and also against
the fall in demand. The oligopolized and cartelized market both protected
against the threat of price wars and made such a policy viable. But to
the extent that price hikes increased above the current rate of inflation,
they were no longer merely a response to increased costs, but became
a cause of the acceleration of inflation.

Pressuring the government to increase spending (despite the rhetoric
of private initiative) was another perfectly natural defense mechanism
of the private sector. Faced with a sharp decline in private consumption,
businesses had no alternative but to try to convince the government to

increase purchases. For instance, the coffee growers pressured the government to buy their surplus production at the highest possible prices, and the government readily yielded. An inherent aspect of the development process of underdeveloped countries today is the increase in government's responsibilities, to the extent that the *laissez-faire* state has become obsolete, because the private sector has shown itself incapable of assuming primary responsibility for development, and economic planning and increasing state intervention in the economy have become universally accepted realities.

The growth of government spending brought about by private sector pressures, without a corresponding increase in tax revenues, immediately provoked a deficit in the government budget and consequently new issues of money. It should be pointed out that the autonomous increase in private sector prices, especially in those areas that directly supplied the government (which are among those most easily organized into cartels), caused inflation directly but also aggravated the governmental deficit even further. Thus the government, which had begun each fiscal year with the goal of balancing the budget, was pressured to buy more than it had planned and at prices higher than it had foreseen, and ended up being forced to issue great amounts of money in order to solve its budget problems.

Finally, in order to defend themselves against existing inflation, enterprises pressured the government and the banking system for more credit. Greater credit was fundamentally important to them for two separate reasons. First, the largest possible volume of credit would tend to reduce the necessity for working capital, particularly short-term liquid assets minus inventories. In an already inflationary situation, in addition to the price increases needed to defend real profit from inflation, making it diverge as little as possible from apparent book profit, it was also necessary to reduce to the minimum (or, if possible, make negative) the difference between short-term liquid assets such as cash and accounts receivable (but not including inventory) and accounts payable. In other words, it was important to reduce to the minimum needed for security the ratio between "quick" current assets and current liabilities, because in the final analysis what really suffers the effect of inflation in an enterprise is the difference between cash and receivables on one side and accounts payable—that is, liquid assets minus inventory—on the other side.[13] It is natural, therefore, that businesses did everything in their power to increase their credit. To the extent that they succeeded, the economy suffered immediate inflationary effects.

Second, the credit obtained implied a negative real interest rate, in spite of carrying the nominally higher interest charged by the banking system, which benefited from its privileged position within an inflationary system. The level of investments in a country depends on the level of income and, given this, on the relation between the marginal efficiency of capital and the market's current interest rate. In the depression in which businesses found themselves, after a long period of prosperity, at the time when the Brazilian crisis arose, the marginal efficiency of capital, that is, the profit expectation, was very low. Only a negative interest rate, made possible by inflation, would allow them to continue to invest, and even then at the risk of increasing their idle capacity. The alternative for new investments (other than, of course, the purchase of foreign exchange) was to increase the liquidity of each enterprise, but, as has been demonstrated, this solution was totally unfeasible in an inflationary situation.

The corporations then pressured the banking system for more credit, in addition to working out new forms of financing with private financers. This amplification of credit, added to the autonomous price increases already mentioned and the pressure put on the government to increase its expenditures, was transformed into the basic cause of inflation in the mid-1960s.

*Corporate Profits and Cost-Push Inflation.* The entire Brazilian inflation in the mid-1960s was basically cost-push inflation. When the Costa e Silva government took power, its team of economists under the leadership of Delfim Netto immediately and very correctly defined the inflation as being primarily a matter of costs. However, the team did not define these costs very completely. Naturally, wages were not mentioned. Although they are a typical cause of cost-push inflation, they were on the decline in real terms at the time in Brazil. Three costs were pointed out: excessive interest rates, the rise in public service rates, and the increase in the tax burden. Doubtless these costs are partially responsible for inflation. However, the most important cost, whose increase constituted the basis of the entire inflationary process, was not pointed out: corporate profit.

It is necessary to remember that profit is nothing more than a type of cost. Like interest, although in different terms, profit can be considered as the cost of capital itself. When enterprises, faced with crisis, automatically began to raise their prices at a time when demand was diminishing instead of growing, they were directly provoking cost-push inflation as they sought to defend their profit rate. It is clear that cost-push inflation is possible only in monopolistic situations. The government naturally had a monopoly and thus contributed to cost-push inflation by increasing the tax burden in order to deal with the increased public expenditures demanded by business. The latter also generally had monopolistic market conditions and was thus able to provoke an inflation of costs by trying to prevent a reduction in profits. This is not to say that inflation tended to make large profits for the entrepreneurs after 1961. On the contrary, during the crisis by all indications the real profit rate declined abruptly, when it did not become negative. What the corporations sought through autonomous price increases was simply to maintain their rates of relative profit so that they would not be totally destroyed.

Viewed in these terms, with profit having been the fundamental cost in the cost inflation that became dominant in Brazil during the 1960s, the problem of the interest rates charged by the banking system can be understood more easily. In the first phase of galloping inflation the banks, which received deposits at nominal interest rates, demanded an elevated rate from businesses. The latter paid because even so, the real interest rate was negative for them. Thus we see a typical case of demand inflation. The banks charged such high rates, and were not very concerned about their own operating costs, because the enterprises' demand for credit was so enormous. When the inflation rate began to decline, the real interest rates went from negative to positive. The demand for credit tended to diminish. It would have been natural for the banks to reduce their interest rates, in order to increase the number of applications. Because of their high costs, however, they were unable to lower rates in proportion to the fall in demand. And even if some of them had been better administered and therefore in a better position to make decisive cuts in their interest rates, they would not have done so because of a tacit agreement among the banks to avoid an interest rate war. Once again it was cost-push inflation, motivated by the profit factor, and made possible by the imperfect organization of the market.

In summary, during the Brazilian crisis, when import-substitution possibilities were severely restricted, enterprises found themselves with growing idle capacity, aggravated by the concentration of income. In order to defend their declining profit rates they began to provoke a cost inflation that was possible because of the monopolistic nature of the market. Thus, during a period of declining demand, they began to raise their prices autonomously, directly provoking inflation, to pressure the government to increase its expenditures, and to pressure both the government and the banking system to provide more credit. The government, in response to these pressures, increased its expenditures and acquired a growing deficit, resolving the situation initially by issuing new currency and later by increasing taxes, which came to be a new focus of cost-push inflation.

Inflation, although it still played a certain role in the Brazilian economic system, could no longer be considered a factor favoring development. Its major merits continued to be the creation of forced savings, the transfer of these savings to the government and to industry, the creation of greater demand (even an artificial one) for durable consumer goods, and the stimulation of investment by resources transferred from wage workers to the private sector, a stimulation made more significant by financing and negative interest rates. On the other hand, these savings were continually diminishing as the classes affected by inflation, especially the workers, succeeded in readjusting their wages more frequently. The distortions in investments provoked by inflation were accentuated. The idle capacity of some industrial sectors increased. Accounting and financial control became more difficult and less precise, to the point that many enterprises effectively lost control. The social injustices provoked by redistribution of income were heightened. Inflation became a permanent focus of social instability. Thus it is typically considered to be a medium-range cause of the Brazilian economic crisis.

Thus there are three general and interrelated medium-range causes of the economic crisis: the lack of investment opportunities, limitations on import capacity, and inflation. Directly related to the reduction of investment opportunities are the narrowing of import-substitution possibilities, idle capacity, the lack of markets, and political insecurity.

## Medium-Range Causes of the Political Crisis

If one were to seek the long-range causes of the political crisis it probably would be necessary to go back to the Paraguayan War, the proclamation of the Republic, and the system of social stratification and political control at that time. Then we would have the agitated 1920s, the Revolution of 1930, the formation of political parties, the passage from the stage of clientele politics to a populist and then to an ideological style, the struggle between industrialism and agriculturalism and its waning importance in the face of the rise of an autonomous left, and finally, the medium-range causes of the crisis. The former elements have already been discussed in Chapter 4, which analyzes the structural transformations in Brazilian politics. Thus the present discussion can be limited to the more recent causes of Brazil's political crisis.

As in the case of the origins of the economic crisis, there are both personal and structural aspects of these causes. In this case the personal causes are probably almost as important as the structural ones. Among these personal causes the resignation of Jânio Quadros is obviously the first. Quadros, who had obtained one of the most remarkable political victories in the history of Brazil, represented many classes and social groups and incarnated the hopes of millions of Brazilians. This president, incapable of resolving the conflicts and inherent contradictions in the coalition of forces that had elected him or of making the compromises the presidency demands, resigned overnight, dramatically deepening the existing crisis of representation in Brazilian politics.

The vice-president, João Goulart, sworn in only after an abortive coup by considerable sectors of the armed forces, succeeded only in making the situation worse. Representativeness was not the only thing lacking in his government. Its instability, its lack of goals and policies, its lack of seriousness and political authenticity, its systematically demagogic approach to problems, the left image it presented—all these factors, which were accentuated with time, could only worsen the political crisis.

Among the medium-range structural causes we will touch briefly upon only three, though this topic is worthy of much more lengthy analysis. First, there is the emergence of the left as an autonomous political force, and its lack of maturity. It was only after the Kubitschek government that the left relegated industrialism and nationalism to a secondary plane and became autonomous in relation to the industrial entrepreneurs. This victory, however, had to be paid for with the price of immaturity. Suddenly the left not only gained autonomy but also won some electoral victories and saw in the federal government a president who would allow it to operate freely—who up to a certain point even opened up some doors for the left. These facts gave rise to a serious error in calculating the left's real political strength, and thus to a policy of agitation that, by the end of the Goulart regime, brought some of the most extreme left groups to begin to prepare for the revolution. Some even imagined that in a country like Brazil, where industrial capitalism was already a well-established fact and where the middle classes were an indisputable political reality, they could gain power and socialize the country by means of a simple government coup.

Second, there was the alarmism of the right. Since the first days of the João Goulart government, alarmism had obviously been the great political strategy used by the most radical elements of the right to bring together the middle classes and the productive classes. The theme was always the same: Communism is knocking at the door, the government is dominated by communists, the communist conspiracy has a foothold and is moving forward. The rightists repeated this so often that finally many left elements also began to believe what the right was saying and acted correspondingly, with the result that alarmism began to have some base in reality.

Third, within the armed forces there was a growing influence of the graduates of the Escola Superior de Guerra (National War College), who were better prepared and better organized than the rest of their colleagues, and who had developed a specific ideology and military strategy based on the inevitability of a third world war and the necessity for Brazil to be linked to the U.S. bloc.

Finally, as a medium-range personal cause, there is the death of President Kennedy, whose progressivism, idealism, and courage had transformed the world political scene and opened new political, economic and social perspectives, particularly for the Latin American countries, and the succession of Lyndon Johnson, who hardened foreign policy, reviving, in the attempt to affirm U.S. continental leadership, methods that had long since died and been buried.

The convergence of these personal and structural factors made possible the Revolution of 1964, whose victory came to be the dominant short-term cause of the political crisis.

## Short-Range Causes of the Economic Crisis

The short-range causes of the economic crisis, and particularly of the recession that began in early 1965, are directly related to the economic policy of the Castello Branco government. This policy will be dealt with here only briefly so as not to give it greater importance than it deserves in relation to the Brazilian crisis.

The *Government Economic Action Program: 1964–66* very correctly placed as its first objective "the acceleration of the country's tempo of economic development," and as the second objective "to progressively contain the inflationary process during 1964 and 1965, aiming for a reasonable price equilibrium after 1966." Then it cited three other objectives. On the next page the priority given to development was even more strongly emphasized in the depiction of a model in which the objective of accelerating development was located in the center and those of countering inflation, assuring full employment, correcting deficits in the balance of payments, and doing something about sectoral and regional inequalities were circled around it as if they were the means toward this goal.[14]

However, there was a contradiction between theory and practice. In the *Economic Action Program* itself there was mention of the "urgency" of combatting inflation.[15] And in reality this policy was given full priority, whereas development was relegated to a secondary position. The whole emphasis of governmental policy, as expressed in the speeches and statements of those responsible for the concrete actions taken, was put on the fight against inflation.

Thus it is necessary to examine the government's economic policy through this prism, which shows a more general contradiction in the very heart of the *Economic Action Program*. The program stated that a "shock treatment" would be inadvisable.[16] Nevertheless it aimed to reduce the rate of inflation, which was 92 percent in 1964, to 25 percent in that year and 10 percent the next year.[17] Although some people might say that this is merely a question of semantics, only a shock treatment could achieve such a drastic reduction.

This drastic approach, which received the name "progressive containment,"[18] was put into practice. It took off from a strictly monetarist analysis of inflation,[19] although later it presented price indexes in which the agricultural deflator grew from 66 in 1949 to 456 in 1960, whereas the industrial deflator increased from 72 in 1949 to only 333 in 1960. The contradiction was even more obvious in light of the following statement from the program:

> If the historically observable tendency of agricultural production for domestic consumption persists, the potential demand for foodstuffs in Brazil derived from a regular annual economic growth of 3.4 percent per inhabitant (which would be quite a favorable rate) and an average elasticity of demand of 0.49 would result in an average annual difference of 5 percent in the rhythm of expansion between supply and demand whose cumulative effect would represent an increasingly intense inflationary pressure.[20]

Nevertheless, this structuralist position, which contradicts the monetarist position adopted earlier in the same document, had no effect on the solutions that were adopted. The anti-inflation strategy was strictly monetarist, erroneously defining inflation as if it were exclusively a demand-pull type of inflation, and was based on three fundamental points: reduction of the budget deficit, reduction of demand, and combat against the psychological and speculative causes of inflation.

The reduction of the budget deficit was carried out through increased taxes, decreased government expenditures and investments, the elimination of government subsidies, and an increase in public service rates. A reduction in demand was again sought through an increase in the tax burden, thus reducing the disposable income of the general public, through credit restrictions limiting enterprises' investment possibilities, and through a wage policy aimed at reducing consumption. Finally, the attack against the psychological and speculative causes of inflation was attempted by means of instruments such as the establishment of price controls (Resolution 71), the Stimulus Law, numerous speeches and appeals, and the Campaign in Defense of the Popular Economy carried out by the Women's Civic Union (União Cívica Feminina) with the collaboration of the government agency for controlling consumer prices, developed around the idea that inflation was in fact over and Brazil was now in its "corrective" phase.

This was the strategy to combat inflation, but government economists were sufficiently realistic to admit that a reduction of investments and consumption would threaten the country with recession. Therefore various compensatory mechanisms were suggested in order to counterbalance the negative effects of the deflationary measures. The major ones were a housing plan, an increase in public works, an increase in exports, and the acceptance of foreign investments.

All of these compensatory mechanisms failed. The housing plan, which was supposed to create many jobs because of the low capital-labor ratio in the construction industry, did not have much effect, as members of the government themselves recognized. It was unrealistic to think that the expected results would be attained in the short term, especially since the whole plan was based on the simplistic and idealistic notion that the problem would be resolved merely by proclamation of a law permitting monetary correction (price indexing) for real estate financing and the creation of means for financing. It was also naive to think that occupational mobility was so great that people working in the metallurgical or textile industry would be able to transfer to the construction industry when they lost their original jobs.

With respect to the increase of public works (among which projected highway construction was especially important), in addition to the difficulty already mentioned in connection with the housing plan, there was also a conflict with the government's objective of reducing the budget deficit. It can thus be easily seen that this compensatory mechanism did not have much chance of success.

There was an increase in industrial exports but it did not have the desired effect, because Brazil's industrial exports are so negligible that a large increase in them makes very little difference in the total list of either exports or industrial activity. For example, in 1964 Brazilian exports of manufactured goods rose only $63.1 million, amounting to 4.6 percent of exports.[21]

Finally, the great influx of direct foreign investment, which was expected when the conservative Marshal Castello Branco took over the presidency and modified the law for the remission of profits, never materialized. Once again it was demonstrated that foreign investors were much less interested in the question of legal restrictions on the remission of their profits than in real opportunities for profitable investments.

All the deflationary measures, which had so aggravated the fundamental problems of the Brazilian economy such as the lack of markets and insufficient demand, together with the nonfunctioning compensatory mechanisms, necessarily resulted in crisis, unemployment, and a general reduction in economic activity.

Another very simple factor contributed further to this situation. Inflation, despite all the distortions it had provoked in the economy, still had a role to play within the economy: to maintain, albeit artificially and only to some extent, the level of demand. The anti-inflationary measures, although they partially succeeded in countering inflation (according to figures from the Getúlio Vargas Foundation, the cost of living in Guanabara rose 45 percent in 1965, 40 percent in 1966), also caused inflation to lose its efficacy for this purpose. Suddenly a vacuum was created in the economic system. Inflation no longer stimulated demand, and nothing arose to take its place. On the contrary, the inflationary practices previously referred to had a negative effect on the economy.

And as if this were not enough, not only was the artificial demand provoked by inflation eliminated, but what could be called the normal demand also shrank. Foreseeing this reduction, if not the absolute stagnation of the inflationary process, businessmen immediately began to reduce their stocks. This is a typical attitude for entrepreneurs to adopt when there are prospects of monetary stabilization. Thus a lowering of inventory was added to the reduction of demand caused by increased taxes and credit restrictions. However, reduced inventory itself is only one of the factors that helped to bring about the reduction of intermediary demand. It is not the only one, as some governmental spokesmen claimed when confronted with the crisis.

Additionally there was a reduction in final demand on the part of the consumers. For they also naturally reduce their spending—especially for durable goods—when there are prospects for the stabilization of the economy. On the other hand, the government's wage policy, particularly the establishment of the minimum wage, had negative effects. The new minimum wage at the beginning of 1965 represented a drastic drop in workers' real wages (see Table 5.3) and, naturally, had a negative effect on the final demand for consumer goods. Later, with the decree of new minimum wage levels at the beginning of 1966 and 1967, the government maintained the policy of reducing real wages, always allowing for an inflationary margin that was lower than the one that ought realistically to have been foreseen. It was only in 1968 that the government of Costa e Silva began to reverse this policy.

July 1965 was the high point of the crisis. Unemployment in São Paulo reached 13.5 percent. After June, however, the unemployment rate had begun to diminish. This tendency was probably the result of the large agricultural harvests of 1965, which sustained the rural population's purchasing power. On the other hand, although the government itself was making only trifling investments, the state enterprises were continuing to buy intensively in the private sector. In July a very fortuitous governmental measure was adopted: a temporary reduction in the retail sales tax. The consequent price reductions had a favorable psychological effect on the public. Confidence began to be shown again. Investments took on a new impulse, especially those made through the recently created National Machinery and Equipment Fund, which made possible generous financing for the purchase of domestically produced machines and equipment. Foreign investments also became more frequent, although still of a lower volume than the government hoped for. Consumers began to spend again; unemployment was reduced. The indexes of bankruptcy and moratoriums dropped, as well as the Labor Department's legal approvals for dismissing workers. The economic crisis was far from being overcome, however. It had lost its strong impulse, but continued in the already existing unemployment, idle capacity, unsatisfactory investment opportunities, and slowdown in industrial investment. In late 1966, however, the crisis returned in full force, and economic recession continued until mid-1967.

The policy that fought inflation by reducing demand when the inflation was in fact caused by costs resulted in economic stagnation or, more precisely, economic recession. An intermediate result of this policy that acted as a fundamental cause of the economic crisis was the reduction in private consumption, which dropped from 69.2 percent in 1960 (a year when Brazil was in a full process of economic development) to 65.6 percent in 1965 (see Table 5.4). This reduction in consumption, basically a fruit of wage policies and the concentration of income, did not result in growth in the rate of gross formation of fixed capital. On the contrary, the latter declined from 17.3 percent to 14.9 percent, basically because of the reduction in private investment. What did increase was inventories—a fact that illustrates the basic nature of the crisis. To the extent that enterprises were accumulating stock in their warehouses because of workers' lower purchasing power, there was no stimulus to production.

## Short-Range Causes of the Political Crisis

The short-range causes have already been touched upon in the discussion of the symptoms of the Brazilian political crisis. First there are the general problems that constituted the long- and medium-range origins of the crisis: lack of representativeness, denial of voting privileges to illiterates, the leadership elite's intransigency and refusal to engage in dialogue, the immaturity of the left, and the political instability of the Goulart government. Then we have the Revolution of 1964, which to some extent dealt with some of these problems, especially that of

TABLE 5.4
Real Product by Type of Expenditure
1956-1965   (Selected Years)

Billions of Cr.$ at 1960 value
Percentages of Total Gross Product

| Activity | 1956 | 1960 | 1961 | 1962 | 1963 | 1964 | 1965 |
|---|---|---|---|---|---|---|---|
| Total Investment | 14.0 | 18.1 | 18.1 | 19.7 | 17.4 | 18.1 | 18.9 |
| Gross Formation | | | | | | | |
| of fixed capital | 12.3 | 17.3 | 16.8 | 17.8 | 16.5 | 16.1 | 14.9 |
| a) Public[2] | 3.5 | 7.4 | 7.6 | 8.2 | 7.0 | 6.7 | 7.2 |
| b) Private | 8.8 | 9.9 | 9.1 | 9.4 | 9.4 | 9.4 | 7.7 |
| Inventory Variation | 1.7 | 0.8 | 1.4 | 1.8 | 1.0 | 2.0 | 4.0[1] |
| Total Consumption | 87.6 | 84.6 | 83.5 | 82.2 | 83.7 | 82.2 | 79.9 |
| a) Government | 14.7 | 15.3 | 15.5 | 15.5 | 16.3 | 15.4 | 14.3[1] |
| b) Personal | 72.9 | 69.2 | 68.0 | 66.7 | 67.4 | 66.7 | 65.6 |
| Exports of Goods and Services | 8.5 | 7.2 | 7.4 | 6.4 | 7.2 | 6.3 | 6.9 |
| Imports of Goods and Services | 10.1 | 9.9 | 9.1 | 8.3 | 8.3 | 6.6 | 5.7 |
| Gross Domestic Product | 100.0 | 100.0 | 100.0 | 100.0 | 100.0 | 100.0 | 100.0 |

[1]Estimates made by the CEPAL/BNDE Center.
[2]Includes mixed enterprises.

Source: Cf. "A Evolução Recente da Economia Brasileira," Desenvolvimento e Conjuntura, April 1967, p. 28. Differences between this table and Table 2.4 are due to differences in criteria. These differences, however, are not significant enough to alter the conclusions.

political instability, but which also, and more importantly, aggravated them.

In particular, the already acute problem of the government's lack of representativeness became worse. The executive office became the fruit of a *coup d'etat*; the legislature, which had been truly representative, lost what little representativeness it had had and became totally subservient to the executive branch because the latter revoked the political rights of those congressmen it considered a threat to its power.

But this is not all. The left was severely repressed, the authentic left as well as the more demagogic elements. In the revocation of political rights, opportunists were confused with leaders of integrity, moderates with extremists. This revocation almost totally destroyed the dialogue among the progressive forces in the country. And nothing jeopardizes the nation more than the suspension of dialogue.

There are other short-term causes of the political crisis, but these factors also had a direct economic influence and can hence be dealt with as general short-term causes of the Brazilian crisis. These causes are a direct function of the ideological position and social framework of the Castello Branco government.

## The Social and Ideological Framework
## of the Castello Branco Government

Obviously, the men who governed Brazil from 1964 to 1967 were military officers. But there were others working together with the military whose power was almost as great, especially in matters relating to the economy—the technocrats. They were almost all economists. During the Castello Branco government they occupied every key economic position in Brazil except for the presidency of the Bank of Brazil. There were economists in the Treasury Ministry, in the Planning Ministry, in the presidencies of the Central Bank and the National Bank for Economic Development, all technocrats who left their positions as technical advisors to take over command of the government.

Brazil had never had a government socially and professionally defined in this manner. The other groups that have usually participated in power in other countries, or at other times in Brazil, were absent from this government. There were no politicians. The government was set up with almost all politicians in a subservient position. Even members of the now extinct National Democratic Union, who would appear to have been the major beneficiaries of the Revolution of 1964, were more instruments than agents of the government. The labor unions were absent. One fact is self-evident, without need of further proof: The old Brazilian aristocracy and the traditional Brazilian economic system based on agriculture did not receive economic benefits from the new government policy. The 1966 coffee policy, which was very hard on the coffee growers, proves this point. Thus it cannot be said that this government was representative of the old Brazilian aristocracy, at least the rural aristocracy. Finally, the entrepreneurs (using a broader definition of this term, rather than Schumpeter's) were also missing, particularly the industrial entrepreneurs. Together with the industrial workers they were the ones who suffered the greatest losses from government policy. They did not participate in policy making. At the most they were called upon on certain formal occasions to applaud, receive instructions, and collaborate with the government. The significance and consequences of their minimal role will be discussed further on.

The Castello Branco government was thus basically a government composed of military men and technocrats only. In other words, it was a government of the middle class. More specifically, it was a government of the traditional middle class, the old middle class, the middle class of professional liberals, public functionaries, priests, and military officers as they had existed before the Brazilian industrial revolution. It was a government in which other Brazilian social groups, especially the industrial entrepreneurs and financiers, did not participate. This government's ideological position was an almost direct consequence of the social outlook of the traditional middle class.

In philosophic terms, it was an idealist government, in the sense that it believed in ideas more than in reality. It was idealist in that it denied reality, or at least never managed to come to grips with it. It was idealist because it believed that it had to change attitudes before it could change structures, that it was more important to "convert" or persuade someone than to set up conditions for social change. The Castello Branco government's idealism can be illustrated by a very significant statement by one of its representatives, who expressed the following ideas in discussing the economic crisis of early 1965:

> The economic situation is really difficult, but there is one compensation. The most important thing now is to change the attitude of the industrial leaders, to make them become concerned with costs and increasing productivity. The time has passed when it was enough merely to sell and to make big profits. Now they either change their attitudes and begin to compete effectively in a free market or they will not survive.

This is a typically idealist approach. Attitudes do not change overnight; concern for costs is not created in the midst of economic depression when the question is not to cut costs but rather to reduce output, fire employees, and struggle to survive.

Another facet of the philosophical idealism of the Castello Branco government was its faith that economic development could be brought about by means of laws. Few governments have promulgated laws so prolifically. And there is no question that many of them were good, well made from a technical point of view. This is the case with the laws concerning rents, the Council on Foreign Commerce, real estate incorporation, the creation of the Central Bank (although this was not really bank reform), and tax reform. One may not agree with all aspects of these laws, but it must be admitted that they are the fruits of the work of intelligent and capable technical experts. The whole problem was in thinking that laws could resolve Brazil's short-term problems, that changes made in the laws concerning the remission of profits would bring foreign capital showering down on the country, that the law concerning capital markets would produce greater public participation in the savings and capital markets, that the housing plan laws would cause houses and more houses to spring up in every corner of the country. This is an attitude completely divorced from reality, comparable to the theories that education is necessary before development can take place, or that the main task is to change attitudes. This is a type of idealism typical of the traditional middle class, stemming from the fact that it is made up basically of independent professionals, military men, and educated public functionaries, and consequently of people who are not integrated into the country's productive process.

If this government was philosophically idealist, in the economic sphere it was immobilist and anti-industrialist. It was immobilist, not because it desired economic stagnation for Brazil, but because it placed monetary stabilization as its primary objective and was ready to sacrifice development to the fight against inflation. It was anti-industrialist not in the sense that it sought to check Brazil's industrial development, but rather because it viewed industrialists and entrepreneurs in general through the typical moralism of the middle class, mistrusting them, suspecting them of seeking to earn maximum profits, of speculating, and therefore of needing government supervision. It was also anti-industrialist to the extent that in its fight against inflation, the government did not hesitate to sacrifice industry, restricting its credit, for example, more than that of agriculture.

Finally, the Castello Branco government was internally conservative, seeking to preserve the status quo; moralist, in that it saw the solution of Brazil's problems in the honesty of its politicians; and anticommunist, to the point of being almost paranoid. Internationally this was a colonialist government, to the extent that it placed the country under the total domination of a foreign power, increasingly servile, a political cover for this power's international activities. It was also colonialist because it believed that Brazil's development could be realized only with foreign aid, that the country did not have conditions for autonomous development.

Conservatism, paranoiac anticommunism, and colonialism are not ideological positions confined to the traditional middle class, but doubtless they form a general part of this class's world view. Moralism is essentially an ideology of the traditional middle class.

## The Industrial Entrepreneur and the Crisis

Thus we see the Castello Branco government as a government of military men and technocrats, a government of the traditional middle class, defined by an immobilist economic policy alienated from reality. It was a government from which workers, peasants, students, and entrepreneurs were excluded.

A government that lacked the participation of these socioeconomic groups could not promote the economic and social development of the country, because it lacked the minimum of representation necessary. All the economic and social development that took place in Brazil after 1930, especially during the terms of Getúlio Vargas and Juscelino Kubitschek and through the influence of the Brazilian Workers Party and the Social Democratic Party, was the result of a complex alchemy of compromises and mutual concessions. This was possible because a range of social interests was represented in the power structure, from industrial laborers to entrepreneurs and even the aristocracy. The only socioeconomic group that was always maintained on the periphery of the Brazilian political process was the rural poor, the peasants.

The generalized exclusion of the most representative groups in Brazilian society, particularly those most directly involved in the productive process, such as industrial workers and entrepreneurs, was an extremely serious error and without a doubt the general and most important cause of the Brazilian crisis. In the short term, however, yet another distinction can be made. The most serious omission, within the framework of a capitalist regime, was that of the industrial entrepreneurs.

In fact, to the extent that Brazil continued its economic development within the framework of a mixed capitalist model by means of the entrepreneurial activity of the state and of private enterprise, it was necessary that industrial leaders, as well as businessmen and financiers, take an important, even a main role, though not an exclusive one, in the control of the government. It is possible for a country to develop rapidly in capitalist terms only if the state represents the interests of the capitalists. It is possible to pursue industrialism only if the industrial entrepreneurs have a hand on the reins of the government. The Castello Branco government tried to maintain capitalism in Brazil but sought to exclude industrial entrepreneurs from participation in the government, creating an inherent contradiction.

Thus the question arises, Why were industrial entrepreneurs and the productive classes in general excluded from participation in the government? It will be answered here only with respect to the entrepreneurs, in accordance with the more general focus of this book.

On the part of the Castello Branco government, this exclusion was a natural occurrence, probably not the result of deliberate calculation. The industrial leaders were initially excluded because the Revolution of 1964 was a revolution of the middle class, led by military men of the middle class, and taken over by technocrats from the middle class. The next question then becomes, Why did the industrial leaders allow themselves to be excluded? There are two answers.

First, the industrial leaders had always been silent and lacking in political organization. One of the typical characteristics of Brazilian entrepreneurs had been their lack of political participation and presence, the fact that they limited themselves to the narrow boundaries of their enterprises and the profit motive. When Brazil's economic policy was focused totally on industrialization, as in the Kubitschek years, the government represented the industrialists almost in spite of them. It was not the industrial leaders who brought Kubitschek to power, nor were they the ones who kept him there. On the contrary, especially in São Paulo, when they did manifest themselves politically, it was often in opposition to Kubitschek.

This leads us to the second reason. When the industrial leaders did begin to participate actively in politics, especially in more recent times, it was only after they had begun to realize that industrialization was already an established fact, that the battle of industrialism against agriculturalism had been won, and they acted in an increasingly conservative manner. They did not perceive the importance of keeping open the dialogue with the left. They did not see that it was fundamental to the maintenance of the democratic process and the country's political stability for workers to continue to organize and to express their demands. Instead they let themselves get involved with the conservatives, becoming their pawns, and thus abandoning themselves to the immature alarmism that predominated in the year before the Revolution of 1964, maintaining a totally intransigent attitude, unwilling to make any compromise. Thus they identified themselves with the Revolution of 1964, which later ignored them or worked against them.

# 6
# The Viability of
# Capitalist Development

Development and crisis were the two key-words of the Brazilian historical process between 1930 and 1968. Despite intermittent political and economic crises, throughout the first 31 years the emphasis was on development. In this period Brazilians witnessed what one might be tempted to call their industrial revolution, but today it has become clear that these years constituted only the first great phase of this revolution. In 1962 began the period here called the Brazilian crisis, characterized by permanent economic, social, and political crisis that worsens from time to time, later returning to its natural state of chronic crisis.

Now the question is, Is capitalist development viable for Brazil? Can we continue our economic growth and overcome the inhuman conditions of our underdevelopment within the limits of a basically capitalist society?

This question is important because we live under a capitalist system that, at least in the intermediate term, was consolidated by the Revolution of 1964, following the industrial development of the 1930s, 1940s, and 1950s. Though it was led by the traditional middle class, and particularly by the military, rather than by the capitalist class, this revolution ended up adopting a basically capitalist ideology. The fact that the traditional middle class in command of the Revolution of 1964 adopted a capitalist ideology can be explained by the very nature of the middle class and its receptivity to ideology. It has no ideology of its own. Aside from idealism (which is more of a philosophical characteristic, stemming from this class's special kind of insertion in the concrete reality) the traditional middle class is generally alienated from the productive process, and is defined by conservatism. Thus it is not surprising that when maintaining security required an alliance with capitalism, this was the path it chose.

The left movement, which had begun to constitute an autonomous force only in the 1960s, suffered a violent blow with the Revolution of 1964. Its immaturity led it to expose itself too much, when it was still too weak and disorganized to stand up to groups of the right and center. As a result, the main effect of the revolution was to consolidate the capitalist system in Brazil, in the intermediate term. The possibilities for the left to regain any sort of power are very slim in Brazil in the second half of the 1960s. Conditions for a socialist revolution are even more remote. Both economic and military power are too well organized to permit any severe breach in the existing institutional framework. A class of entrepreneurs appears, which, though not very active politically, has strong economic power. As we saw in Chapter 3, the middle class and particularly the new middle class show a great development, and end up assuming power with their technocrats and bureaucrats, who soon show their conservative nature. Finally, within the international context Brazil is located in the United States' sphere of influence. This superpower, with its typically imperialist perspective, has since the Cuban experience made it increasingly clear that any left revolution in Latin America would invite American intervention. (History has shown that it is sufficient to be a great power to be imperialist.) The case of the Dominican Republic, which was hardly a left revolution, showed that this is not a position backed up merely by words. In light of the economic power of the entrepreneurial class, their numbers, their conservatism, the military and political power of the middle class, and the pressure from North America, it is difficult to imagine that any other alternative to the capitalist one would have any chance to dominate in Brazil, at least in the intermediate term.

## Industrial Revolution and False Analogy

The degree of industrial development that took place in Brazil from 1930 to 1961 was so great that it has led many observers to believe that the Brazilian industrial revolution was complete.

In fact, during this period, Brazil saw a vast diversified and integrated industrial park established within its borders. Consumer industries, making both durable consumer goods and lighter products were installed. In 1961, the percentage of imported consumer goods was minimal. Basic industries—ironworks, aluminum, copper, chemicals, lye—were also largely established. Though there was still work to be done in these areas, especially in the industrialization of chemicals, the most important part had been accomplished, making use of the subproducts of oil refineries. This was also true of the capital goods industry. It saw an intensive development in the 1950s, so that at the end of the decade, two-thirds of the equipment for national industry was being domestically produced.

These facts might lead one to the conclusion that Brazil had in fact completed its industrial revolution. I came to believe this and put it down on paper. All indications pointed to the fact that the nation had reached a stage in which investment and reinvestment had become an integral part of the economic system itself; investments were stimulated by the profit motive and also were the condition for obtaining new profits, so that development had become automatic and necessary. However, in affirming these facts, we are making an analogy to the development of developed countries. Today we see that this is a false analogy, based on facts that do not directly correspond to our situation.

In reality, when the three nations that first underwent industrial revolutions—England, France, and the United States—had reached a degree of industrial development more or less comparable to that of Brazil in 1961, they came to have a self-sustained development. This analogy leads to the conclusion that the Brazil of 1961 (despite eventual crises it might suffer) roughly corresponds to Europe at the end of the Industrial Revolution, and that both these social systems then entered a period of self-sustained development.

However, this analogy omits an elementary but fundamental fact. Brazil's industrial development took place under very different conditions than that of England, the United States, and France. There are three factors that determine these basic differences:

1. Brazilian industrial development occurred through import substitution, whereas this process did not define the Industrial Revolution of today's developed nations. On the contrary, they participated in the international market of manufactured goods as exporters.

2. The industrial development of the developed countries was realized by the integration of a series of techniques that were being perfected at the time, adapted to the economic needs of each country. On the contrary, Brazil utilizes imported technology that is often ill-suited to our needs and provokes serious distortions in our economy, particularly in terms of unemployment.

3. Finally, Brazil's industrial development takes place under the supervision of an imperialist superpower that, like all superpowers, would like to orient and control the country's political and economic development. The distortions that these factors produce in both the economy and the national society are so serious that unless they are overcome, Brazil's industrial development will not be definitively consolidated. It will present that appearance, yet without having reached a phase that can legitimately be considered self-sustained, that is,

automatic and necessary. Consequently, one must conclude that Brazil has not yet completed its industrial revolution.

## The Definitive Proof:
## Exportation of Manufactured Goods

The distortions caused by the process of import substitution suggest the first definitive proof that the Brazilian economy will have to face in order to overcome these distortions. I am referring to the exportation of manufactured goods. One of the essential conditions for considering Brazil's industrial development as self-sustained is that it has come to have an increasing participation in the international commerce in manufactured products.

There are two reasons to support this thesis. First, the opportunities for import substitution and reduction of the import coefficient have basically been exhausted. Thus, Brazil's only alternative is to increase its national product, that is, increase its exports concomitantly and proportionally. If it is no longer possible to reduce the import coefficient (that is, the percentage of imports in the national product), when the national product increases, industry's need to import machines and raw material will also increase. And soon, the domestically oriented development we had experienced until recently will no longer be possible. Increased importations are imposed upon the economy.

Second, we have already seen that we cannot increase our total exports by increasing the exportation of primary products, for a number of reasons: low income-elasticity of demand for agricultural products, increasing competition among the underdeveloped countries, use of artificial substitutes by the developed countries, unstable prices for primary products, etc. Thus, we are forced to shift our emphasis to the exportation of manufactured goods.

In 1966, exports of manufactured goods, which had been showing a gradual increase, represented 5.9 percent of Brazil's total exports, compared with 6.8 percent in 1965. In absolute terms, this represented a decrease from $109.5 to $104.4 million.[1] In 1967, exports began to recover.

We can consider that manufactured products represent 6 percent of Brazil's exports. If we planned for a 6 percent growth rate for the national product (which would be the minimum acceptable) this would mean that exports would also have to increase 6 percent in order for the ratio of imports to remain constant. If we wanted this increase to be based on the increase of our manufactured exports alone, we would have to increase our exportation of these products by 100 percent in the first year. In the following years, this percentage could be reduced by 50 percent, 33 percent, and so on until the theoretical 6 percent limit was reached, when our exports would be exclusively of manufactured goods. Now it is obvious that such rapid growth is impossible. Therefore, while directing our efforts toward the increased exportation of manufactured goods, we would also have to try to increase the exportation of primary products. The difficulties implicit in these two tasks are enormous, and again pose the question of whether capitalist development is viable for Brazil.

Because both these tasks are essential, the Brazilian economy can meet this challenge only to the extent that it effectively exports manufactured goods. Eventual favorable conditions in the market, external to the Brazilian economy itself, could cause a new boom in the exportation of raw materials. But such a boom would not be any proof of the capability of the Brazilian economy, because the impulse would be the result of outside conditions. Brazil would continue to be an underdeveloped country, exporter of primary products, at the mercy of the typical fluctuations in the international market for these products. It would be subject to the competition of other producers of the same product utilizing cheap labor, as well as to competition from producers of synthetic subsitutes in the industrialized countries. Even more serious is the fact that in the production of prime materials, the introduction of advanced production techniques is not called for. As a result, there is no need to train specialized workers, productivity continues to be low, and underdevelopment continues to be a permanent phenomenon on the Brazilian economic scene. Thus we can meet this great challenge only to the extent that Brazil participates significantly in the international commerce of manufactured goods and its role is acknowledged by the industrialized nations.

Naturally we cannot expect to compete in every industrial sector. Rather, enterprises should make choices as to the sectors where their major efforts should be directed and receive incentives from the government. There are two criteria for the choice of these sectors: the existence of cheap national prime materials (as in the classic case of instant coffee); and a lower ratio of capital to labor. The reasons for this second criterion are obvious. Since underdeveloped countries have an abundant and cheap labor force, according to the theory of economic development, they should concentrate their industrial efforts in labor-intensive sectors rather than capital-intensive ones. While it is obvious that there are a series of qualifications that should be made to this statement, they are not appropriate at this moment, nor do they alter our basic argument.

However, it is important to point out that there are two types of labor-intensive industries. The first is almost craftsmanship, such as the clothing industry, leatherwork, and furniture making. When labor-intensive industries are mentioned, one usually thinks only of these types of industries, characterized not only by a low capital-labor relationship but also by a low level of technological development. These kinds of manufactured products should definitely continue to be exported. Yet to remain only with this type of product is another way of expressing a colonial inferiority complex, and more seriously, of remaining underdeveloped while at the same time exporting manufactured goods.

There is another kind of industry, also labor-intensive, but requiring a high level of technological development. The example *par excellence* of this type of industry is the production of electronic or mechanical equipment by special order. Because it is by special order, such production cannot be standardized and consequently cannot be highly mechanized, much less automated. Each product calls for a special project. Only some of the pieces can be standardized, whereas others have to be specially made and individually assembled. Thus the relationship of capital to labor in this kind of industry has to be low. However, the manual labor is highly specialized. It is at this point that the antinationalists with their latent inferiority complexes will ask, But are we capable of developing a specialized labor force equal to the task? I am certain that we are. It is much easier and cheaper for underdeveloped countries to import technology, pay royalties, contract foreign technical experts, and send scholarship students abroad to study than to import equipment.

It is these sectors, either with easy access to prime materials and/ or with a low capital-labor relationship (which does not mean a low level of technology) that should be stimulated to produce for exportation. At any rate, once the more favorable sectors are chosen, it is essential to lower production costs, that is to say, to increase productivity decisively so that we are able to compete in the international market. However, at first we will have to keep our costs and prices lower than those of our richer competitors (as occurred in the case of Japan), because we have neither an established name nor a tradition in the international commerce in these products.

Once this decisive point in the Brazilian economy has been reached, Brazil will have finished its industrial revolution and reached the stage of self-sustained development, and will consequently have shifted the emphasis of its exportation from primary to manufactured goods. This change would go together with an aggressive commercial policy applying modern principles of marketing, along with direct government intervention to stimulate certain exports. These measures would result in a decisive increase in industrial output and consequently in lower costs.

**Three Possible Capitalist Ideologies**

At the end of the 1960s, as the economic crisis is being overcome, I perceive three possible ideologies for Brazil. By "possible" I mean that they are ideologies that could be put in practice, be defended by their supporters, and eventually become the government ideology, to the extent that they become politically victorious. These three possible ideologies are classic neoliberalism, technocratic-military interventionist liberalism, and developmentalist nationalism.

*Classic neoliberalism.* Classic neoliberalism is bourgeois ideology *par excellence.* It comes close to the idea of *laissez-faire,* but cannot be equated with it for the simple reason that pure liberalism is dead and buried today. It favors the least possible state intervention in the economy, and would like basically to leave the responsibility as well as the main fruits of development in the hands of the capitalist class. In the underdeveloped countries it is a systematically colonialist ideology to the extent that it has no faith in the national capitalist class's ability to develop the nation and thus eventually appeals for foreign assistance. It is an ideology that defends the democratic order, individual liberties, and the representative system, but its proponents are always ready to abandon or limit these ideas when they feel that the system is endangered, as occurred in 1964. This ideology presupposes that the nation will basically be controlled by two groups: the capitalist class, which holds the economic power and will occupy key positions in the government determining economic policy; and the professional politicians, who function not merely as representatives of the capitalist class, as some hasty observers would like to believe, but also as participants in a relatively autonomous social status group, who defend their private interests. Their role is to serve as intermediaries among the state, the capitalist class, the middle class, and the population in general, in that order of priority.

This is the ideology that is probably supported by the great majority of the Brazilian entrepreneurial class, and also by a significant part of the middle class. I do not find this ideology workable for Brazil's economic development for three fundamental reasons. It is a colonialist ideology, and I believe that Brazil's development can be realized only through a well-defined national project. It is liberal, minimizing the role of the state, and I affirm that currently there is no economic development without state intervention, that the problems that an underdeveloped country has to face today are so large that only careful planning and deliberate and intelligent state intervention in the economy can lead to development. Finally, it is strictly capitalist, the ideology of a small group only that seeks the advantages of development for itself alone. This may have been politically acceptable in the nineteenth century, but in the twentieth, and particularly in Brazil, it no longer is. In addition, the effects of the concentration of income implicit in this ideology are disastrous.

*Technocratic-military interventionist liberalism.* Technocratic-military interventionist liberalism is the ideology that came to dominate Brazil in the years 1964 to 1967. This phenomenon was examined in the last chapter, which looked at the socioeconomic background of the military officers and technocrats who came to power with the Revolution of 1964. This ideology, as the name I have chosen indicates, is based on a contradiction: It is both interventionist and liberal. Really, it is a whole tangle of contradictions, to the extent that technocrats and military men dominate it. As members of the traditional middle class, detached from the productive process and receiving no benefits from the industrial development that took place between 1930 and 1961, they are characterized politically by idealism and alienation from reality. They seek to change the world by laws and decrees and moralism, by personalizing problems and attributing personal or even collective responsibility. Their ideology has a strong moral content, rather than a focus on the existing structures. They are characterized by conservatism, with policies that appear to be substantial reforms, but in fact are only superficial ones.

In addition to these traits, technocratic-military interventionist liberalism is also a capitalist ideology. However, it is a capitalist ideology whose authors and principal defenders are not capitalist entrepreneurs (who were excluded from power by the Revolution of 1964), but rather military men and technocrats. For them, capitalism is not an internalized phenomenon, an organic part of their lives, but rather a label to be placed on their opposition to communism, which frightens them because they are conservatives. Their capitalism is thus not very authentic but rather the fruit of contradictions. They call themselves capitalists yet are averse to private profits they do not share in. They defend liberalism, yet have established a rigid system to control enterprises, often including strong policing measures that Brazil has never known until recently. All the documents state that they intend to strengthen the private sector rather than the public, yet they nationalize foreign hydroelectric corporations and progressively increase the state's participation in the economy.[2]

*Developmentalist Nationalism.* There is still a third possible capitalist ideology for Brazil. It is what I shall call developmentalist nationalism, since its fundamental characteristics are that it is nationalist and that it sets national development as its most important objective. Nationalism, defined by the belief in a country's potential for self-development, is opposed to colonialism. It affirms that economic progress occurs only to the extent that the nation itself sets this progress up as its goal, makes the necessary sacrifices to attain it, and is fully aware that its success will depend upon its own efforts in this direction. Barbosa Lima Sobrinho well expresses another dimension of this concept: "The substance of nationalism is not antagonism of interests or ideas."[3] The idea of conflict is not essential to patriotism, yet it is impossible to speak of nationalism without expressing an explicit or implicit conflict of interests. Thus antagonism and a belief in Brazil's potential, in its values as a nation in the process of formation—these are the essential characteristics of nationalism.

This antagonism can take many forms, depending on the epoch and the situation in which determined nationalist attitudes or ideologies appear. In Brazil today, this antagonism has its origin in the fact that the national interests of Brazil as an underdeveloped country are not in agreement with those of the industrialized countries and that the interests of the capitalist groups in the developed countries (though we will qualify this below) are not necessarily the same as those of the Brazilian people. In fact, the interests of developed countries and their enterprises are often clearly in conflict with Brazil's interests. This is especially true in relation to the United States, which, as an imperialist superpower directly dominating the Latin American countries, is the source of the greatest conflicts of interests.

An acknowledgement of this conflict is essential to the self-definition of a nationalist in Brazil today. But such an acknowledgement does not necessarily mean that one must see conflict in all areas, point out the contradictions in each and every sector. In fact, it was this kind of attitude that led nationalism as an ideology to a phase of decline in Brazil. Chapter 4 has shown how at the end of the 1950s and beginning of the 1960s, nationalism ceased to attract the Brazilian capitalist class. Consequently, it also ceased to be the fragile yet essential link between the left and the entrepreneurs, who had tried to form a united front around the nationalist ideology in the 1950s.

When this united front was no longer viable, the nationalist ideology was monopolized by the left. It is clear and understandable that the left radicalized nationalism, mixing up its economic arguments with political ones. As a result, the economic arguments favoring nationalism became weak and imprecise. And nationalism as an ideology entered a period of decline, to the extent that working class groups, the middle class, and, naturally, the capitalist class were not predominantly tied to the left.

Foreign capital was a focal point in this debate. In general, the nationalist position was radically opposed to foreign capital. However, its theoretical arguments were based on insufficient economic analysis.

It is true that there were and are enormous series of isolated cases of foreign enterprises (especially in public services) whose actions are highly antinationalist. Barbosa Lima Sobrinho's work on the activities of the electric companies is a classic in this area.[4] But when the left tried to prove that foreign investments, or at least the majority of them, were disadvantageous for Brazil, its nationalist economic theory showed its marked limitations, and nationalism became demoralized.

In reality, a position that opposes all foreign investment is not economically feasible in Brazil. Doubtless there are political arguments that could support this position. If our goal is to establish socialism within a relatively short time, then in fact it makes little sense to permit the entry of foreign capital into Brazil. However, apart from these political motives, in economic terms it is difficult to deny the important role that foreign capital plays. If one accepts the argument that in underdeveloped countries the great problem is the lack of investment capital; if one admits that investment, especially in industry, has multiple effects, producing revenue not only directly for the foreign proprietors of capital, but also for wage workers, the government, and other enterprises; if one concedes the great importance of know-how in industrial development, then it is hard to make firm economic arguments against foreign capital.

These arguments do, however, exist, and suggest a nationalist policy of selective rigor with respect to foreign investment and controls on the activities of foreign enterprises (such as regulation of the remittance of profits, and an obligatory process for gradual nationalization). This position has a solid theoretical basis. The explanation of this theoretical basis for the selection of foreign capital deserves a chapter of its own. However, in a quick summary, the argument is as follows. Really the claim that the underdeveloped countries' greatest problem is their lack of capital is only a half-truth. There is a lack of capital in some sectors where the underdeveloped country does not have appropriate technology or the understanding of that technology, and where the necessary investments would be very high. However, in a great number of other sectors, there is sufficient capital and often extra capital. Enterprises function with idle capacity. Entrepreneurs and isolated capitalists don't know what to do with their profits, rents, and interest, and end up consuming them, sending them abroad, or investing them unproductively and increasing idle capacity.

Yet this is absurd as an economic analysis, some would say. And in fact it is, if one assumes an integrated market with highly developed capital, able to channel savings to investors, with perfectly mobile production factors and, especially, capital; if one assumes the existence of essentially rational behavior befitting *homo economicus.* It is impossible to imagine that within this same economy there could exist isolated sectors, some with abundant capital and some lacking capital.

In Brazil, however, this is definitely not the sort of economy that exists; and in fact, in certain sectors there is an effective excess of capital. Thus it makes no sense to allow foreign capital to enter these sectors, and in those where it has already penetrated, or in new sectors, it should be carefully controlled. Indiscriminate opposition to multinationals makes no sense, but neither, in a country like Brazil, does the inverse attitude of welcoming them in any circumstances.

# 7
# The Post-1966 Expansion and the New Model

Starting in 1967, the Brazilian economy entered a new expansion, repeating and trying to outdo the expansive performance it had showed in the second half of the 1950s. The economic crisis had been overcome, whereas the political crisis marked by the authoritarianism of the military government continued to worsen.

The economic expansion that began in 1967 coincided with General Costa e Silva's rise to power. The reforms made during the previous crisis established the bases for this recuperation. Among these, the reform of the banking system, the reform of the capital market, tax reforms, and the institution of price indexation were fundamental. All of these reforms had been more or less defined before 1964, but had not been implemented for lack of political power. Roberto Campos and Octávio Gouvea de Bulhões implemented them with notable intelligence between 1964 and 1966, while at the same time adopting a short-term monetarist economic policy based on the restriction of aggregate demand and on the wage squeeze, which are both analyzed in Chapter 6.

However, as this chapter will show, the basic reason for this new expansion is the middle class's increased capacity to purchase durable consumer goods, especially automobiles. This was possible because of the concentration of income, not only within the upper bourgeoisie, as in the previous expansion cycle, but also from the middle class on up. It is also a function of the large-scale development of direct consumer credit, which was made possible by the institution of price indexation. The 1967 policy of minidevaluations in the exchange rate stimulated exportation and served as another important factor in the economy's recuperation. Finally, there was also a shift in short-term economic policy, and inflation was no longer blamed on demand. Rather, an emphasis on its cost component resulted in an economic policy geared to the situation at the time, based on the expansion of demand and administrative price control.

## The 1967–1971 Period

The Costa e Silva government, which began in 1967, maintained many of the negative aspects of the previous Castello Branco regime that had aggravated the crisis. Yet at the same time, it signaled a series of political changes that clearly set it apart from the previous government.

### Political Changes

This epoch is divided into two different periods: the two years before Institutional Act Number 5, and the period after this act was made law. In the course of this first period, there was a breakdown in the unity and ideological firmness of the first moments of the military government. When the military first took power, they assumed a typically idealist attitude, imagining that the nation could be rapidly transformed. However, once in contact with the reality of the situation, they slowly perceived that this reality was not as adaptable as they had expected. They soon understood that Brazilian society has a structure, character, and rhythm all its own that cannot be changed overnight through various superficial reforms, the repealing of political rights, and the suspension of political freedoms. As a result, two of the pillars of the idealist military-revolutionary ideology—moralism, expressed as the fight against corruption, and anticommunism, as the struggle against subversion— lost much of their strength. This trend was emphasized even more when it became clear that the government leaders' fight against subversion and, especially, corruption was not quite what it seemed. The suspension of certain political leaders' civil rights makes it very clear that under the pretense of the fight against subversion or corruption, the government adopted measures ensuring that it would remain in power.

So the military became disillusioned, losing their enthusiasm for the revolution and also their unity around it. This ideological dilution and vacillation resulted in a relative diminution of their power, to the extent that they became divided, discouraged, and disorganized. In this way, though still occupying a typically subordinate position in the first months of the Costa e Silva government, civil groups gradually increased in power and influence. Their relative regaining of power is apparent in the attention that Costa e Silva paid to public opinion, an element completely disregarded in the previous government.

A superficial analysis of the personalities of the two presidents also demonstrates the evolution of the Revolution of 1964. Whereas President Castello Branco was a cold, deliberate aristocratic man characterized by his lack of respect for the people, President Costa e Silva showed himself to be a passionate, emotional man, actively involved in life. It is obvious that the two different personalities imply very different styles of government. Yet more important was the education and training of these men. Whereas General Castello Branco was one of the intellectual leaders of the *Escola Superior de Guerra*, General Costa e Silva was a typical "barracks military man," only superficially influenced by the abstract and alienated models of the *Escola*.

Finally, as the Castello Branco government came to an end, the institutional-juridical panorama was modified. The institutional acts with their discretionary powers were replaced by a new constitution, new electoral laws, laws concerning political parties, and the national security law. These measures were hardly examples of democracy in their origins and context, and represented a serious backward step in the long-term political situation. However, in comparison to the Castello Branco government's dictatorial regime, they represented a short-term weakening of the Revolution of 1964.

It was probably as a reaction against this weakening of military power that Institutional Act 5 was enacted in December 1968. The government again assumed full power; political rights were suspended; the president received dictatorial powers that enabled him to enact laws, put people in prison, cancel the mandates of representatives, establish censorship of the press, and exclude professors from universities. The country's redemocratization was paralyzed. To some extent this was a response to the timid increase in civil power, the reorganization of the left, and the student revolt that took place in Brazil as well as in many other societies during this period. But more than anything else, it was an attempt by the leading military group to retain power and unite its forces to carry out the tasks that were still unfinished.

Here appears the great problem of the Revolution of 1964, revived again by Act 5. These tasks had not yet been defined. The Revolution of 1964 adopted as its starting point an essentially negative ideology: the fight against subversion and corruption. It also theoretically established positive goals: national security and economic development. However, the first of these ended up being redefined in negative terms, in terms of the fight against subversion. Another positive ideological element, the affirmation of a nationalist ideology, never came to be fully defined. It made much more progress in the Costa e Silva government, that of Castello Branco having been clearly colonialist. Economic development was defined only in the most general terms. While one could not justly say, as of the Castello Branco government, that it subordinated economic development to a policy designed to fight inflation, the Costa e Silva government was never able to define objectives that could unite the nation's efforts. Despite the undeniable successes of its economic policy, the country still lacked a true national project that would affect broad sectors of the population.

At a certain point it seemed that this project would eventually be defined in nationalist and developmentalist terms, yet this possibility never materialized. When Act 5 was enacted, the country began a new chapter in the evolution of its political crisis without a national project promising optimistic perspectives for the future. The democratic dialogue that had been interrupted in 1964, but was being encouraged little by little, ended abruptly in 1968. As a result, another wave of radicalization reverberated, with groups of the extreme right and, especially, the extreme left operating illegally, once institutionalized channels were closed to them. Once again the features of the Brazilian crisis stood out in sharp relief.

## Changes in Economic Policy

There were also significant changes in economic policy. The government's preliminary plan made a diagnosis of the Brazilian economy, with an implicit criticism of the Castello Branco government. The document makes the following summary:

I. Weakening of the Private Sector, a Result of:

    (1) more serious problems with monetary liquidity;
    (2) decreased demand in many sectors.

The reduction of monetary liquidity made it difficult to maintain production at full capacity, which in turn was a result of:

    (a) the rapid expansion of certain costs, especially financial ones (interest), public service rates, the tax burden, and social responsibilities;
    (b) the quantitative control of credit;
    (c) the increase in average production costs, linked to the falling demand in various sectors;
    (d) the massive sale of very attractive public bonds in the capital market.

The decrease in demand in a great number of sectors was provoked by:

    (a) the reduction in average real wages;
    (b) the decrease in disposable income, as a result of increased taxes (without a corresponding increase in public spending);
    (c) the autonomous increase in the prices of certain services important to the make-up of wage workers' expenses;
    (d) the drop in agricultural production in 1966;
    (e) the reduction in the level of private investments.

Sectors were affected in varying degrees by the insufficiency of demand or circulating capital: Those sectors most dependent on governmental demand present relatively better conditions in terms of sales and liquidity; those sectors more dependent on private demand, mainly that of wage workers, face serious problems in the present situation, making the difficult long-term perspective even worse.

II. Excessive Pressure Exerted by the Public Sector, in Various Forms.

The previous government's efforts to correct distortions in the economy and prepare the public sector for large investment programs seem to have been excessive for the economy as a whole. While it is true that the government's participation in terms of budget expenditures represented a smaller percentage of the national product, drastic increases in prices and the rates of public enterprises and the creation of new contributions (such as the Guarantee Fund for Time of Service) transferred a volume of resources from the private to the public sector in a relatively short time period, excessively reducing consumers' disposable income and enterprises' liquidity.[1]

This gloomy picture, which was aggravated by the previous government's economic policy, resulted in the formation of a strategy to fight inflation. It was an intelligent plan created by a new group of technical experts who were responsible for the control of the economy.

Basically they defined the problem as cost-pushed inflation, rather than as demand-pulled inflation, which was how it had been defined under the Castello Branco government. The government plan affirms that this analysis explains the most recent features of the inflationary process in Brazil, which has shifted from a stage characterized by expanding demand with a high utilization of productive capacity to a stage characterized by expanding costs with marked levels of idle capacity. Despite the contraction of demand, inflation continued in this last stage, because of the autonomous increase of certain costs, increased interest rates, the increase in average costs because of a drop in sales, and inflationary expectations.[2] Mr. Delfim Netto, treasury minister, and apparently the inspiration behind this reformulation, had previously stated:

The current Brazilian inflation cannot be understood in terms of theoretical schemes of pure demand-pulled inflation or pure cost-pushed inflation. Experience has shown that these two tensions alternate in predominance over the economy. In fact, the autonomous pressure of costs has always been present in the inflationary process yet was often obscured by the importance of the effects resulting from demand. These tensions are increased by the very nature of the fight against inflation.[3]

The basic thrust of the diagnosis cannot be denied, yet the analysis could have been more profound. The government's political involvements must have hindered its perspective. For example, the government made a point of stating that its changes in strategy in the fight against inflation were a result of the present economic situation, and did not imply a criticism of the previous government's policy. While it was clear that the economic situation had undergone changes, these changes were fully apparent when General Castello Branco and his Planning Ministry took office. The economy had already functioned with idle capacity since the beginning of the Brazilian crisis. Again, among the costs that cost-pushed inflation implies, the most important factor was profit, that is, the "cost" of each enterprise's capital. This cost was not taken into account in the official analysis.

At any rate, the Costa e Silva government has the distinction of being the first officially to diagnose inflation in Brazil as cost-pushed inflation, and to take measures coherent with this analysis. The majority of these measures were designed to stimulate demand, rather than limit it, as in the previous government.

Delfim Netto's economic policy showed good results. In defining inflation as caused primarily by costs, and only secondarily by demand, the government did not hesitate to take measures (though often limited ones) to stimulate demand. In this way, wage policies were reformulated in an attempt to make up for the losses wage workers suffered from the inadequate application of the formula of wage indexation. Credit guidelines became more flexible, and government investments continued in substantial amounts. Once demand was stimulated, enterprises increased their production and the employment level was again stabilized. Thus the economy entered a cumulative process of prosperity in which increased demand stimulated production, which, in turn, stimulated demand. Corporate profits rose so that enterprises were no longer pressed to raise prices in order to cover their costs.

In accordance with its definition of the causes of inflation, the government established strong administrative controls on industrial prices. If inflation resulted from costs, this was a sign that prices were being set monopolistically. This being the case, it made no sense to try to fight inflation by severe restrictions on demand. Demand should be liberated while at the same time a strict control over industrial costs and prices was established. Modern auditing techniques should be adopted, rather than the old system of price controls, which could easily be evaded. In this way cost variation could be verified so that the authorities could decide whether to grant price hikes or not. This policy was implemented through the creation of the Interministerial Price Council (CIP), which controlled costs and prices in the 350 largest

Brazilian enterprises, precisely the oligopolistic sector of the economy. The government's deficit was also held within strict limits and credit was controlled, so that at the same time as we entered a period of relative prosperity, inflation was reduced to almost half of that verified in 1965 and 1966. In 1967 and 1968 it floated around the 25 percent mark, and it was even further reduced in 1969.

It should be pointed out that the reduction of the government's deficit and of its issuing of currency was in part made possible by the financial reforms of the Castello Branco government. Castello Branco's mandate was strongly antidevelopmentalist. However, even though its anti-inflation strategy was both mistaken and exaggerated (because it was unable to differentiate cost-pushed inflation from demand-pulled inflation), and worsened the economic crisis, standing in the way of development, this regime facilitated the Costa e Silva government's control over the budgetary deficit. But the most important measures for holding the deficit in check originated from the Costa e Silva administration. On one hand, taxes were increased, and on the other, the new prosperity made it possible to collect more taxes, so that the deficit could be reduced. It should be pointed out that the government's deficit is a consequence of inflation, rather than a cause. To the extent that the government was able to reduce the inflationary rate (of costs) by stimulating demand and controlling prices, it also became easier to control the budgetary deficit and the issuing of new currency, so that the inflationary spiral was prevented from gaining force.

One other positive aspect of the economic situation during the Costa e Silva government was the increase in exports. The export picture got better in 1967, setting a record of $1,890 million in 1968. By all indications, it appeared that exports would reach the two million dollar mark in 1969. Aside from the favorable international economic situation, another positive influence upon exports (and especially manufactured exports) was the finance minister's policy of a mobile exchange rate. He established minidevaluations of the exchange rate that not only limited speculation, but also gave better guarantees to exporters, who would no longer run the risk of seeing their export costs (in cruzeiros) rising above their export prices.

*The Economic Recuperation*

The national income's growth rate, which had maintained extremely high indexes until 1961, began to fall starting in 1962. As Table 7.1 shows, the 1963–1965 period was one of serious economic crisis. Per capita income showed negative growth rates during these three years. In general, the Brazilian economy showed a quite unfavorable performance from 1962 to 1967. However, in 1968 the nation began a decided

TABLE 7.1
Growth Rate of the GNP

| 1960 | 9.7% |
|------|------|
| 1961 | 10.3% |
| 1962 | 5.3% |
| 1963 | 1.5% |
| 1964 | 2.9% |
| 1965 | 2.7% |
| 1966 | 5.1% |
| 1967 | 4.8% |
| 1968 | 8.4% |
| 1969 | 9.0% |
| 1970 | 9.5% |
| 1971 | 11.3% |

Source: Data gathered and revised by
the Fundação Getúlio Vargas. See
Conjuntura Econômica, Jan. 1970 and
Jan. 1971. The data for 1971 is an
estimate from the Treasury Ministry,
made in December of this same year.

economic recuperation. In this year, 1969, and 1970, revenue increased
8.4 percent, 9 percent, and 9.5 percent respectively.

Despite the recession in the United States, Brazil's economic activity
was strong in 1971. Investment remained high; exports were estimated
at three million dollars; the exportation of manufactured goods showed
a marked improvement; the government's budget deficit was under
control; and prices increased at a slower pace. The growth rate was
estimated at 11.3 percent.

## The Weak Democratic Tradition

Though the crisis had been overcome in the economy, one could not
say the same of the political situation. At the end of 1969, the nation
was shaken by the death of President Costa e Silva. His successor was
General Garrastazu Médici, chosen by a military council. The country
continued under an authoritarian regime. Facing this dictatorship, the
most radical of the left groups, disoriented and lacking perspective,
responded with terrorism. The police often responded with violence
and torture. The highest echelons of government attempted to diminish
this phenomenon, but were unable to overcome the resistance of the

police. Despite successive defeats that revealed its weakness and lack of mass support, terrorism continued to be active, though it gradually became debilitated. On the other hand, the youth, intellectuals, and political leaders continued in silence. No possibilities of democratic dialogue existed. The dictatorial military regime, which had not yet been clearly defined, finally showed its true colors in 1968. We lived under the effects of Act 5.

Nevertheless, as we can see from the government party's victory in the 1970 elections, the government gradually managed to build a favorable image in the eyes of the masses. Brazil's victory in the 1970 international soccer championship helped that process along. But there are two other much more important factors: the Brazilian people's weak education in democracy, and the government's attempt to formulate a national project.

The Brazilian population's lack of experience in democracy makes it easy prey to strong governments. This phenomenon occurs not only among the lowest classes. These, the illiterate, miserable, and marginalized, are not even taken into account in the political process. The industrial working class and the lower urban middle class show a similar lack of democratic beliefs. This problem is related to the artificial origins of Brazilian political liberalism. The liberal tradition in Brazil never involved the majority of the population, as in the case of the United States or Europe. Liberalism has always been an imported ideology.

Until 1930, the nation was dominated by an agrarian-commercial oligarchy. Its economic and political ideology was liberalism, though in fact this ideology never had political consequences. However, it was adopted in the sphere of economics as a way to maintain the colonial *status quo* in Brazil. Economic liberalism, *laissez-faire*, prevented the government from adopting interventionist and protectionist policies and hindered any project for the nation's industrialization. In this way, economic liberalism became a powerful arm at the service of the agrarian-commercial oligarchy to keep Brazil as a model of economic dependency, an exporter of primary products the benefits of whose system were reserved for this oligarchy and for the imperialism of the industrialized countries.

Political liberalism was only a secondary aspect of this model. The political system was effectively oligarchical, based on the power of large *latifundiários* and the large-scale exportation of primary products and importation of manufactured goods. There was room for economic liberalism, but political liberalism did not fit in well. So it survived only artificially, idealized in the law schools that educated the sons of the middle and upper classes. It managed to hold sway to the extent that it was the dominant ideology in Europe, and because it was coherent with economic liberalism. Yet it was not representative of the nation's interests nor its most profound convictions, nor even of its most significant sectors.

The economic, political, and social changes that began in 1930—the period I am calling the first stage of Brazilian revolution—did little to change this perspective. The new political approach that emerged from this revolution denounced the antinationalist character of economic liberalism and tried to exclude its defenders from the country's economic and political process. In this sense, this movement shares common characteristics with the Revolution of 1964. However, while both processes negated economic liberalism, they also negated political liberalism. Thus it is not surprising that Brazil has little experience in democracy. In the period between 1930 and 1964, both political and economic liberalism were defended by the social and political groups that had dominated the nation until 1930. Thus political liberalism received its strongest defense from the most reactionary elements, who nevertheless did not hesitate to forget that ideology when it conflicted with their interests, and to appeal to the armed forces.

Of course there were also defenders of political liberalism among the progressive groups that emerged in this period. In fact this emergence created the elements for a period of democratic government between 1945 and 1964. But these groups—the working class, industrial entrepreneurs, students, intellectuals, the new middle class—were much more concerned with defining a nationalist ideology geared toward industrialization and economic intervention than with the defense of democratic freedoms. Until 1964, the intellectuals of the Brazilian left had little concern with formulating and defending a liberal political ideology in which political freedoms were an essential value. In fact, these freedoms had few defenders until 1968. Thus one can understand the lack of a democratic spirit in the Brazilian population and the reasons why a strong government could receive popular support.

Yet besides this negative factor, there is also a positive element that explains the popularity of the military government. This was the attempt to formulate a national project for the country's development. After 1964, the Castello Branco government adopted two watchwords, both negative: the fight against subversion and the fight against corruption. This kind of conservative and moralist appeal elicited little enthusiasm among the popular classes. After the transitional phase represented by the Costa e Silva government, the Médici government shifted the emphasis of its discourse from this negative approach to a more positive one. Though still incipient and imprecise, nationalism began to make its voice heard in the political-economic arena. This tendency received support from the military, whose traditional nationalism had received little stimulus from the Castello Branco–Roberto Campos government.

This new nationalism was mixed with a strong current of patriotism. It can be noted in the attention given to the flag, the national anthem, and moral and civic programs. These elements often became indistinguishable from the government's new development plan, which placed the building of an economically great and powerful nation above all other goals. This emphasis was expressed in its foreign policy with respect to coffee and instant coffee, marine freights, and the fishing industry. The Transamazônica Highway is another clear expression. It was built to ensure the nation's sovereignty over that area, as well as to mobilize the Brazilian people. The construction of Brasília and the Belém-Brasília Highway had the same goals.

In this way, the first outlines of a nationalist ideology and a national project began to be traced. The Brazilian military again emphasized nationalist ideals. But this nationalism was not yet clearly defined; it lacked a clear position on foreign capital and the nation's economic, political, and cultural dependence on the United States and Western Europe. Under the influence of technobureaucratic leaders, the government adopted a basically pragmatic attitude during this period, making it difficult to formulate an effective nationalist ideology. In fact, the strategy of the ruling technocratic group was clearly based on an alliance between the government and national and international capital. However, the government did not play a subordinate role in this alliance. Instead, it was an active element that sought to increase its rate of economic growth through the alliance.

## Concentration of Income and the Economy's Recuperation

As Chapter 5 has shown, the reasons behind Brazil's economic crisis of 1962–1967 are clearly related to the way income was distributed.[4] Starting in the 1950s, there was a strong tendency for income to be concentrated in the hands of the capitalist class. This tendency was caused by the increasingly capital-intensive nature of the investments made, and resulted in a permanent state of underconsumption. It was difficult to make up for the weakness of aggregate demand by private investments because the latter, in the final analysis, are related to the population's capacity for consumption. In a closed economy (as ours was from the point of view of industrial production) every investment, either short or long term, resulted in an increased supply of consumer goods that would have to find a market. The exhaustion of the possibilities of import substitution took place at the same time as the concentration of income, and severely limited the growth of the consumer goods market necessary to keep aggregate demand high.

TABLE 7.2
Profile of the Global Demand in Brazil

| Groups | % of the population | Population (1,000) | Per Capita income in $s | Total income ($1,000) | % of the income |
|---|---|---|---|---|---|
| 1st | 50% | 45,000 | 130 | 5,850 | 18.6 |
| 2nd | 40% | 36,000 | 350 | 12,600 | 40.1 |
| 3rd | 9% | 8,100 | 880 | 7,128 | 22.7 |
| 4th | 1% | 900 | 6,500 | 5,850 | 18.6 |
|  | 100% | 90,000 | 350 | 31,428 | 100.0 |

Source: Celso Furtado, Um Projeto para o Brazil (Rio de Janeiro: Editora Saga), 1968, p. 38. Based on data from CEPAL, Estudios sobre la Distribución del Ingresso em America Latina (Santiago, 1967).

Celso Furtado described this phenomenon in *Subdesenvolvimento e Estagnação na América Latina*,[5] in which he developed the bases for the "Latin American stagnation thesis." I adopted a part of this thesis in analyzing the structural vicious circle of Brazilian underdevelopment. Later, as a sequel to his previous diagnosis, Celso Furtado made a proposal aimed at overcoming the economic crisis. *Um Projeto para o Brasil*[6] is based on a plan for greater state participation in the economy and in the distribution of income.

Celso Furtado provides information, based on data from the CEPAL, on the distribution of income, that is, the profile of global demand, in Brazil. We see a population of 90 million inhabitants, with a per capita income of $350. Table 7.2 demonstrates that the concentration of income is an outstanding characteristic of the Brazilian economy. Fifty percent of the population live practically at the subsistence level, with a per capita income of $130. These same 50 percent have a share in the national revenue equal to that of the richest 1 percent of the population (this data being only approximate, of course).

On the basis of this data, which confirms that the then recent income concentration process was responsible for the economic crisis, Celso Furtado proposed an economic policy that would redistribute the income. This policy would be implemented by increasing the tax burden on the richest 10 percent of the population. This would imply a reduction of 25 percent in the per capita income of the fourth group, whose income would fall from $6,500 to $4,875, and a 10 percent reduction in that of the third group, whose per capita income would be reduced to $792. On the other hand, Celso Furtado estimates that the fourth group has an 80 percent marginal propensity to consume, and the third group a 100 percent propensity. Therefore, from the $1,625 dollars per capita taken from the fourth group in taxes, the corresponding liquid savings would be 80 percent, that is, $1,300, since the remaining $325 would no longer be saved by the fourth group. In other words, the government would save $1,625, but the fourth group would no longer save this $325. As to the third group, the 10 percent tax would be entirely transformed into government savings, that is, there would be a savings of $88 per capita. Given the population of the two groups (900,000 for the fourth group and 8,100,000 for the third), we would have an increased savings of $1,882,800 ($1,300 x 900,000 plus $88 x 8,100,000), corresponding to approximately 6 percent of the national income.

These savings, which would result from increased taxes, would be invested in large, highly labor-intensive projects. In this way employment would increase, as well as wages in the first and second groups. With their increased share in the national revenue, these groups would increase their demand for simple consumer goods, which are generally produced by labor-intensive methods. The consequent further increase in employment would put an end to open and hidden unemployment.

Celso Furtado's proposal is very attractive. It is based on an objective analysis of the Brazilian economic crisis and presents socially favorable solutions favoring a redistribution of income. It is an economically feasible project, though a quite radical one. It would not have to be implemented abruptly. It would be necessary to consider the reactions of private investors, who would have to reorient their investments. Nevertheless, this proposal has one fundamental limitation. It is politically very difficult to implement because it requires an extremely strong government independent of economic interest groups. Nor does it consider the negative effects that this redistribution would have on the expansion of the most technologically dynamic industries, which cater mainly to the third and fourth groups. While it is clear that these unfavorable effects could be bypassed, it would not be an easy task. Swimming against the tide is always more difficult. The most technologically sophisticated industries set the pace of Brazilian economic development. These are also the industries where the most active political-economic interests are concentrated.

It was probably because of these potential problems that Antônio Barros de Castro began to study another alternative for the Brazilian economy.[7] He views the profile of global demand in much the same was as Celso Furtado. Castro, also a CEPAL economist, observed that the first group was completely marginalized from the Brazilian market, and the second group participated only minimally. On the other hand, the history of Brazil's industrialization is marked by the production of more and more technologically sophisticated goods, intended for an increasingly small minority of the population. In the process of import substitution, it was initially simple general consumer goods that were substituted, such as textiles and food products. However, as this process evolved, those industries that remained dynamic, with greater growth

potential, began to produce more expensive and technologically sophisticated goods intended exclusively for the high-income classes, such
as automobiles or high fidelity equipment.

Antônio de Castro posited that if these premises are correct, in order
for Brazil to overcome the crisis, the nation would have to concentrate
income rather than redistribute it. This concentration, however, would
not be limited only to the fourth group, the capitalist class. We have
already seen that this kind of concentration was one of the basic causes
of the crisis. Rather, the third group, the middle class, should also be
included, and also the top layers of the second group, which could be
making progress toward entering the third group. The first group and
the majority of the second would be kept at their stagnated income.
Increases in income would be directed toward those of the intermediate-
and high-income groups. Though Antônio de Castro says he is not fond
of this solution on the social level, he sees it as potentially highly
successful from the strictly economic point of view. Benefiting these
groups, he argues, would maintain a high level of demand for sophisticated
goods, and consequently sustain the nation's dynamic industries.

From all indications, it appears as if this was the path chosen for
the Brazilian economy after 1964, rather than that proposed by Celso
Furtado. This policy can be pointed out as one of the basic factors in
the nation's economic recuperation after 1967. This was not a solution
formulated by the government economists and consequently was not
the result of a deliberate and conscious economic policy. There are no
definitive studies on this subject. Yet there is a firm basis for the
hypothesis that Brazil's recovery and further development was built
upon the concentration of income among the middle and upper classes.

Two kinds of evidence support this thesis. First, the post-1964 Brazilian
government of technocrats and military men is a middle-class government. Consequently, whether consciously or unconsciously, it formulated
an economic program that would benefit its class. The program of the
*Banco Nacional de Habitação* is one of the most obvious examples.
The *Plano Nacional de Habitação* was formally established to build
popular housing. In practice, however, it became an excellent means for
constructing houses for the middle class. Another important example
is the government's wage policy, which rigidly controlled working class
wages while liberating middle-class salaries. Furthermore, as industries
became more automated and capital-intensive, the natural tendency of
the market was to favor the intermediate groups, to the detriment of
the lower classes. Directly or indirectly, this type of industry demands
workers with an intermediate level of qualifications in much greater
proportion than labor-intensive indusry.

But there is more than indirect data and inferences to indicate that a concentration of income took place that benefited middle- and high-income groups. A 1969 *Banco do Nordeste* study shows how this process occurred in various capitals of the Brazilian northeast. According to this research:

- In Recife, the poorest 40 percent of the population, who had received 16.5 percent of the total income in 1960, received only 11.5 percent in 1967;

- In Salvador, the poorest 20 percent, who had received 5.3 percent of the total income in 1960, received 3.8 percent in 1966;

- In Fortaleza, the poorest 20 percent of the population, who had received 8 percent of the income in 1962, received only 5.3 percent in 1965.

This same phenomenon was repeated in Natal, Joâo Pessoa, Maceió, Campina Grande, and Sâo Luiz. Table 7.3 shows the complete results of this study.

The relation between the minimum wage and the average wage is another indication of this concentration process. Whereas the minimum wage in real terms fell each year, the average wage was rising. The real minimum wage showed a steady decline throughout the decade. Using May 1969 prices, the real minimum wage, which was 331.50 cruzeiros per month in 1959, systematically fell each year until it reached 187.20 in 1970. Table 7.4 shows this constant drop, which was especially pronounced between 1964 and 1965, showing a 20 percent decrease in that year alone. On the other hand, the real average wage rose during the 1965–1970 period in the state of Sâo Paulo. Using February 1969 prices, the real average wage, which was 405.66 cruzeiros in 1965, increased to 534.05 in 1970, as Table 7.5 shows.

The 1970 census definitively confirms the existence of income concentration. Whereas in 1960 the richest 5 percent of the population received 37 percent of the national income, in 1970 this figure grew to 45 percent.

The obvious conclusion is very simple and confirms our original hypothesis: A concentration of income was taking place, starting from the middle class and continuing on up. The minimum wage is an indication (though not always the most accurate one) of the remuneration received by the poorest sectors of the population. According to the Labor Ministry's data, in Sâo Paulo, the richest city in Brazil, 30 percent of the working population receives the minimum wage. The average wage is influenced on one hand by the minimum wage, and on the

TABLE 7.3
Distribution of Income by Fifths of the Population
(percentage)

|  |  | 1st (lowest income) | 2nd | 3rd | 4th | 5th (highest income) | Total |
|---|---|---|---|---|---|---|---|
| Recife | Oct. 60 | 16.5 | | 14.5 | 21.9 | 47.1 | 100.0 |
| | Mar. 67 | 3.2 | 8.3 | 10.9 | 21.2 | 56.4 | 100.0 |
| Salvador | 62 | 5.6 | 8.5 | 13.6 | 21.8 | 50.5 | 100.0 |
| | Aug. 66 | 3.8 | 7.7 | 13.9 | 23.6 | 51.0 | 100.0 |
| Fortaleza | 62 | 8.0 | 11.2 | 16.0 | 15.0 | 49.8 | 100.0 |
| | July 65 | 5.3 | 8.8 | 14.4 | 22.5 | 49.0 | 100.0 |
| Natal | Nov. 64 | 5.2 | 8.6 | 15.0 | 22.2 | 49.0 | 100.0 |
| | July 66 | 4.2 | 10.9 | 13.2 | 20.9 | 50.8 | 100.0 |
| Maceió | Apr. 64 | 15.4 | | 12.0 | 20.1 | 52.5 | 100.0 |
| | Mar. 68 | 3.0 | 7.3 | 12.6 | 21.3 | 54.9 | 100.0 |
| J. Pessoa | Nov. 64 | 5.6 | 8.1 | 14.8 | 20.7 | 50.8 | 100.0 |
| | July 67 | 2.8 | 6.5 | 12.9 | 23.7 | 54.1 | 100.0 |
| S. Luiz | Sept. 63 | 5.6 | 11.7 | 15.9 | 22.9 | 43.9 | 100.0 |
| | Feb. 67 | 4.6 | 8.5 | 13.2 | 21.4 | 52.3 | 100.0 |
| C. Grande | May 62 | 16.2 | | 13.8 | 21.3 | 48.7 | 100.0 |
| | July 67 | 2.7 | 5.7 | 11.2 | 20.9 | 59.5 | 100.0 |

Source:  Banco do Nordeste do Brasil, Distribuição e Níveis da Renda
Familiar no Nordeste Urbano (Fortaleza, 1969), p. 22.  Research
carried out by the BNB/ETENE-SUDENE.

TABLE 7.4
Real Minimum Wage

| Month and Year | Nominal Minimum Wage in Cr.$ | Cost of Living Index 1965/67: 100 | Real Minimum Wages in Cr.$, May 1969 prices |
|---|---|---|---|
| 1/1959 | 5.90 | 4.04 | 331.50 |
| 10/1960 | 9.44 | 7.08 | 302.65 |
| 10/1961 | 13.216 | 10.1 | 297.02 |
| 01/1963 | 21.00 | 16.3 | 292.55 |
| 02/1964 | 42.00 | 34.1 | 279.55 |
| 03/1965 | 66.00 | 64.9 | 230.80 |
| 03/1966 | 84.00 | 90.1 | 211.60 |
| 03/1967 | 105.00 | 122.0 | 195.36 |
| 03/1968 | 129.60 | 151.0 | 194.83 |
| 05/1969 | 156.00 | 187.0 | 189.37 |
| 05/1970 | 187.20 | 227.0 | 187.20 |

TABLE 7.5
Average Wage in the State of São Paulo

| Month and Year | Nominal Average Wage in Cr.$ | Deflator | Real Average Wage in Cr.$ Feb. 1969 prices |
|---|---|---|---|
| 3/1965 | 119.7 | 64.9 | 405.66 |
| 3/1967 | 219.55 | 122.0 | 466.00 |
| 3/1968 | 267.82 | 147.0 | 400.66 |
| 5/1969 | 400.48 | 187.0 | 470.96 |
| 2/1970 | 534.05 | 220.0 | 534.05 |

other by the higher wages that are paid to specialized workers, trade masters, technical operators, office personnel, engineers, and all the bureaucratic and technical employees typical of the middle class from its highest to its lowest sectors. So if the minimum wage falls and the average wage continues to increase, it is clear that this occurs as a result of a redistribution of income favoring those who receive higher wages.

To a certain extent, this phenomenon could be explained by the hypothesis that the minimum wage has become less and less important to the extent that industries pay their workers more than the minimum wage. However, while this is in fact the case in many enterprises, the minimum wage continues to be the base or point of reference in setting wages for unskilled and semiskilled workers. Thus, aside from being coherent with the analysis I am making, the hypothesis of the concentration of income among those receiving higher wages or salaries seems to be the most adequate to explain the inverse tendencies of the minimum and average salaries.

## Development of Dynamic Industries

This concentration of income ensured a large market for the most dynamic, technologically up-to-date industries. For example, the automobile industry was one of the foundations for the recuperation of Brazilian economic development. Automobile production showed a 5.6 percent growth in 1969, producing 112,844 automobiles in 1968 and 183,367 in 1969.[8] An increase in the first group's income has absolutely no effect on the automobile industry. Rather it is the income growth of the third group, and certain elements of the second group, that influences the market for these products.

There was another factor that sought to increase revenues, and also investment, without the constant pressure for a redistribution of income.

This was the government's policy giving incentives for the exportation of manufactured goods. This measure made concentration of income and development economically compatible by making investments possible without an increase in consumption. The final products were exported, rather than having to find a domestic market. The importation derived from this exportation process was focused on the purchase of prime materials and equipment intended to increase exportable production. And in this way the economy entered a cycle in which the capitalist system maintained its dynamism independently of income, redistribution, and an expansion of the internal market.

Thus the recuperation of the Brazilian economy resulted from these two phenomena related to the distribution of income. On one hand there is the phenomenon predicted by Antônio de Castro, the concentration of income in the hands of the middle class. On the other, there is the stimulation of the export economy, making development compatible with the concentration of income. Both phenomena could be considered negative from the social point of view. However, this book is not making a social critique, but rather an analysis of Brazilian economic development. Development is an historical phenomenon that should not include valorative connotations. Yet economic development is often erroneously defined as a process that benefits society as a whole through the redistribution of income. Unfortunately (if I may be permitted this valorative intervention), this definition is not a precise one. It is a product of idealist rather than historical reasoning. For example, the English Industrial Revolution was an historical process of great economic development. Yet it was also a period characterized by the concentration of income and the impoverishment of the peasants, which forced them to become industrial laborers. A century was necessary for this tendency to be reversed, so that the English working class would experience an effective rise in its standard of living.

This does not mean that here and now, in the twentieth century, two centuries after the Industrial Revolution, Brazilians should be repeating the same experience. I believe that no concentration of income took place in the 1930–1955 period. Yet all indications are that in the mid-1950s, Brazilian economic development came to be based on the process of concentrating income in the hands of the middle and upper classes. And this process was one of the main factors responsible for the recuperation of the Brazilian economy after its period of crisis.

Finally, one must admit that this model based on the concentration of income and the abandonment of the poorest Brazilians, the first group, in spite of its social injustice, is economically viable for a long period. As long as it is possible to increase the incomes of the third and fourth groups and transfer elements from the second to the third group, the economy can maintain its dynamism, despite the misery of more than 50 percent of the population.

## The New Political Model

In fact, it appeared that Brazil was setting up a new historical model of economic and political development.[9] Throughout the nineteenth century and up until 1930, Brazil developed according to the primary-export model. It was a development model geared to the external market, a product of the enormous development of international commerce and the international division of labor that started in the middle of the nineteenth century. Beginning in 1930 with the crisis of the international capitalist system, a new development model appeared in Brazil: the import-substitution model.

Industrialization followed this development model in Brazil, with the economy oriented to the domestic market. The import coefficient, that is, the ratio of imports to the national income, abruptly decreased. It maintained a level of about 22 percent at the end of the 1920s and fell to about 7 percent at the beginning of the 1960s. Industrialization was realized by substituting domestic products for goods that had previously been imported, whereas exportation remained relatively stagnant.

The last chapter examined the crisis of the import-substitution model, making a detailed investigation of its causes. At first I thought that it was a permanent structural crisis. However, it now appears obvious that the crisis was only transitional. The point at which the import-substitution model reached its maximum distortions and exhausted its possibilities coincided with a series of short-term, nonstructural economic problems as well as a political revolution. All these factors set off an economic crisis that lasted from 1962 to 1967 and served as a transitional phase to a new model for economic and political development in Brazil.

I have already outlined the underlying dynamic of this new economic model, in identifying the structural reasons for the economy's recuperation as related to the concentration of income among the upper and middle classes. I shall now summarize its main characteristics.

Brazil had definitely moved beyond the import-substitution model. The new development model had entirely different economic characteristics. The import coefficient was no longer decreasing; in fact it tended to increase. Our exports were no longer stagnant, either quantitatively or qualitatively. On the contrary, our exports increased dramatically, starting in 1966, and rapidly diversified, with marked growth in the export of manufactured goods. While some imported products were still being replaced by domestic production, the dynamic factor in Brazilian industrial development was no longer based on setting up new industrial sectors and consequently on the process of import substitution. It was now based on growth in the domestic market and the further development of already established industrial sectors.

The political model for Brazilian development in the 1930–1961 period was based on an alliance among the emerging national bourgeoisie, populist currents, and left sectors, centered around industrialism, nationalism, and moderate interventionism. It began to collapse at the end of the 1950s, and the Revolution of 1964 filled the political vacuum caused by the crisis of that political alliance. This revolution initially adopted a liberal project to the extent that it was realized with the participation of the traditional middle class and the oligarchical groups that had represented the opposition in the previous political model. The project announced by the Castello Branco government was quickly to reestablish representative democracy in the nation and establish a liberal capitalist system, reducing the government's participation in the economy. Yet this project was rapidly abandoned.

The political development model taking shape from 1964 until now in Brazil could be called a technobureaucratic-capitalist model. It is based on an alliance between the military and civil technobureaucracy[10] on one hand and national and international capitalism on the other. In its turn, this alliance is based on an economic development model characterized by the modernization of the economy, the concentration of income among the middle and upper classes, and the marginalization of the lower class.

The political and economic models of technobureaucratic-capitalist development constitute an organic unity that demands an integrated analysis. We could also call this development model "state capitalism," yet this denomination seems to detract from the specificity of the phenomenon under study. What we have in Brazil is a development model based on technobureaucratic control of the government by the military, technical experts, and bureaucrats, and also based upon capitalist control of the production process by this same government as well as by national and, especially, international capitalist groups.

The military men who took power in 1964 are a technobureaucratic group *par excellence*. Originating from a modern bureaucratic organization, the armed forces, they have a strong technical background and administer considerable human and material resources. They always adopt efficiency as one of their principal criteria, a preference characteristic of the technobureaucracy. Once in power, they immediately called upon civil technobureaucrats to participate in the government. Especially since the beginning of the Costa e Silva government, these two groups originating from the new middle class have assumed full control of the government and placed economic development and national security as their basic objectives.

Starting in 1964, national and international capitalism were invited to participate in the system. The 1964 revolution's early liberal economic tendencies explain this fact. The initial idea was actually to hand over power to the capitalist group, in accordance with the classic patterns of liberal capitalism. Nevertheless, the technobureaucratic group soon realized that it had sufficient strength and technical-organizational capacity to maintain control in its own name. It also saw that it could establish a developmentalist policy closely allied with national and international capitalism.

Thus the foundation was laid for the technobureaucratic-capitalist development model in Brazil. It is based on large technobureaucratic government and the large capitalist enterprise. The technobureaucratic government controls an immense part of the national economy; plans development; establishes fiscal, monetary, finance, wage, and housing policies; and intervenes directly in the economy through large public enterprises. The large capitalist enterprises and the large public enterprises are responsible for production. They utilize modern technology, and receive fiscal incentives and credit subsidies from the government. They have a large part of the national savings at their disposal because they obtain large profits and have access to the capital market.

The large technobureaucratic government and the large capitalist enterprise complement one another. Aside from its general control of the economy, big government also provides electrical energy, transportation, steel, oil, and communications. Large capitalist enterprises, mainly the international ones, control manufacturing industries, particularly automobiles, capital goods, durable consumer goods, electronics, and petrochemicals. It is in this latter sector, and also in mining and international finance, that the alliance between the government and international capitalism is most explicit. The financial agreements signed by Petrobrás, Vale do Rio Doce, and Banco do Brasil are clear examples of this phenomenon.

This alliance establishes the basis of a new kind of dependence: technical and political dependence. It is no longer a colonial dependence, opposed to industrialization, like the alliance of the agrarian-commerical oligarchy with international capitalism in the nineteenth century and the first part of the twentieth century. After international capitalism set up its own industries in Brazil in the 1950s, its opposition to Brazilian industrialization naturally disappeared. Yet a series of limitations were imposed upon our industrial development, especially when there was a conflict between the matrix and a Brazilian subsidiary or branch. There also continue to be groups (such as the U.S. instant coffee industry) that, because they are denied the opportunity to set up production in Brazil, are opposed to our industrialization. However, as a rule, international capitalism is interested in Brazilian industrialization to the extent that this implies profits and accumulation.

A second characteristic that distinguishes this new alliance from the old is that the former does not place the Brazilian partner in a clearly subordinate position, as was the case in the agrarian-commercial oligarchical relationship with international capitalism. In the present alliance, national capitalism is still the subordinate element in relation to both international capitalism and the technobureaucratic government. This latter, however, is an equal partner. It participates in the alliances that serve its interests, where it makes concessions, but it does not necessarily occupy a subordinate position. The Brazilian government of today is sufficiently strong, and represents the interests of the new middle-class technobureaucracy with enough coherence and concordance, that it plays its political role in the balance of power in its own name.

The government is no longer a simple representative of capitalist economic power, as in the orthodox Marxist analysis of the question. The unprecedented geometric progression of technology in general, and of administrative techniques for the management of large enterprises, has transferred power to the government technobureaucracy. On the other hand, the extraordinary growth of the state apparatus and its direct control of an enormous and continuously increasing portion of the means of production makes the technobureaucratic system even more autonomous.

In this way, the large technobureaucratic government is today in a position to be a partner in and even, to a certain extent, to control the activities of international capitalism within Brazilian borders. Outside the limits of this alliance, it can also take nationalist measures, as occurred in the case of the instant coffee industry, the international shipping freight policy, the 200-mile limit on its territorial waters, the Transamazônica Highway, and the restrictions placed on international capitalism's control of banks.

Yet despite the fact that this alliance is made between two relatively equal partners, this model does not go beyond dependent development. It is a new kind of dependence that, instead of being colonial and opposed to industrialization, has developmentalist characteristics. Development is realized by integrating Brazil into the international capitalist system, in which it becomes an appendage with neither technological autonomy nor autonomy in its accumulation of capital. Because foreign enterprises have no interest in developing a national technology, there is naturally a strong technological dependence. On the other hand, because foreign enterprises reap high rates of profit, an increasing portion of the national savings escapes our control, at the same time that a permanent process of denationalization of the economy takes place.

## The New Economic Model

In terms of supply, that is, in terms of the organization of the productive system, the new model of Brazilian economic development is characterized by what Maria Conceição Tavares and José Serra have called the "progressive heterogeneity" of the Brazilian economy.[11] Since the exhaustion of the import-substitution model, we can divide the economy roughly into two sectors: the modern sector and the traditional sector. The modern sector is made up of large capitalist and public enterprises, in the industrial, financial, and commercial sectors. It is especially, though not exclusively, characterized by technologically dynamic industries that use highly capital-intensive imported technology. The traditional sector includes not only a large part of the agricultural sector and the crafts industry, but also small and medium-sized industry. This sector produces relatively simple goods, using a relatively basic technology. It also includes the small businesses and consumer services oriented toward the low-income classes.

The modern sector differs from the traditional mainly in employing more advanced technology. The consequent productivity differential, as well as its larger scale, allows it to appropriate considerable savings and consequently permits it to control a large part of the accumulation of capital, together with the government. In the areas where the modern and traditional sectors coexist, involved in the same kind of production, the productivity differential does not necessarily drive the traditional producer out of the market, but it does ensure a high rate of profit for the modern producer.

This modern sector, which has the advantage of more advanced technology in production techniques as well as in administration and organization, also receives a whole series of incentives from the government. In accordance with its policy of basing the nation's development upon the growth of large industries, the government encourages and facilitates mergers, offers fiscal advantages, provides special credit, and develops the capital market. As a result, in the short term (and as I shall explain later, also in the long term), the economy becomes progressively more heterogeneous.

The other side of this model is the restructuring of demand examined earlier in this chapter. Aggregate demand may also be divided into two sectors, roughly, though not exactly, corresponding to the two productive sectors. They would be the upper and middle classes on one hand, containing about 30 percent of the Brazilian population, and the lower class, representing the other 70 percent, on the other hand. The first sector consumes mainly luxury goods—automobiles, durable consumer goods, and services produced by the modern technologically dynamic sector. The concentration of income among the upper and middle classes favors an even greater development of large national and international corporations as well as public enterprises. In turn, these large enterprises, highly capital-intensive and technologically sophisticated, increase the demand for specialized and administrative personnel, rather than non-specialized workers. Middle-class employment increases at the same time as lower-class workers become increasingly marginalized. Thus this circle of development is completed, as development of the modern sector permits concentration of income among the upper and middle classes, and this concentration, in its turn, stimulates the modern sectors' growth. Both the traditional productive sector and the lower classes are excluded, marginalized from this process.

There is another aspect of demand that has not yet been analyzed. Besides the concentration of income among upper- and middle-class conspicuous consumers, there is another phenomenon that reinforces the model, making the concentration of income compatible with development. This factor is exportation, which has increased rapidly in Brazil in the last years. Not only is the country passing the definitive test outlined in Chapter 6, but it is also finding a way to avoid the necessity for internal consumption of the consumer goods it produces. They are exported in exchange for machinery and raw materials. Thus it is no longer necessary for consumers' acquisitive power to increase in proportion to increased production.

This development model was recently the object of a simulated econometric study made by professors Samuel A. Morley and Gordon W. Smith. They concluded that "the more regressive the distribution of income is, the greater the rate of industrial development, in large part due to the importance of durable consumer goods, especially automobiles and the industries that supply them—rubber, machinery, metals, and gasoline."[12] Nevertheless, they also verify that the negative effect of a more equalitarian distribution of income on the nation's growth rate would be small. A simulation they made with a more progressive distribution pattern shows a difference of only 8 percent from that with the most regressive or concentrated pattern.

Though it confirms the theory that concentration of income is positively associated with Brazil's recent economic development, this analysis also gives impetus to Celso Furtado's distributionist thesis. The former verifies that even without the plan for state intervention in the economy that Celso Furtado proposes, the rate of industrial growth would hardly be reduced by a fairer distribution of income.

Nevertheless it is clear that it is not Celso Furtado's model that is in effect, but rather the model that concentrates income among the upper and middle classes. Representatives of these classes, confronted with this model, commonly affirm that it is only for the short or intermediate term. The way the story goes, in the long term, income will necessarily be redistributed, the marginalized populations integrated within the system, and the traditional sector homogenized with the modern sector, as in Europe and the United States.

Unfortunately, this approach is not necessarily true. In simplified and abstract terms, if Brazil's population were 100,000,000, with 70 percent making up the lower class with a per capita income of $214.30, and the other 30 percent making up the middle and upper classes, with a per capita average of $1,000, we would have a general per capita income of $450. To simplify further and identify the lower class with the traditional sector and the middle and upper classes with the modern sector, the traditional sector would have an income of $15 billion and the modern sector, $30 billion.

Now imagine that the population increases at the same rate in both sectors, and that income increases by 3 percent in the traditional sector (which would mean that the traditional sector would be kept marginalized, with a stagnant per capita income). It would be sufficient for the modern sector to grow by 9 percent for the economy as a whole to show a 9 percent annual rate of growth.

However, in order to grow by 9 percent, the modern sector does not necessarily have to resort to the market and labor power of the traditional sector. I have already described the effects on the market of the concentration of income among the middle and upper classes, that is, in the modern sector. In relation to labor power, the situation depends entirely upon the technology that is utilized. Imagine that we have an annual investment of $9 billion, of which 90 percent will go into the modern sector. I shall also postulate that the supply of labor in the modern sector (which includes middle class specialized workers) increases 3 percent per year, and that this supply constitutes 50 percent of the sector's population (the half actively involved in production). Thus 450,000 young people from the modern sector enter the labor market every year. Given an annual investment of $8.1 billion, if the marginal relation of capital to labor were $18,000, the modern sector would not have to contend for labor power with the traditional sector. In other words, according to this model, if $18,000 or more were needed to employ a new worker, it would not be necessary to transfer labor from the traditional to the modern sector, and the former would be permanently marginalized.

There are no available studies that measure this marginal capital-labor relation. It is important to remember that this relation includes not only direct employment created by the investment, but also indirect jobs in the service sectors. This is why, though it is apparent that the relation is quite low, we cannot make definitive conclusions in this respect.

Nevertheless we can make some general observations. Today investments in the modern sector are highly capital-intensive. They use much less labor power per unit of capital than the developed nations used in the corresponding phase of their economic growth. Therefore it is reasonable to suppose that the modern sector will not need labor from the traditional sector if the present tendency continues. The high intensity of investments being made is no longer a reason for underdevelopment and crisis, as I had previously believed, but now constitutes the cause of development with a consequent economic and social marginalization.

This technobureaucratic-capitalist development model, based on the concentration of income and the permanent marginalization of a large part of the population is therefore economically viable. However, I do not know to what extent it is politically viable. Clearly, it is not economically, much less politically necessary. The most one can say is that the alliance between the large technobureaucratic government and the large capitalist enterprise, and the process of income concentration, actively facilitate the development process today. Yet they also create profound social distortions and an economic and political dependence that sooner or later must be reevaluated. This is why it is not difficult to imagine that this development model will be reevaluated as on one hand, social pressures from the marginalized groups increase, and on the other, the government technobureaucracy begins to question the advantages of this alliance with national, and especially international, capitalism. There is no guarantee that this will happen, and in fact, the present tendencies point in the opposite direction. Yet there is no structural factor to impede this change in tendency.

## Industrializing Technocracy, the Fourth Alternative

The preceding chapter examined three possible ideologies for Brazil—classical neoliberalism, technobureaucratic-military interventionist liberalism, and developmentalist liberalism. The first two ideologies are not suited to a national project for economic development. The third is not politically viable on the one hand because of the absence of organization, independence, and political consciousness among the industrial entrepreneurs, and on the other hand, because of the colonialism, conservatism, idealism (alienation from reality), and moralism of the technocrats and military officers who assumed power in 1964. Yet these latter traits are not necessarily intrinsic to technobureaucrats and military officers. Rather, they are characteristics of the traditional middle class from which the Castello Branco government's military and civilian leaders were recruited. Leaders, however, may also be chosen from the new middle class, the product of Brazil's industrialization since 1930.

The new middle class is similar to the traditional one whose origins date back before the industrial revolution, in that it is conservative, cautious, and concerned with its own security. It differs from the traditional middle class to the extent that it is integrated into the productive process, and therefore has a more realistic perspective. The new middle class depends fundamentally upon economic development. It is a product of this development, its power and prestige increasing in direct relation to industrialization. The latter is responsible for the emergence of large public and private bureaucratic organizations in which elements of the new middle class, professional managers and technical experts, slowly but surely assume power.

On the assumption (still strongly denied by orthodox Marxists, but becoming increasingly true in a substantial number of countries, including Brazil) that middle-class groups are becoming politically dominant, one can suppose that Brazil will come to be governed by technobureaucrats and military men of this new middle class. It is characterized by its strong orientation or necessity to promote economic growth, this being the source of its power and prestige. If this were to occur, one could predict that the Brazilian military would begin to leave their colonialist and authoritarian ideas behind, and that the technocrats would begin to develop an economic theory adapted to the real necessities of Brazilian development. In order to become more politically representative, any national development project would have to include other groups in the government, especially the industrial entrepreneurs. Such a government could also reopen the dialogue with the left, as well as restore the unions' autonomy. On the other hand, this government would soon perceive that Brazil's economic development can take place only on nationalist terms and with increasing state intervention. Only in this way can the structural vicious circle of Brazilian underdevelopment be overcome. Since their interests are not organically tied to the liberal capitalist system, the technocrats and military officers of the new middle class will have no difficulty adopting positions favoring state control as they become necessary. Nevertheless, in adopting these measures they are not opting for socialism. What characterizes this new middle-class technocratic and military government is its ideological indefinition. Its fundamental interest is in maintaining its own power and security, which are essentially linked to the need for technological and industrial development, because technical knowledge (today the strategic factor of production, historically replacing land and capital) is what legitimates technobureaucratic power. If greater state control is necessary to ensure this development, then measures for state control will certainly be adopted.

Initially, I did not indicate this alternative because it is not typically capitalist. Nevertheless, within the existing institutional framework, it seems to be a viable alternative. There is no guarantee that this model will be adopted, nor do I consider it to be an ideal solution. Yet if one were to imagine an alternative for the economic, political, and social development of Brazil that was not strictly socialist, it would probably be the model just described.

An appropriate question here is whether socialism can lead Brazil to development. Here, of course, one can only hypothesize. My personal conviction is that a basically socialist system, with certain qualifications, would be ideal for Brazil. The qualifications are that certain sectors that are not easily dealt with through planning (such as small business, agriculture in general, where family farming tends to be the more efficient solution, and a large part of commerce and industry that demands a constant adaptation to the market) would be reserved for private initiative. All basic industry, a good deal of heavy industry, the banking system, and public services would remain under state control. Both private and state enterprises would function with considerable autonomy. They would be controlled in part by planning, by subsidies, and by economic sanctions, but also in part by market mechanisms, still in effect.

This book, however, is not geared toward creating political and economic theory, much less the author's ideal economic and political system for Brazil. Rather, it intends to make a global analysis of Brazilian society in this critical phase of its history, beginning in 1930 and continuing until the present. And this factual analysis verifies the diagnosis of a crisis, and more importantly, of the structural vicious circle in which Brazilian development is caught. One must therefore conclude that capitalist development is not a very viable solution for Brazil today. Neither the existing economic structure nor its present leadership permits one to predict a long-term future for Brazilian development along capitalist lines.

Nevertheless, for other reasons, starting with the economic and numerical strength of the entrepreneurial and middle class, and also the subordinate situation we occupy in relation to North American imperialism, any kind of socialist solution also faces serious obstacles.

Brazil is thus faced with an impasse. The period of Brazilian history analyzed here is characterized between 1930 and 1961 by development, and later by crisis. This crisis, which at first appeared to be temporary, has now shown itself to be persistent, profoundly rooted in the economic, social, and political structure of Brazil. Alternative solutions become less and less satisfactory. After the Revolution of 1964, the crisis became worse, and today Brazil is a divided nation, without long-term prospects. Yet though they may be difficult, there are alternatives that can lead Brazil on the path to economic and social development. Eventually a solution will be found that also respects civil liberties. This is why I would like to affirm confidently that in one way or another this crisis will be overcome. I have no crystal ball, nor do I intend to state how the crisis ought to be overcome. I admit that the prospects are not very bright. Nevertheless, I do not feel that pessimism is justified. Brazil is very big and very young. The world is undergoing a profound political, social, economic, and technological transformation. The technological revolution, with its immense potential for reform, and the student revolution, marked by idealism and a sense of personal responsibility, are taking place in Brazil as well as the rest of the world. Thus I am certain that any chance reader who may come upon these pages a few years from now will see that the Brazilian crisis as it is defined here has been overcome. There will be other problems, new challenges to be met. The period of development and crisis from 1930 through 1971 that I have analyzed here will have become part of history.

# 8
# The Crisis of the 1970s

The expansion that began in Brazil in 1967 reached its high point in 1973. Starting in 1974, an economic slowdown set in, reaching its culmination with the great recession of 1981. Between 1967 and 1973 the gross domestic product grew by an average of 11.3 percent per year, whereas between 1974 and 1981 the growth rate was only 5.4 percent. Industrial output suffered a more marked drop: In the first period it increased 12.7 percent annually, whereas between 1974 and 1981, the average annual increase was only 5.4 percent.

Thus Brazil was going through a second industrial cycle. Since the 1950s the Brazilian economy had attained sufficient industrial density to reflect the classic economic cycles. The existence not only of a complete consumer goods industry, but also of capital goods and basic inputs industries, created the conditions for the economic cycles of overaccumulation and underaccumulation of capital to become endogenous, closely linked to the internal dynamic of the Brazilian capitalist system. Brazil's economic cycles were no longer merely a reflection of the central economic cycles, repeated in Brazil by means of the rise and fall in the prices of export products (especially coffee) and the volume of our exports in dollars. Thus the Brazilian export cycle was no longer an exogenous one corresponding to the primary export model, but rather became a result of the internal dynamic of the Brazilian capitalist system. Yet at the same time, the internal economic cycle continued to reflect the cyclical movements of international capitalism, to which the Brazilian economy is naturally and increasingly tied. Table 8.1 shows the evolution of Brazilian output in the last two industrial cycles.

The first question to be asked is why this reversion of the economy took place in 1974. One should also examine what happened to the rate of inflation, the foreign debt, and the distribution of income, at the point when the economy entered this cyclical slowdown. The answers to these questions naturally lead to a closer examination of the economic policy practiced during this period.

TABLE 8.1
Output in Relation to Industrial Cycles
(annual growth rates)

| Periods | GDP | Industry | Agriculture | Services |
|---------|-----|----------|-------------|----------|
| 1955–62 | 7.1 | 9.8 | 4.5 | 6.8 |
| 1963–67 | 3.2 | 2.6 | 4.2 | 3.7 |
| 1967–73 | 11.3 | 12.7 | 4.6 | 9.8 |
| 1974–81 | 5.4 | 5.4 | 4.9 | 6.6 |

Source: National Accounts, Fundação Getúlio Vargas, and
Conjuntura Econômica, 35 (May 1982) for 1981 GDP.


**Reversion of the Cycle**

The first question about the crisis that began in 1974 is whether it is in fact a cyclical phenomenon. According to the neoclassic or monetarist economists, capitalist economies tend to balance out automatically, so there is no reason to speak of cycles. In fact the neoclassic economists encounter great difficulties in formulating a theory concerning economic cycles. They may admit that such cycles occur, but their explanation is always related to exogenous factors. In the case of Brazil, the exogenous factor pointed to was the oil crisis that began in the second half of 1973. Accordingly, one of the most significant representatives of this school said of the economic slowdowns between 1962 and 1980: "The recessions in Brazil's growth were influenced by external crises," later specifying that "in the most recent years of growth recession—1975 and 1977—we have the obvious direct and indirect effects of the oil crisis . . . and to complement this fact we had the finance crisis of the 1970s,"[1] that is, the large increase in interest rates that began in 1979.

Although these exogenous factors are undoubtedly important, it is obvious that they explain very little about the cyclical fluctuations in the economy. The latter are always caused by overaccumulation in the expansive phase, followed by a drastic reduction of investments in the slowdown phase. This phenomenon can be systematically observed in all capitalist economies. It is true that the 1973 oil crisis helped provoke the cycle's reversion, but it is also clear that the extraordinary accumulation then realized would also necessarily lead to crisis. As Table 8.2 demonstrates, industrial investment grew at an annual rate of 26.5 percent between 1967 and 1973, taking a vertical drop to only 0.1 percent between 1973 and 1980. Obviously, such an absolutely incredible growth rate could not be maintained for very long.

TABLE 8.2
Industrial Output and Accumulation Throughout the Cycle
(annual growth rates)

| Periods | Investment in Manufacturing | Manufacturing Industry | | | | |
|---|---|---|---|---|---|---|
| | | Non-durable Consumer Goods | Durable Consumer Goods | Capital Goods | Inter-mediary Goods | Total |
| 1955–62 | 17.4 | 6.6 | 23.9 | 26.4 | 12.1 | 9.8 |
| 1962–67 | -3.5 | 0.0 | 4.1 | -2.6 | 5.9 | 2.6 |
| 1967–73 | 26.5 | 9.4 | 23.6 | 18.1 | 13.5 | 12.7 |
| 1973–80 | 0.1 | 4.4 | 9.3 | 7.4 | 8.3 | 7.6 |

Source: José Serra, "Ciclos e Mudanças Estruturais na Economia Brasileira do Após-Guerra," Revista de Economia Política, no. 2 (April–June 1982).

Nevertheless, overaccumulation explains the reversion of the economic cycle only to the extent that it lowers industry's expectations of profit, and subsequently investments. In principle, a reversion of the economic cycle occurs by virtue of a reduction in the rate of capital accumulation, which in turn results from a drop in projected profit rates in relation to interest rates.

In 1974, the global rates of profit and accumulation still continued to increase, but probably the rates expected by the consumer goods industry (Department II: wage goods, and Department III: luxury consumer goods) were already on the decline, implying a subsequent decrease in the rate of accumulation. Only the Department I investments (capital goods), promoted by the second National Development Plan (NDP), were maintained.

Starting in 1974, the reduced rate of accumulation occurred particularly in the durable consumer goods industry (and especially in the automobile industry), which had led the expansive cycle. This was thus a classic crisis of underconsumption. The only difference, as I have previously observed,[2] is the fact that not only workers' wages, but also and principally the technobureaucratic middle class's salaries increased less than did profits in the expansive phase of the cycle. If consumption is considered to be a function of wages and salaries, and investments (and consequently industrial output) to be a function of profits, then it is easy to see that though the purchasing power of workers and the salaried middle class (which served as the basic market for the automobile industry) was growing, the production of durable consumer goods was increasing much more rapidly. In the years 1967–1973, the durable consumer goods industry grew at the explosive annual rate of 23.6 percent, whereas average wages in the same period (statistics are not available differentiating wages from salaries) increased at an annual rate of only 3.1 percent, as one can deduce from the data in Table 8.7. Even considering that the consumption of durable goods is also partly a function of profits, it is apparent that this overaccumulation in the durable consumer goods industry could not be sustained. Overaccumulation and consequently overproduction thus occur in relation to consumers' purchasing power.

Consumers' purchasing power was being artificially stimulated by the institution and generalization of direct consumer credit, made possible by the establishment of the price indexation in 1964 (which in practice partly annulled the Usury Law, removing the 12 percent annual limit on interest). By 1973, however, consumers were no longer able to go further into debt. Since the great majority of them already were in debt, direct consumer credit was no longer causing demand to increase more than income.

It should be observed that this interpretation, which attributes the reversion of the cycle to underconsumption, is not one commonly accepted by the neo-Marxist and post-Keynesian economists who represent an alternative vision to neoclassical monetarism.[3] Though the theory of underconsumption as an explanation for the economic cycle has solid bases not only in reality but also in the thinking of Marx, Rosa Luxemburg, Keynes, Baran and Sweezy, and Celso Furtado, it is frequently criticized, especially by orthodox Marxists, who consider it to be "reformist" because it presupposes that an adequate income policy and administration of aggregate demand could to some extent neutralize the cycle. The orthodox economists seek to explain the cycle in terms of the tendency (which has become a question of faith) of the organic composition of capital to increase, the decrease in the output-capital relation, and finally the decrease in the rate of profit. Nevertheless, I know of no Brazilian economist who has seriously used this theory to explain the reversion that occurred in 1974. In fact, though this theory has a certain logical consistency, it is of little help in explaining the short-term economic cycles (lasting about ten years) that I am examining here. In reality, what tends to happen is a certain increase in the organic composition of capital when the cycle is approaching its high point, because capital accumulation increases more quickly than wages and salaries. However, this fact is compensated for by the growth in the rate of surplus value, because the volume of profits is also increasing more quickly than the volume of wages and salaries, so that the rate of profit does not fall as a function of the increase in the organic composition of capital. It only falls in terms of expectations when enterprises no longer have consumers to buy their products.

A third explanation, also adopted by contemporary Marxism, and with a solid basis in Marx's thinking, is that the rate of profit decreases during the high point of the cycle as a result of the exhaustion of the industrial reserve army and the increased wage rate. Though this theory is of great value in explaining the cyclical reversions of the central countries with their strong unions, it explains far less in a country like Brazil where, aside from open unemployment, there is a large and permanent contingent of underemployed workers. However, at the cycle's peak in 1973, when there was a much lower level of unemployment, there was an increase in real wages that may have had some influence in the cyclical reversion.[4]

The perception that both the theory based on the increase in the organic composition of capital and that based on the exhaustion of the industrial reserve army were inadequate, together with a curious resistance to the theory of underconsumption (which can be explained only by the virulence of the orthodox Marxists' critiques of this theory) led various Brazilian economists to adopt another theory concerning economic cycles. This theory, advanced in 1976, was based on the concept of disproportion.[5] Nevertheless, these authors finally ended up with a position based on the underconsumption theory. This is clearly and correctly stated by Maria Conceição Tavares: "The recessive tendencies appear first in the nondurable goods sectors, given the fact that the majority of wages increase much less than output."[6]

The disproportion theory is really a theory of the economic cycle with Marxist origins, and in the final analysis is also a theory of underconsumption. This theory divides the economy into two sectors—Department I, producer of capital and intermediary goods, and Department II, producer of consumer goods—and assumes that because profits increase faster than wages in the expansive phase of the cycle, then Department I will also increase more rapidly than Department II in this phase. In Keynesian language, it is the accelerator mechanism that is at work. This disproportionate growth in the output of capital goods finally leads to their overproduction in relation to the consumer goods industry. Thus profit expectations in the capital goods sector are reduced, cutting off investments. This reduction has a multiplier effect on the economy as a whole, setting off a cyclical slowdown. Though it differs from and complements the original underconsumption theory by dividing the economy into two departments (or three—Department II being separated into durable consumer goods and wage goods), the disproportion theory is also a theory of underconsumption.

However, its originators did not perceive this fact. They saw only that Brazil's industrialization had entered a period of serious intersectoral and intrasectoral disequilibrium between 1967 and 1973. This basic disequilibrium was a result of the durable consumer goods industry's having grown more rapidly than the capital goods industry, and it was to this fact that they attributed the crisis.

A more rapid growth of the consumer goods industry could not lead to a crisis of disproportion. That is to say, decreased profit expectations and a consequent fall in investments in this department could not lead to such a crisis because they do not lead to reduced production and investments in Department I. What happens is merely that pressure is placed upon the trade account, with a greater importation of capital goods and basic inputs (which in fact occurred). A crisis of disproportion occurs when there is overaccumulation in the capital goods industry in relation to the consumer goods industry because of the insufficient growth of the latter, and when, as a result, Department I is suddenly forced to paralyze its investments. This was definitely not the case in the years 1967–1973 in Brazil. At this point, there was not insufficient growth in Department II.

### Increasing Inflation

Once the economic slowdown began, the rate of inflation, which had been falling up until 1973, again began to rise. Table 8.3 shows this increased inflationary tendency throughout the entire 1974–1981 period. It is true that in the years in which the GDP's growth rate fell even more because of monetarist policy measures (1975, 1977, and especially 1981), the rate of inflation also fell slightly. Yet the general tendency of the inflation rate was clearly to increase in the slowdown period (1974–1981), when it reached an average rate of 60.0 percent in contrast to 19.5 percent between 1967 and 1973 (Table 8.3). On the other hand, it is important to note that whereas in the first period the means of payment increased on the average at a rate almost double that of inflation (35.6 percent versus 19.5 percent) and this showed a declining tendency, in the second period, although the average growth rate of the means of payment was less than the average rate of inflation (53 percent versus 60 percent), the latter increased.

The theory developed by Ignácio Rangel to explain the increased inflation rate in the slowdown phase of the previous cycle is in complete agreement with this observation.[7] The cyclical slowdown provokes an increase in the rate of inflation, to the extent that inflation becomes a mechanism to defend the accumulation process. In reality, the more general cause of inflation is the class conflict over distribution. In Brazil, because of the political weakness of the working class, inflation is fundamentally a fruit of continuing attempts by the capitalist class to

TABLE 8.3
Inflation, GDP, and Means of Payment
(annual percentage variations)

| | Gross Domestic Product | Inflation (General Price Index) | Means of Payment (M$_1$) |
|---|---|---|---|
| 1967 | 4.8 | 28.3 | 45.7 |
| 1968 | 11.2 | 24.2 | 39.0 |
| 1969 | 10.0 | 20.7 | 32.5 |
| 1970 | 8.8 | 19.3 | 25.8 |
| 1971 | 12.0 | 19.5 | 32.2 |
| 1972 | 11.1 | 15.8 | 38.3 |
| 1973 | 14.0 | 15.5 | 47.0 |
| 1967/73 | 11.3 | 19.5 | 35.6 |
| 1974 | 9.5 | 34.6 | 33.5 |
| 1975 | 5.6 | 29.4 | 42.8 |
| 1976 | 9.7 | 46.2 | 37.2 |
| 1977 | 5.4 | 38.8 | 37.5 |
| 1978 | 4.8 | 40.8 | 42.2 |
| 1979 | 6.8 | 77.2 | 73.6 |
| 1980 | 7.9 | 110.3 | 70.2 |
| 1981 | -1.9 | 95.1 | 73.0 |
| 1974/81 | 5.4 | 60.0 | 53.0 |

Source: Fundação Getúlio Vargas and Banco Central.
Indice Geral de Preços, Conjuntura Econômica.

increase or at least maintain its rates of profit during the cyclical slowdown.

Starting in 1974, two mechanisms were put into practice that increased the rate of inflation while serving to maintain capitalist accumulation: "administered inflation" on the part of oligopolistic enterprises and "compensatory inflation" on the part of the state.[8] By means of administered inflation large oligopolistic enterprises increase their profit margins (profit over sales) in the slowdown phase in order to compensate for decreased sales and maintain their rate of profit (profit over capital). Yoshiaki Nakano demonstrates this fact definitively with data from the great recession of 1981. When inflation was 105 percent, as measured by the General Price Index, between February and July 1981, the competitive sectors increased their prices about 60 percent, whereas the average increase in prices in the oligopolistic sectors was 170 percent.[9]

But this kind of inflationary behavior on the part of the oligopolistic enterprises dates back to 1974. In fact, inflation and recession, that is, stagflation, can be understood only in the context of an oligopolized and indexed economy.

Administered inflation is apparent in the effects that domestic prices suffered as a result of the first two oil crises (1973 and 1979). Though these crises did not have the excessive importance that monetarist economists assigned to them, the "imported inflation" administered by the OPEC cartel doubtless contributed to the increase in inflation.

Compensatory inflation has its origins in the state's economic policy. It can be the Keynesian policy of increasing state expenditures in general in order to restimulate aggregate demand, or it can also be, as recently in Brazil, the establishment of an enormous system of subsidies for industrial export items, the consumer goods industry, agriculture, and the state enterprises' accumulation. These subsidies, paid out of the monetary budget, destabilize the state's global budget (the fiscal budget remains balanced, but this is of little importance). The deficit leads to the issuing of new currency, which naturally accelerates inflation if certain sectors of the economy are functioning at close to full employment. This compensatory increase in the amount of circulating currency is not exogenous to the economic system, as the monetarists claim, but rather strictly endogenous to the extent that it is a result of the very dynamic of capitalist accumulation.

Administered and compensatory inflation explain the increased rate of inflation. Three related factors explain why once a determined level of inflation is reached, this level tends to be maintained. In the first place, the propagation mechanism is strengthened by the oligopolized and cartelized nature of the economy. When a recessionary economic policy seeks to fight inflation, if businesses, especially oligopolies, are not able to increase their profit margins, they manage at least to pass on their cost increases and therefore to maintain their existing margins. A decrease in the inflation rate requires decreasing profit margins. Second, the system of indexing debts and credit, wages and rents, ensures continuing inflation, while at the same time it to some extent neutralizes those effects that are distortionary and lead to the concentration of income. Finally, because the real quantity of currency decreases with inflation if it is not nominally increased, the government is forced to issue new currency and increase credit in order to maintain the economy's level of liquidity, thus creating a deficit and sanctioning the existing inflation.

In the case of Brazil, starting in 1974, the public deficit (and the resulting nominal increase in the supply of currency) served to maintain the existing level of inflation (thus sanctioning it) rather than to accelerate inflation, because at no point did the economy return to an approximation of full employment.

## The Foreign Debt

Another consequence of the cyclical reversion was a disequilibrium in Brazil's balance of trade and current account at the time, which in turn resulted in an explosive growth in foreign debt. By assuming this debt, the country sought to postpone or bypass the economic slowdown. In turn, the external disequilibrium now became a cause of the crisis (in the same way as inflation), to the extent that it forced the government to adopt recessionary measures to reduce importations.

The foreign debt had already begun to accelerate during the "miracle." As Table 8.4 shows, the gross foreign debt almost quadrupled between 1967 and 1973. Since the reserves also increased greatly, the new foreign debt almost doubled in this period, increasing from $3,173 million to $6,155 million. As the increase in reserves shows, the debt during this period was based on increased international liquidity, that is, on the increased availability of Eurodollars for foreign loans. The government's strategy was to increase the gross foreign debt as much as possible while at the same time maintaining its own guarantees with increased reserves.

The debt was used to finance deficits in the trade account, which in turn would permit an increased rate of accumulation. However, though consumer goods were not directly imported, the commercial deficits also led to increased consumption, to the extent that prime materials and machinery were imported for the domestic production of consumer goods.

The trade account, which was usually favorable (in order to compensate for the deficit in services: freight, insurance, tourism, and interests), began to show a deficit in 1970. Between 1960 and 1969, the surplus in the trade account was $2,103 million, which is considerable in light of the small scale of Brazil's foreign trade at the time. Yet in the first years of the 1970s, even before the first oil crisis, Brazil began to finance its expansion with foreign loans. In the period between 1970 and 1973, the trade account's surplus turned into an accumulated deficit of $346 million.

When oil prices quadrupled at the end of 1973, it would have seemed natural for this policy concerning commercial deficits and foreign debt to change. However, it did not. The euphoria of the miracle had a contagious effect on Brazilian economic policy. We declared ourselves an "island of prosperity" and began to formulate grandiose projects for the second National Development Plan (NDP). These were centered around the development of the basic input industry, which would be

TABLE 8.4
Balance of Payments and the External Debt
(in millions of $)

| Year | Exports | Imports | Trade Balance | Net Services[1] | Interest | Current Account Balance | Gross Debt | Reserves |
|---|---|---|---|---|---|---|---|---|
| 1967 | 1,654 | 1,411 | 213 | -270 | -184 | -237 | 3,372 | 199 |
| 1968 | 1,881 | 1,855 | 26 | -328 | -144 | -508 | 3,780 | 257 |
| 1969 | 2,311 | 1,993 | 318 | -367 | -182 | -281 | 4,403 | 656 |
| 1970 | 2,739 | 2,507 | 232 | -462 | -234 | -562 | 5,295 | 1,187 |
| 1971 | 2,904 | 3,247 | -343 | -560 | -302 | -1,307 | 6,622 | 1,723 |
| 1972 | 3,991 | 4,232 | -241 | -730 | -359 | -1,489 | 9,521 | 4,183 |
| 1973 | 6,199 | 6,192 | 7 | -1,010 | -514 | -1,688 | 12,572 | 6,415 |
| 1974 | 7,951 | 12,641 | -4,690 | -1,532 | -652 | -7,122 | 17,166 | 5,269 |
| 1975 | 8,670 | 12,210 | -3,540 | -1,429 | -1,498 | -6,700 | 21,171 | 4,040 |
| 1976 | 10,128 | 12,383 | -2,255 | -1,574 | -1,809 | -6,013 | 25,985 | 6,644 |
| 1977 | 12,120 | 12,023 | 97 | -1,576 | -2,103 | -4,037 | 32,037 | 7,256 |
| 1978 | 12,659 | 13,683 | -1,024 | -1,720 | -2,695 | -5,927 | 43,511 | 11,895 |
| 1979 | 15,244 | 18,084 | -2,839 | -2,378 | -4,185 | -10,742 | 49,904 | 9,689 |
| 1980 | 20,132 | 22,955 | -2,823 | -3,120 | -6,311 | -12,807 | 53,847 | 6,913 |
| 1981 | 23,293 | 22,091 | 1,213 | -2,837 | -9,179 | -11,717 | 61,411 | 7,507 |

[1]Net Services do not include interest, profit and dividends.

Source: Banco Central and *Conjuntura Econômica.*

handled fundamentally by state enterprises, and the capital goods industry, under the control of national entrepreneurs. Between 1974 and 1976 we accumulated a commercial debt of $10,485 million.

This development strategy, which shifted the emphasis from Department III, the production of durable consumer goods, to Department I, the production of capital goods and basic inputs, was theoretically correct. But it was overly ambitious for the times, inviable in the new international situation. Within this context of developmental euphoria, in 1974 alone our trade account showed a deficit of $4,690 million and our gross debt increased almost 50 percent, whereas our reserves began to decline. The next years of the second NDP, 1975 and 1976, continued to be years of very high deficits, and only in 1977, when we came to our senses and abandoned the plan, did we show a trade surplus.

However, during this same year our foreign debt had reached such a high level that it tended to snowball. We were $32,037 million in debt, with interest alone amounting to two billion dollars. In 1979, when the United States initiated the restrictive monetary policy it still maintains today, generating dramatically increased interest rates, Brazil paid more than $4 billion in interest. In 1981, with a gross debt of $61,411 million, Brazil paid out $9,179 million in interest, which represents 39 percent of the value of our export products. In fact, it is interest rather than the trade deficit or services that has become the main element responsible for this snowballing debt, which got out of control and no longer has any positive effect on the rate of accumulation or even the rate of consumption. At first, between 1970 and 1976, Brazil borrowed money to increase its rates of accumulation and consumption. Later, between 1978 and 1980, Brazil borrowed money to maintain its level of consumption. Since 1981, we borrow not to maintain consumption, but almost exclusively to pay interest.

In the first years of the 1970s, the strategy was reasonable to the extent that the domestic rate of return was higher than foreign interest rates. The only problem at this point was that not everything we imported by borrowing was used for investment. A large part of our imports were used indirectly for consumption. This is why, even though we systematically increased our exports (at 20 percent per year during the 1970s) they were not sufficient to ensure a trade surplus. In fact, there were two factors that made a surplus in our trade accounts increasingly difficult to attain. On one hand, the increasing foreign debt had only a secondary effect on our export capacity. On the other hand, there was a serious deterioration in our terms of trade starting in 1977, which was further aggravated by the second oil crisis in 1979. As Table 8.5 shows, the price index for Brazilian exports in relation to our imports fell from 112.7 to 65.1 between 1977 and 1981. And beginning in 1979,

TABLE 8.5
Foreign Rates

| Year | 1<br>Import<br>Coeffi-<br>cient | 2<br>Import<br>Coeffi-<br>cient<br>(minus oil) | 3<br>Terms of<br>Trade<br>Index<br>(1970=100) | 4<br>Net Debt/<br>Exports | 5<br>Debt/<br>GDP<br>% | 6<br>Exchange<br>Valuation<br>Index<br>(1970=100) |
|---|---|---|---|---|---|---|
| 1970 | 5.4 | 5.0 | 100.0 | 1.50 | 9.0 | 100.0 |
| 1971 | 6.1 | 5.5 | 92.8 | 1.69 | 9.2 | 94.0 |
| 1972 | 6.7 | 6.1 | 98.2 | 1.34 | 8.6 | 92.4 |
| 1973 | 7.4 | 6.7 | 107.9 | 0.99 | 7.4 | 91.0 |
| 1974 | 11.5 | 9.1 | 88.3 | 1.50 | 10.8 | 87.0 |
| 1975 | 9.3 | 7.3 | 85.5 | 1.98 | 13.1 | 85.2 |
| 1976 | 7.8 | 5.7 | 96.0 | 1.92 | 12.3 | 85.5 |
| 1977 | 6.7 | 4.7 | 112.7 | 2.04 | 13.8 | 81.7 |
| 1978 | 6.6 | 4.6 | 94.5 | 2.50 | 15.2 | 75.6 |
| 1979 | 7.7 | 5.0 | 89.1 | 2.64 | 17.2 | 65.2 |
| 1980 | 9.2 | 5.4 | 70.2 | 2.33 | 18.8 | 56.8 |
| 1981 | 7.7 | 4.0 | 65.1 | 2.31 | 18.8 | 68.9 |

Source: (1) Banco Central do Brasil, Annual Reports 1980 and 1981.
(2) Banco Central do Brasil, Annual Reports 1980 and 1981,
and April 1982 Monthly Bulletin.
(3) Ibid.
(4) Banco Central and Conjuntura Econômica.
(5) Ibid.
(6) Banco Central do Brasil, Fundação Getúlio Vargas.

international interest rates increased rapidly, whereas domestic profit rates fell. At this point, the foreign debt not only snowballed uncontrollably but became a heavy burden on the Brazilian economy as a whole.

Thus the foreign debt became the main obstacle to the country's economic development. Because Brazil was heavily in debt and paying high international interest rates, it was to be expected that the international bankers would call for greater and more specific austerity measures and that the Brazilian government would have to adopt a more restrictive economic policy. As occurred in 1981, the international bankers have imposed a recessionary monetarist economic policy that seeks to control inflation and reduce imports. The Brazilian government, paralyzed and with little or no bargaining power, is incapable of proposing an alternative administrative economic policy and must give in to the bankers' demands.

The result of this situation is that it becomes more and more probable that Brazil will be forced to renegotiate its debt. (For futher discussion of renegotiation, see "The Total Crisis of 1983" in Chapter 10.) It will probably not happen until our reserves reach a very low level because of the refusal of the international banks to renew our credit. In the final analysis the decision to renegotiate the foreign debt, which will cause the Brazilian economy even greater losses, will not be Brazil's, but that of twenty or thirty big banks which dominate international finance.

## The Second National Development Plan
## and the Limited Slowdown

The beginning of the economic slowdown in 1974 could be clearly observed. At its peak in 1973 the GDP grew 13.9 percent, whereas in 1974, it dropped to 9.8 percent. But the slowdown between 1974 and 1979 was very gradual. Really it can be considered a slowdown only in comparison to the great expansion immediately preceding it. In fact, the GDP grew at an annual rate of 6.9 percent between 1974 and 1979, an average rate that equals that of Brazil's growth since the 1940s. This moderate slowdown, which ended in 1980 with an 8 percent growth rate, was possible because on one hand inflation served as the economy's defense mechanism against the crisis, and on the other, the foreign debt permitted the rate of accumulation to remain relatively high, even though the rate of profit was falling.

In fact, the rate of accumulation, propped up by the foreign debt and by state investments under the second National Development Plan, continued to rise in 1974 and 1975, although the cycle had already turned around. The fact that the rate of accumulation was maintained at such a high level after the cycle's reversion is surprising. Usually it is the drop in the rate of accumulation (provoked by reduced rates of profit anticipated in relation to interest rates) that begins the slowdown. This was not the case in Brazil because the state, giving priority to the capital goods and basic input industries through its second NDP, continued to make large investments itself and to stimulate investment in Department I. However, as Maria Conceição Tavares observes, though the economy practically doubled its productive capacity between 1973 and 1975, "the relative scale of the capital goods sector is insufficient to create an 'autonomous demand' that is able to stimulate its own demand and that of the entire production goods sector."[10]

On the other hand, in the durable and nondurable goods industries, which are the most important in terms of total output, the rate of accumulation dropped very quickly as consumers, already in debt and well-stocked with durable goods, no longer continued to increase their consumption as fast as during the "miracle." José Serra observes that "this variation in the cycle is not due to problems of demand in terms of aggregate investment nor to restrictions in the supply of import products. The difficulties arise in terms of the current demand for durable and nondurable consumer goods."[11]

TABLE 8.6
Basic Variables

|  | (1) | (2) | (3) | (4) |
|---|---|---|---|---|
| Year | Profit Rate | Investment Rate | Marginal Output/ Capital Ratio | Growth Rate of GDP |
| 70 | nd | 21.7 | 0.36 | 8.8 |
| 71 | nd | 22.5 | 0.47 | 12.0 |
| 72 | nd | 22.7 | 0.44 | 11.1 |
| 73 | 18.3 | 23.4 | 0.50 | 14.0 |
| 74 | 21.4 | 24.9 | 0.29 | 9.5 |
| 75 | 18.2 | 26.8 | 0.17 | 5.6 |
| 76 | 20.8 | 26.6 | 0.33 | 9.7 |
| 77 | 18.0 | 24.9 | 0.20 | 5.4 |
| 78 | 14.3 | 25.2 | 0.16 | 4.8 |
| 79 | 10.7 | 24.7 | 0.26 | 6.8 |
| 80 | nd | 24.3 | nd | 7.9 |
| 81 | nd | 22.0 | nd | -1.9 |

Sources:  (1) Bonelli and Guimaraes, "Taxes de Lucro de Setores
Industriais no Brasil, 1973–1979," Estudos
Econômicos 2, no. 3, pp. 93–114.
(2), (3), and (4) Brazil's National Accounts,
published by the Fundação Getúlio Vargas.

Starting in 1976 when it became apparent that the second NDP was inviable and had to be abandoned, the rate of accumulation began to fall. The incremental output-capital ratio, which serves to measure investment productivity, was already in full decline, as Table 8.6 shows.

This decrease in the output-capital ratio reflects the fact that the GDP's growth rate fell more quickly than the rate of accumulation. While the second NDP's economic policies continued to stimulate accumulation in its high-priority sectors, they also sought to control aggregate demand through monetary and credit restrictions. As a result, the rate of accumulation was maintained, whereas the growth rate decreased. But the most important factor in the reduced output-capital relation is the long maturation of the large state investments made at the time. These include the Itaipu hydroelectric plant, the steel railway, Usiminas, Açominas, and Tubarão port, some of which are still unfinished today (October 1982). When these projects were halted or slowed down, because Brazil simply did not have the resources to support investments

of such megalomaniac proportion, available resources were squandered
and the output-capital ratio was even further reduced.

Carlos Lessa observes that the second NDP was an authoritarian
strategy that, in the depths of the cyclical reversion, was based on the
premise that "the state is the subject, society and the economy are the
object."[12] The euphoria of the "miracle" and technobureaucratic vol-
untarism joined together to accomplish the project *"Brasil potência."*
Brazil was to pay the price for this optimism at the beginning of the
1980s, when other more serious errors came together with those already
made. Yet it should be pointed out that the basic strategy of the second
NDP—giving priority to basic inputs and the capital goods industry—
was correct. Furthermore, the use of state enterprises to produce the
most important inputs—oil, electrical energy, steel—and giving local
consumer goods industries special orders for machinery and equipment
were also appropriate strategies. The plan's most serious mistake was
that it did not take into consideration the cyclical nature of capitalism.
We did not recognize that the expansion cycle would necessarily exhaust
itself in Brazil and throughout the capitalist system, and that our
fundamental problem was now to bring our ambitions down to size
and adapt to the crisis (made even more serious by the energy problem)
rather than simply ignore it.

### Economic Policy, 1974–1979

The economic policy developed in Brazil starting in 1974 had its
high points and low points, and serious errors were made in an attempt
to carry out a grandiose development project in the middle of a cyclical
reversion and finance it with foreign debts that finally got out of control.
Yet until the second half of 1979, as long as Mário Henrique Simonsen
was in command of the national economy, if Brazil did not succeed in
managing the economy through a firm administrative control over prices
and economic aggregates, at least no large errors were made in terms
of the economy as a whole. Most importantly, none of the orthodox
monetarist policies that proved so disastrous in Chile, and principally
in Argentina, were adopted.[13] Though the monetary authorities adopted
a basically neoclassic and monetarist discourse in theory, their practice
was more moderate, combining basically Keynesian monetary and fiscal
instruments of macroeconomic policy with instruments of administrative
control such as price controls through the Interministerial Price Council
(CIP), control of exchange rates through the minidevaluation policy
(which had its successful start in 1967), control over interest and rents
through indexation, and wage control. The discourse was monetarist,

but the practice was a mixture of monetarism, Keynesianism, and price administration.

This eclectic practice was the fruit of societal pressures and counterpressures, particularly from the industrial bourgeoisie, which began to become powerful in the 1930s, and after the 1950s definitively became the dominant class in Brazil. From this position, it felt it could demand an economic policy that would serve its interests. Obviously this policy could not be limited to pure neoclassic orthodoxy.

Generally what we had between 1974 and 1979 was a Keynesian stop and go policy, which tried on one hand to adapt to the two great oil crises (1973 and 1979) through inflation and increased foreign loans, and on the other, to meet society's demands for accumulation (and consumption). Although this policy was not ideal, it was far superior to the orthodox monetarism that deindustrialized Chile and Argentina.

The Geisel government administered the economy by means of this stop and go process. In 1974 monetary restrictions began that were later abandoned in 1975. Because of the six- to nine-month lag between the monetary contraction and its effect on the GDP, the latter's growth rate fell rapidly to 5.7 percent in 1975. But in 1976, it again increased explosively, by 9 percent. In 1977, the GDP contracted again, this time to a 4.7 percent growth rate, because of a contraction in the means of payment in real terms of 6.2 percent in the previous year. Yet in 1978 and 1979, the GDP again grew by 6.0 percent and 6.4 percent respectively.

Given increasing inflationary pressures caused by the second oil crisis, and the finance crisis characterized by increased international interest rates, 1979 should have been a year of economic contraction. But when Simonsen left the government in August of 1979, he did not have time to carry out the new stop he had planned. Rather than his medium-term policies, which though they did not resolve the country's problems, at least did not dramatically worsen them, we would have a new economic policy administered by Antônio Delfim Netto.

## A Contradictory Policy

Brazil's economic policy from 1974 to 1979 was marked by a basic contradiction. On the one hand, the president's second NDP made great efforts at investment—efforts that in the final analysis were anticyclical, led the country into debt, and produced inflationary pressures. On the other hand, the Treasury and Central Bank sought to restrain these processes by restrictive but short-lived policies. As Dércio Munhoz[14] points out, there was an ongoing contradiction in the bosom of the government itself, which supported a developmentalist, interventionary policy on one hand and a conservative monetarist policy on the other.

This monetarist position, however, was never radical and at any rate never entirely prevailed. This contradictory economic policy generated serious distortions: increased real interest rates, increased financial speculation, and the increased appropriation of economic surplus by the expanding financial sector.

Domestic interest rates bore two kinds of contradictory pressures. On one hand, price indexation, which was lower than the rate of inflation, brought about a decrease in interest rates. On the other hand, the government placed restrictions on the supply of currency and sought to cover its deficits without provoking further inflation by selling bonds. This policy resulted in higher domestic interest rates.

The most serious consequence of the domestic debt, which, in real terms, increased 105 percent from 1970 to 1980, was that it facilitated extraordinary financial speculation, raising interest rates. Open market transactions, stimulated by a system that guaranteed the full liquidity of private sector bonds, accelerated the velocity of money and were an additional source of inflationary pressure. This process was finally corrected to some extent in 1979 when a series of regulatory measures were implemented by the Central Bank. These measures (through the creation of the Liquidation and Custody System, a clearing system for trading in public securities) made speculation in private bonds more difficult. They did not, however, prohibit a significant profit increase for the financial system, as well as an increase in its share of the national income.

Although the foreign debt increased heavily in this period, Brazilian foreign credit was good because the terms of payment were maintained at a reasonable level, as were the reserves.

It should be observed that, contrary to the general belief, the cruzeiro was deliberately devalued throughout this period. As Table 8.5 shows, the cruzeiro was devalued by 13 percent between 1974 and 1978. This policy was aimed toward making our manufactured exports more competitive, as well as facilitating the reduction of export subsidies. The devaluation resulted in slight inflationary pressures and eventually stimulated the deterioration of the terms of trade. Yet in principle this policy was correct; we exported a great deal more, especially manufactured goods, during this period.

However, despite the increasing devaluation of the cruzeiro, the government was unable to take away export subsidies when faced with the deterioration of our terms of trade (as a result of the international crisis as well as the second oil crisis in 1979). That is why the government formulated its late 1978 plan for an additional 25 percent devaluation of the cruzeiro that would be spread out over four years. This additional devaluation would be accomplished by accelerating the minidevaluations and would make it possible to eliminate all export subsidies. Nevertheless, many observers interpreted this plan as a sign that the cruzeiro was being valorized, when in fact just the opposite was taking place. The mistaken December 1979 maxidevaluation confirmed this wrong impression. In fact, if we take the year 1970 as our parity base for the cruzeiro, in 1978 the cruzeiro had been devalued by 24.4 percent. With the maxidevaluation, this percentage jumped to 43.2 percent in the middle of 1980.

### Expansion and Recession: 1980 and 1981

In the beginning of 1979, when President Figueiredo began his mandate and Mário Henrique Simonsen moved from the Treasury (where he had been since 1974) to the Planning Ministry, the Brazilian economy showed serious signs of crisis, some of which were being diagnosed by the government at the time:

- inflation had reached dangerous proportions (77.2 percent in 1979);

- the foreign debt was out of control, exacerbated by the oil crisis and increased international interest rates;

- the federal budget, burdened by growing compensatory subsidies and the state enterprises' cash deficit, made up 5.3 percent of the GDP in 1978 and 8.1 percent in 1979;[15]

- the cruzeiro was excessively valued;

- some of the state enterprises' prices (especially the public service enterprises) were artificially low.

In order to deal with this situation, Simonsen proposed (*a*) accelerating the minidevaluations; (*b*) reducing state expenditures and subsidies; (*c*) consolidating the fiscal and monetary budgets; and (*d*) provoking a new recession that would reduce imports and keep the inflation rate under control.

The entrepreneurs were dissatisfied with their falling profits. They put pressure on the government to name Antônio Delfim Netto, administrator of the "miracle," as planning minister, and forced Simonsen to resign.

Delfim Netto took up his post in August of 1979, imagining that he could repeat his success of 1967. He developed an expansionist strategy, correctly based on the premise that the cost push, or the administrative component, was what continued to be high. By expanding the economy at the same time as it administered prices, the government could induce enterprises to lower their profit margins (profit over sales), reducing inflationary pressure without decreasing their rates of profit (profit over capital) because sales would increase.

But the situation in 1979 was far different from the one in 1967. Whereas in 1967 the state budget was balanced and the foreign debt reduced, the picture in 1979 was exactly the opposite. In 1967, we were coming out of a cyclical crisis naturally, whereas in 1979 we were in the depths of crisis. In 1967, the neutralization of workers facilitated a wage squeeze policy; in 1979 important union movements were being consolidated in São Bernardo do Campo. In fact, the only common factor between these two periods was the cost component of inflation.

On the basis of this erroneous evaluation, several serious mistakes were made in economic policy. In the second half of 1979, the state enterprises carried out what was called "corrective inflation," raising their prices, which in turn pushed other prices upward. Contrary to the government's expectations, these inflationary effects were not limited only to 1979 but extended well into 1980.

In December 1979, the cruzeiro was devalued by 30 percent. This maxidevaluation created insecurity among those who had taken foreign loans, and caused the state enterprises serious losses. It also had strong inflationary effects. After this measure, the government preestablished the indexation of the exchange rate, as well as the economy's general indexation, at levels much lower than that of inflation. It sought to "reduce the enterprises' inflationary expectations" with this measure, thus placing price increases under control. This monetarist concept of inflation as based on expectations, like that adopted in Argentina, was obviously not appropriate to the situation. Whereas inflation increased 120 percent, the price and exchange indexation remained less than 60 percent.

As a consequence, the real interest rate of both domestic and foreign loans fell rapidly. This fall did not respect the law of value and caused immediate distortionary effects. There were no longer incentives for individual savings, and speculation and the black market became an integral part of the finance market. Inventories were increased, the economy entered into euphoria, the GDP increased by 8 percent, imports increased beyond measure, the trade deficit grew to $3.4 billion, and the gross foreign debt reached $53.8 billion by the end of the year.

In the second half of 1980, this irresponsibility on the government's part was curbed by the international banks, which suspended the automatic roll-over of Brazil's debt. After a series of unsuccessful trips abroad, and because of the international banks' increasing pressure for a stabilization plan, Minister Delfim Netto announced drastic policy changes in November 1980. The money supply, contracted since August of that year, was even further reduced, investments in the state enterprises were cut, interest rates and commodity prices were liberated, and the preestablishment of price and exchange indexation were lifted. The only policy elements that did not comply with the demands of the International Monetary Fund (IMF) were the maintenance of the 1979 wage law and continued subsidies to export manufacturers and agricultural producers; the government lacked political conditions to retract these measures.

Severe monetary contraction, as well as a dramatic increase in interest rates, paralyzed investments. Domestic interest had been artificially controlled by an underestimated preestablishment of price indexing and by the official fixation of bankers' interest rates. When these measures were lifted, at a point when real international interest rates had risen to almost 10 percent and the money supply had been curtailed, domestic interest rates rose rapidly to an average of 30 percent in real terms.

Studies show that minor fluctuations in interest rates have little effect on investments when rates of profit are high.[16] But when real interest reaches such a high level, and especially in a moment of cyclical slowdown, investment becomes inviable and is paralyzed. This is what took place in 1981 when the slowdown finally became a recession—the most severe in this country's industrial history. For the first time since 1930, the GDP's growth rate was negative. The industrial employment level fell 10.3 percent and industrial output decreased 9.9 percent. On the other hand, inflation also dropped, though only moderately—from 110 percent in 1980 to 95.1 percent in 1981. The trade account finally showed a surplus because of the reduction of imports provoked by recession. The international banks renewed Brazil's credit.

The effects of this recessionary and monetarist economic policy were quite modest, especially on inflation, and show a marked contrast with those of the 1964–1965 period, when a much more moderate recession (in 1965, the GDP still grew 2.7 percent whereas industrial output fell 4.7 percent) resulted in a significant drop in the inflation rate—from 91.8 percent in 1964 to 34.5 percent in 1965.

The fact that this later inflation was so resistant to recession can be explained by the economy's high level of indexation. In 1965, only wages were indexed to some extent, and even these were later reduced greatly. Other prices were only beginning to be indexed. In 1981 the Brazilian economy was indexed on a wide scale. Consequently, all cost increases were passed on to wages, interest, the exchange rate, rent, and finally commodity prices. Thus it became much more difficult to lower the established level of inflation.

In reality, the main objective of the recessionary policy was not to reduce inflation, but rather to balance the trade account and appease the international financial system.[17] This policy achieved some reduction in inflation only because the competitive sectors of the economy were unable to pass on all their cost increases. Yet even these paltry results, which were obtained by distorting relative prices (with the competitive sector suffering losses), proved to be of short duration. When the economy began to recover in 1982, structural inflation began to grow again. Exports dropped, however, because of the international recession, reducing the trade surplus even more. Despite the submissiveness of our economic policy, the international banks again began to threaten to cut off our loans.

In other words, the recession didn't resolve a thing. It only deepened the crisis, clearly showing that the government was paralyzed, unable to formulate a viable economic policy that could lead the country out of crisis.[18] Because of their impersonal and indiscriminate character, monetary restriction and recession were merely the simplest solution; it is clear that they were not the most efficient one in view of the oligopolized and indexed nature of the Brazilian economy. In fact, it became that much more obvious that an economy that is highly indexed (and consequently able to neutralize many of the distortionary distributive effects of inflation) must adopt more moderate and gradual policies to control inflation. In fact, its only real alternative is to live with inflation, which, in the final analysis, is relatively neutralized.

## The Distributive Crisis

The slowdown that began in 1974 was not only a financial crisis involving foreign and domestic debt and inflation, but also, and more importantly, a distributive crisis. This crisis originated on the international level. When oil prices rose in 1973 and again in 1979, the terms of trade deteriorated (see Table 8.5), creating an immediate real and potential advantage for oil-producing countries and a disadvantage for Brazil. But the fundamental cause of this distributive crisis was the exhaustion of the expansive cycle and the beginning of the contraction or slowdown phase. During the 1973–1974 cyclical reversion, when the country's terms of trade deteriorated, there was also an immediate reduction of what one might call our "potential ouput." Nevertheless, real income was maintained on one hand by the state's inflationary investments (the second NDP), and on the other by foreign loans. At that point effective income was greater than potential income. Another way to describe this phenomenon would be to say that effective income, that is, the sum of wages and profits, came to be greater than output, and the disequilibrium was "resolved" by compensatory inflation and foreign loans.

TABLE 8.7
Wages and Productivity

|  | (1) | (2) | (3) |
|---|---|---|---|
| Year | Real minimum<br>wage index | Real average<br>wage index | Productivity<br>index<br>(GDP per capita) |
| 70 | 100.0 | 100.0 | 100.0 |
| 71 | 95.7 | 103.2 | 109.3 |
| 72 | 93.9 | 107.4 | 118.5 |
| 73 | 86.1 | 112.7 | 131.8 |
| 74 | 79.0 | 112.7 | 140.8 |
| 75 | 82.5 | 121.5 | 145.1 |
| 76 | 82.0 | 127.2 | 155.3 |
| 77 | 85.4 | 135.8 | 159.8 |
| 78 | 88.0 | 147.2 | 163.4 |
| 79 | 90.4 | 154.0 | 170.1 |
| 80 | 93.4 | 149.4 | 179.0 |
| 81 | 95.5 | 161.3 | 171.4 |

Source: (1), (2) The minimum wage index includes the thirteenth
month's wage that was instituted in 1962. The average
real wage corresponds to the average wage of São Paulo
unions until 1974. (Source: Bacha and Taylor, Models
of Growth and Distribution for Brazil, Washington,
World Bank, 1980). Starting in 1975, the source is
the FIBGE (Fundação Instituto Brasileiro de Geografia
e Estatística) for wages in the manufacturing industry.
All indexes were deflated by the DIEESE's (Departamento
de Estatística e Estudos Socioeconomicos) cost of
living increase.
(3) National Accounts, FGV, Conjuntura Econômica, Dec. 1981.
The data for 1981 is an estimate.

This disequilibrium necessarily implies a distributive conflict. Given
its large scale, in order to resolve this problem, it would be necessary
to reduce wages or salaries or surplus value in some way. The concomitant
reduction of all these income components would result in a classic
recession. The isolated reduction of wages or salaries, interest or rent
dividends, or the corporate profit of various sectors is an alternative
solution, but would require resolving the distributive crisis in favor of
or against particular classes or sectors of the economy.

The classic solution that had been used in 1964 and 1965—reducing
wages—had become politically inviable. The opposition's severe critique
of the concentration of income during the 1970s and the government's
defeat in the 1974 Senate elections made a wage squeeze impossible.
In fact at that point, the government made changes in its wage policy,

TABLE 8.8
Distribution of Income among the Economically
Active Population
(percentage)

|  | 1960 | 1970 | 1972 | 1976 | 1980 |
|---|---|---|---|---|---|
| poorest 20% | 3.9 | 3.4 | 2.2 | 3.2 | 2.8 |
| poorest 50% | 17.4 | 14.9 | 11.3 | 13.5 | 12.6 |
| richest 10% | 39.6 | 46.7 | 52.6 | 50.4 | 50.9 |
| richest 5% | 28.3 | 34.1 | 39.8 | 37.9 | 37.9 |
| richest 1% | 11.9 | 14.7 | 19.1 | 17.4 | 16.9 |

Source:    Data from the 1960, 1970, and 1980 Demographic Census
and the PNAD; data for 1972 and 1976 from the IBGE.

increasing the acquisitive power of the real minimum and average wages,
as Table 8.7 shows. And in 1979, as a result of strong union activity,
a new wage law was enacted. This law provided for cost of living
increases twice a year rather than annually, and for a 10 percent increase
above the cost of living for those earning three times the minimum
wage or less. Those earning lower wages who kept their jobs got real
wage increases that were systematically higher than the increase in
productivity.

As a consequence of the first change in wage policies in November
1974, when all workers received a 10 percent bonus and the wage squeeze
policy was abandoned, two things happened. At the same time that the
cyclical slowdown provoked a decrease in the growth rate of the economy's
global productivity (that is, GDP per capita), there was also what I
have called a "relative reduction of surplus," or a certain deconcentration
of income.[19] Reduced rates of profit, as can be observed in Table 8.6,
resulted not only from the cyclical slowdown but also from the increase
in real wages that began in 1975. Between 1974 and 1979, while
productivity (GDP per inhabitant) increased by 20.8 percent, average
real salaries increased by 36.6 percent. Although the data on real minimum
wages is always questionable, the difference is nevertheless significant.

In a study made in 1976, I confirmed that the concentration of income
was highest in Brazil in 1974. Although the National Household Survey
(PNAD) was not made in that year, the data in Table 8.8, which shows
1972 as the year with the highest concentration, suggests that this analysis
is correct. This process continued and became more pronounced in 1973
and 1974. However, a moderate deconcentration process began in 1975.

Obviously, this slight deconcentration of income was the fruit of
strong distributive conflict. Although such conflict is an integral part

of any economic system, it became extremely pronounced during the slowdown and crisis that lasted from 1974 to 1982. Capitalists and technobureaucrats resisted any relative reduction of their share of income that resulted in inflation and debt. With the enactment of the 1979 wage law, the distributive conflict tended to be resolved against the interests of the middle class, who receive salaries roughly equivalent to 20 times the minimum wage.

The distributive conflict also took place on the level of the various corporate sectors and departments. The sector that benefited particularly during this slowdown was the finance sector. A particularly perverse characteristic of contemporary monopoly state capitalism is that it tends to benefit finance capital in moments of crisis. The decision to fight inflation within the framework of a relatively orthodox economic policy means stimulating increased interest rates. On the other hand, domestic and foreign loans lead banks to increase the volume of their loans in relation to their capital. Finally, inflation itself encourages bank profits to the extent that their cash deposits don't pay interest.

One hears a lot about the emergence and dominance of finance capital in Brazil. Yet in reality, if we define finance capital as the merger of industrial capital with banking capital under the latter's control, this phenomenon never existed in Brazil. Nevertheless, the financial system has grown impressively. Financial enterprises show high profits based on high interest rates, speculation, and privileged treatment by the government. Consequently, the finance system's share in the national income grew 5.7 percent in 1970 and 9.8 percent in 1979, with evident losses for other productive sectors.

The favored productive department between 1974 and 1976 was Department I, producer of capital goods and basic inputs, which was heavily subsidized. Yet though Department III, producer of durable consumer goods, showed a significant decrease in its growth rate (23.65 percent between 1967 and 1973, and only 9.3 percent between 1973 and 1980), as Table 8.2 shows, it was nevertheless the department with the highest growth rate during the slowdown.

In the middle of 1982, with inflation again growing and exports declining for the first time in many years, the Brazilian economy finds itself in the same shape as the central capitalist economy—in deep crisis, perhaps the worst of its industrial history. The fundamental obstacle to Brazil's development is foreign debt, and the international banks' constant threats to suspend the roll-over of our debts if we are unable to balance our trade accounts and maintain reasonable control over inflation.

These two factors are both consequences and causes of cyclical slowdown. It might be said that the economy's decline in the last half of the 1970s is a transitional crisis. The industrialized underdeveloped model, which took the place of the import-substitution model, has reached its end. After this crisis, we may expect that Brazil will define a new pattern of accumulation.

# 9
# The Dialectic of
# Redemocratization and *Abertura*

The Revolution of 1964, which established a military regime in Brazil, consolidated technobureaucratic capitalism in the country, that is to say, a dominantly capitalist yet increasingly state-controlled social formation, based on the alliance between the bourgeoisie and the state technobureaucracy. Ten years later, in 1974, a process began that the government would initially call "distention" and later *abertura*.[1] In order to understand this slow and contradictory political process, through which, to a certain extent, a democratic regime was reestablished during the 1970s, we must first have a clear understanding of the political regime that was established and the social formation that was consolidated by the Revolution of 1964.

From 1974 until the present, the political process has been characterized by the dialectical relationship between the *abertura* directed by the government and the redemocratization demanded by civil society. These two processes are not radically contradictory, but serve different objectives. Redemocratization is not only the actual reestablishment of civil rights and the electoral process, but also the struggle for democracy that takes place within a society. *Abertura* is a process controlled by the military, giving in to the process of redemocratization, yet at the same time postponing it as long as possible in order to preserve military power.

## The New Militarism

Once the authoritarian and modernizing military regime had been set up in Brazil in 1964, several other Latin American nations established military regimes (some of which have lasted until today) that sought to copy the Brazilian "model." This fact has led many analysts to identify the Brazilian military regime on the one hand with such regimes as those in Argentina and Chile, and on the other with those of General Alvarado in Peru or with General Torrijos in Panama.

In fact these regimes have certain points in common. The most important common characteristic is the fact that they are all the product of a "new militarism" that is technobureaucratic, modernizing, and Latin American. It is not the same as the classic militarism of the caudillos, because it emerges from armed forces constituted in the form of bureaucratic organizations, and therefore committed to authoritarian and developmentalist rationality. The Latin American "new military man" who has begun to become dominant in the postwar period in the most advanced countries of the region is a state technobureaucrat in uniform who combines developmentalist rationality and authoritarianism into the concept of national security. He is thus clearly distinguishable from the old Latin American caudillos who are oriented only toward maintaining in power the agrarian-mercantile oligarchies of which they form a part.[2]

The Brazilian military regime, however, has been rather more successful than some of its Latin American compeers, managing to remain in power for more than 18 years and, though it finally experienced a serious economic crisis, achieving high rates of economic growth throughout this period. During these same years, the Peruvian military regime has already fallen, and the Argentine and Chilean regimes have been leading their respective economies to deindustrialization and economic regression.

The failure of these regimes, in contrast to Brazil's success, can be explained in a number of ways. In the case of Argentina and Chile, the lack of a large industrial reserve army of the underemployed makes income concentration and the accumulation of capital difficult. In Peru, the military regime took power when the country still had only a very weak industrial base. The fundamental difference, however, has to do with the class alliances established in each country. In Peru the military technobureaucracy sought to establish an autonomous project (and a little bit later, through SINAMOS [Sistema Nacional de Apoyo a la Movilización Social] unsuccessfully attempted to win popular support). In Argentina and Chile, the military formed an alliance with the old agrarian-mercantile bourgeoisie, to some extent modernized by finance capital. In Brazil, however, the military technobureaucracy sought direct support from modern industrial and banking capital.

The alliance between the military technobureaucracy and industrial capital is the source of the Brazilian military regime's specific nature as well as its political strength, differentiating it from other Latin American regimes. This alliance did not become very well defined until about 1967. The military, under the UDN's influence, initially sought on the one hand to ally itself with the state civil technobureaucracy, and on the other to win support from the traditional petty bourgeois middle classes and the agrarian-mercantile bourgeoisie. But the regime soon realized that industrial and banking capital were in the strongest position, and decisively allied itself with both sectors.

In fact, the military technobureaucracy was unable to stand alone or even together with the new salaried middle classes. In order to remain in power, it had no alternative but to unite with the dominant bourgeois classes. If it had not made this choice, its government, like that of Peru, would soon have fallen. However, it is important to know with which faction of the bourgeoisie one should ally. An alliance with a reactionary faction such as the agrarian-mercantile bourgeoisie, like those made in Argentina and Chile, offers better chances of remaining in power for a long time, but this alliance will not further a true process of capital accumulation and development.

### The Strength and Weakness of the "Tripod"

The alliance between the military technoburueaucracy and industrial and banking capital, which defines the nature of the Brazilian military regime, is also the key to its relative economic and political success. In 1964, Brazil already had a powerful industrial bourgeoisie that had set up a complete industrial park. The multinational industrial enterprises had been solidly established since the 1950s. Banking capital, which served as the link between mercantile and industrial capital, was modernized and integrated into the accumulation process. (I do not call banking capital "finance capital," as is commonly done, because finance capital is a merger between banking capital and industrial capital, under the former's leadership. This merger never occurred in Brazil.)

Yet this dominant bourgeois and multinational class was unable to direct the accumulation process through classic market mechanisms and liberal democracy. At this point, the state technobureaucracy, both civil and military, emerged as a rationalizing force that, allied with this class, consolidated an economic and political form new to Brazil: "state capitalism," or "technobureaucratic capitalism." This phenomenon, which is generalizing to all the industrialized capitalist countries, means a dominantly capitalist social formation that shows increasingly techno-bureaucratic characteristics.

Thus between 1964 and 1968 an authoritarian and exclusive "tripod" political pact was formed, based on the alliance of the state techno-bureaucracy with the local bourgeoisie and multinational enterprises. The strength of this pact lay in the fact that local as well as multinational capital was already dominantly industrial capital, and in the military technobureaucracy's perception of this fact. Its exclusive nature was expressed in the radical exclusion of workers and broad sectors of the salaried middle class and petty bourgeoisie from political and economic power.[3]

Starting in 1974, it became clear that this exclusivity and lack of popular representation was one of the pact's major weaknesses. The other was that the economic and political control of the country was in the hands of the state technobureaucracy (both civil and military) and not in the hands of the bourgeoisie. Thus the social formation, which was dominantly capitalist, did not correspond to the political regime, dominantly military and consequently dominantly technobureaucratic. Though the military technobureaucracy understood that it would have to form alliances with the dominant industrial and banking capitalists, and make them the great beneficiaries of the system, it maintained its political control as the ruling group, also determining economic policy. The military's political tutelage over the bourgeoisie created a fundamental contradiction that, together with the lack of solid popular support due to its exclusivity, set off in 1974 a process of institutional crisis and also a process of partial redemocratization of the nation.

### The Advances and Retreats of *Abertura:* 1974–1978

Starting in 1974, Brazil began to undergo a transition to democracy, yet in the middle of 1982, this process is far from complete. In this sense, the Brazilian *abertura* is *sui generis*. Political scientists who study Latin America have tried to establish relationships and analogies among the democratic transitions experienced in Portugal, Spain, Greece, Peru, and Brazil. Whereas in the beginning of the 1970s most studies focused on the nature of authoritarian regimes, it has now become common for progressivist political scientists to study the nature of the transition toward democracy. Though they seek to establish the similarities among countries involved in this process, Brazil's evolution in this direction is markedly different from that of the aforementioned societies.

There are many reasons for the particular nature of the Brazilian case, starting with the fact that in the other countries I have mentioned, the transition was a rapid one, whereas in Brazil it is very slow and contradictory. In the cases of Greece and Portugal, the transition implied a break with the constitutional order. In the cases of Spain and Peru, the process was planned, as it was also in Brazil. But in these four cases, the transition took place relatively quickly and completely, whereas in Brazil it has already lasted more than eight years.

In fact, while the Brazilian *abertura* is a real process of transition to democracy, it is also a strategy aimed toward the survival of the authoritarian military regime. It is a contradictory process, a dialectic between civil society's demands for redemocratization and the regime's procrastination.

In this process, which opens up a bit and then closes again, the military regime wants to make it appear that redemocratization is a gift it is bestowing upon society. On the other hand, it has to consider the conservatism of the bourgeoisie, so that *abertura* has to be a slow, gradual process. If it were not, there would always be the threat of a regression, because among the military there is a distinction between the "soft-liners" (generally called "Castellists" after the first military president, Marshal Castello Branco) and the "hard liners." What is curious, however, is that it is never possible to tell who's who among the Castellists and the "hard-liners," because, though it may have suffered an occasional superficial split, the bureaucratic unity of the army has remained essentially untouched since 1974.

In fact, this antagonism between the two groups is mostly a fiction created by the regime itself and kept alive by superficial observers. The hard-liners are systematically used by the soft-liners to threaten civil society and maintain the authoritarian regime. *Abertura* must be slow and gradual because it is threatened by the same military men who propose it.

At any rate, after the regime's institutionalization between 1964 and 1968 and the rigorous military dictatorship between December 1968 (when Institutional Act 5 was enacted) and the beginning of 1974 (when General Garrastazu Médici left the presidency), *abertura* was initiated.[4] At this point, a first phase began during which President Geisel made promises of a "distention." However, with the government party's defeat in the November 1974 elections (with the MDB [Brazilian Democratic Movement] winning 14.5 million votes for its senators against the Arena candidates' 10.1 million votes), this process suffered its first crisis and its first closure, marked by the suspension of representatives' mandates in April 1975. The year 1975 was one of crisis, exemplified by journalist Vladimir Herzog's death by torture in October and by the ecumenical mass celebrated by São Paulo Cardinal Dom Paulo Evaristo Arns, the first mass demonstration against the regime.

Once General Ednardo D'Avilla de Mello was removed from the command of the São Paulo Second Army (the military torturers' headquarters), the *abertura* process took its first steps. Yet further suspensions of civil rights and the approval of the *Lei Falcão"* (a law designed to limit opposition candidates' appearances on television during the 1976 municipal elections) clearly demonstrate that General Geisel's intentions in the direction of *abertura* were rather limited.

Despite the *Lei Falcão* the opposition made a considerable showing in the November 1976 municipal elections. It did not take long for the authoritarian regime to respond. In April of 1977, General Geisel closed Congress down for 14 days and enacted a series of amendments to the 1969 Constitution, designed to ensure Arena's majority representation in the 1978 general elections. The most salient of these measures was the creation of "bionic" senators, elected indirectly, which guaranteed Arena's automatic representation in almost a third of all the Senate seats.

This would be the regime's last authoritarian coup until 1981. As a result of the "April political package," the protests within civil society began to increase. The bourgeoisie, who had spoken out against state control since 1975, now began to support democracy directly. The Bar Association, journalists, intellectuals, students, and the Church raised their voices in support of the reestablishment of civil rights. In the 1978 elections, the MDB was again victorious in the Senate and almost managed to win a majority in the House of Representatives. The government had no other alternative but to accept the redemocratization in progress and further accelerate the *abertura*.

The lifting of press censorship between 1977 and 1978 was the first concrete sign of redemocratization. And finally, in June of 1978, President Geisel announced an *"abertura cronogram,"* seeking to influence the elections and the members of the electoral college who were to select the new president of the republic. According to this timetable (as indeed did take place) his government would end by handing over his mandate to his successor, General João Batista Figueiredo. Institutional Act 5, which gave the president dictatorial power to suspend civil rights, censor the press, and close down Congress, was also annulled.

## The Bourgeoisie's Withdrawal from the Authoritarian Political Pact

Once Act 5 was done away with on 31 December 1978, the country took a big step in the direction of redemocratization. This was clearly a victory won by civil society and, within it, the dominant class. Since the 1977 "April political package," the bourgeoisie had finally abandoned its authoritarian stance and opted for the nation's redemocratization. Whereas other sectors of society—the left intellectuals, workers, students, the Church, the salaried middle class, the petty bourgeois professionals— had been demanding redemocratization for a long time, the bourgeoisie's position favoring the restoration of civil rights was a new fact. It was not only new but also decisive, and became the fundamental motive force behind redemocratization.

There is clear evidence that redemocratization was a victory of civil society, whereas *abertura* is an authoritarian strategy rather than the military's approach toward democracy, as they and their organic intellectuals would like to have us believe. A concrete indication of this is the fact that the June 1978 "*abertura* timetable" is, in the final analysis, a trade-off proposed by the military to civil society. Under pressure, the government agreed to do away with Act 5, but in exchange it required João Batista Figueiredo's election by the electoral college— that is to say, a guarantee that the same system would remain in power for at least six more years.

On the other hand, one can see how important the bourgeoisie's support of redemocratization was in making *abertura* inevitable for the government. The 26 June 1978 "Manifesto of the Eight," called the "First Document of the Entrepreneurs,"[5] made room for students, lawyers, the Church, and workers to demonstrate more strongly in favor of the redemocratization for which they had struggled so long.

In fact, as I pointed out in a series of newspaper articles published between 1976 and 1978, what was taking place, particularly in 1977, was the collapse of the alliance between the industrial bourgeoisie and the military technobureaucracy.[6] The basic idea developed in these articles was that redemocratization was inevitable, and not merely as the military regime's strategy to regain its legitimacy, nor as the natural liberalizing tendency of a capitalist regime like the Brazilian one, nor as the fruit of popular struggles for democracy.[7] Though each of these explanations has some basis in reality, the essential new historical fact was the breakdown of the authoritarian capitalist-technobureaucratic pact of 1964, and the definition of a hegemonic political project by the bourgeoisie. Thus a "democratic social pact" was created within civil society, leading the nation toward redemocratization. The stability of the authoritarian regime depended upon the stability of the alliance between the military technobureaucracy and the bourgeoisie. The importance of the struggles for democracy of workers, students, intellectuals, and the *comunidades eclesiais de base* (base communities of the Catholic Church) is indisputable.[8] But the new and decisive historical fact was that broad sectors of the bourgeoisie supported redemocratization.[9]

## The Bourgeoisie and Authoritarianism

The hypothesis that the fundamental reason behind redemocratization is the industrial and petty bourgeoisie's breach of the authoritarian capitalist-technobureaucratic pact stems from a basic presupposition: that even though this class has a long history of pacts and political covenants with authoritarianism, it is incorrect to assume that the bourgeoisie is inherently authoritarian. The hypothesis that the only alternatives available to a capitalist and industrialized society like Brazil are socialism and fascism no longer makes sense. This hypothesis was defended by the proponents of the "imperialist superexploitation interpretation" of Latin America, based on the idea that, given the exploitation to which the central countries subjected the Latin American countries, there was no other alternative for the local bourgeoisies but the authoritarian, fascist superexploitation of workers.

In reality, this interpretation exaggerates the imperialist exploitation of countries that have already reached a considerable degree of industrialization, like Brazil. It ignores the fact that imperialism's capacity to extract surplus from the peripheral countries tends to decrease to the extent that these countries become industrialized and define their own national objectives. In other words, this interpretation does not make a distinction between the old primary export imperialism and the new dependence of multinational industrial enterprises. Nor does it take into account that in an industrialized society like Brazil, the class struggle takes precedence over the anti-imperialist struggle.[10]

The mercantile (speculative and *latifundiária*) faction of the Brazilian bourgeoisie is intrinsically authoritarian. It has always depended upon mechanisms of primitive accumulation in order to appropriate economic surplus. This mercantile bourgeoisie, still dominant in many northeastern and central western states, is and always has been authoritarian, because it needs a strong state to realize its accumulation.

The industrial bourgeoisie, though far from being independent of the state, is not necessarily authoritarian for structural reasons: Its basic mechanism for the appropriation of surplus is surplus value. The entrepreneur's profit is thus realized in the market, through the classic exchange of equivalents, in which workers sell their labor power and capitalists sell their commodities in the market for their respective values. It was the domination of the surplus-value mechanism that enabled the central capitalist countries to become democratic during the nineteenth century. And this same process now makes it possible for a nation in an advanced stage of industrialization, like Brazil, to have an industrial bourgeoisie that is not necessarily committed to authoritarianism.

When pressured by the popular classes, the industrial bourgeoisie tends to adopt or accept a democratic posture, because it is a very numerous dominant class that needs institutionalized mechanisms to alternate power among the various groups and factions whose natural tendency is division. The industrial bourgeoisie is by nature a heterogeneous and divided class that unites and becomes authoritarian only when seriously threatened. And democracy is an institutionalized mechanism that, given the bourgeoisie's ideological hegemony, permits power to move among its various factions without risking its dominance, even when a left party takes power.

## The Military Regime's Loss of Legitimacy

The bourgeoisie began to break its authoritarian alliance with the technobureaucracy in 1975 with a campaign against state control and completed this partial breach in 1977, finally achieving the abolition of Act 5.

The basic reason for this change in the bourgeoisie's political position was the increasing loss of legitimacy on the part of the military regime in relation to civil society. Legitimacy is understood here to mean the support of civil society, which in turn may be defined as that part of the population that is organized into various classes, class factions, groups, and institutions with varying levels of political power. Legitimacy differs from representativity, the support of the "people," or all citizens, equal before the law. The regime's loss of legitimacy began in the early 1970s. The Brazilian military regime was never representative and certainly never democratic, but it did have the benefits of a certain degree of legitimacy until about 1974, to the extent that it could count upon the support of the class with the greatest political weight in civil society: the bourgeoisie. This legitimacy was based on two factors: the bourgeoisie's fear of a left revolution in Brazil and the regime's economic success. The threat of "communist subversion" was a fundamental justification of the 1964 *coup d'état*, because the bourgeoisie was in fact frightened. The economic success of the "miracle" justified subsequent Brazilian authoritarianism.

In the first years of the 1970s the last guerrilla *focos* were eliminated. The left became extremely cautious and took up the defense of democracy with much greater vigor than in the populist period. The bourgeoisie lost its fear of subversion, and consequently the authoritarian system lost a great deal of its legitimacy.

Also, the economic slowdown in 1974 revealed that the leaders' technobureaucratic omnipotence was not all it was thought to be. And finally in 1976 when the second National Development Plan was abandoned, two things became very clear: The state technobureaucracy was unable to overcome the movements of the economic cycle, and it could commit large errors in economic forecasting. The developmentalist legitimacy of the state technobureaucracy had received a severe blow.

Once the authoritarian regime had lost these bases of legitimacy its most obvious faults were clearly revealed: authoritarianism itself, and the concentration of income that had been confirmed by census data and widely analyzed by economists critical of the government. The two thrusts of the opposition in the 1974 election were denouncing the dictatorship and exposing the effects of the concentration of income. The result was Arena's defeat, which took the party entirely by surprise. After the 1970 elections, Arena's leadership had felt that it would play the role of Brazilian PRI (Partido Revolucionario Institucional [Mexicano]). The regime's defeat in the November 1974 Senate elections dealt a deadly blow to the regime's legitimacy by making its lack of representativeness glaringly obvious.[11]

It is no coincidence that the bourgeoisie's campaign against state control began in December of 1974 when liberal economist Eugênio Gudin, the father of neoclassical orthodoxy in Brazil, denounced the continuous growth of state enterprises. This criticism was greatly exaggerated and did not acknowledge the evident fact that the growth of the state enterprises was oriented strictly to stimulate (and never to compete with) private accumulation. Nevertheless, this criticism had its repercussions, was transformed into a political campaign, and became the bourgeoisie's first manifestation of opposition to the regime since 1964. In fact, once it became clear that the military regime was lacking in legitimacy, the bourgeoisie was quite prepared to listen to accusations against it. A classic liberal argument against state control was especially welcome. By fighting against state control, the bourgeoisie showed its dissatisfaction with technobureaucratic tutelage.

This tutelage had become increasingly difficult to accept because there was a decrease in the growth rate of the surplus to be divided up among capitalists' profits and technobureaucrats' salaries. Surplus is understood here as output exceeding necessary consumption, which in turn, in an economy like the Brazilian one, corresponds to total wages. Thus the GDP minus total wages equals surplus, which in turn corresponds to the sum of profits, interest, capitalists' rents, and top-level technocrats' salaries. This decrease in the growth of surplus originated on the one hand in the decreased growth of the GDP per capita, and on the other hand in the increase of workers' wages as a result of the change in wage policies after the November 1974 elections. Starting at that point, the rate of profit tended to decrease.

In a capitalist economy, a reduced rate of profit in a cyclical slowdown is a normal phenomenon. But in Brazil, the fact that the state has a great influence in the division of surplus gives this phenomenon an immediate political connotation. As long as the GDP continued to grow more than 10 percent, the eventual and necessary arbitrariness of state tutelage in dividing up surplus was acceptable. If some corporations received more special orders, or one industrial sector obtained more subsidies, or certain entrepreneurs received more favors, this was all acceptable as long as everyone was making big profits. But once surplus was relatively reduced, the arbitrariness of the state's tutelage became much less acceptable. The 1975 campaign against state control clearly expressed a protest against the favoritism that would certainly be a part of the big second National Development Plan projects. Yet when the plan was abandoned in the second half of 1976, it was the entrepreneurs involved in the production of capital goods and basic inputs who were to form the nucleus of the entrepreneurial opposition to the authoritarian regime. They had received the greatest benefits from the second NDP, and no longer did once it was abandoned.

## The Bourgeoisie's Project for Political Hegemony

It was not only negative reasons related to the government's loss of legitimacy that led broad sectors of the bourgeoisie to break their alliance with the state technobureaucracy in 1977 and support the struggle for redemocratization. At this point the bourgeoisie also formulated its own project for political hegemony—a project that could be carried out only within the framework of a democratic regime. The bourgeoisie, and especially the industrial bourgeoisie, wanted to shake off military tutelage and take command of the nation. The entrepreneurs renewed their efforts in this direction. The bourgeoisie wanted to be not only the economically dominant class, but also the political leadership.

Though this project was to a certain degree naive in that it sought to establish a linear relationship between economic and political domination, it nevertheless had a concrete basis in reality. Capital accumulation had been accomplished at a rapid pace since the 1930s. As a result, an immense entrepreneurial bourgeoisie had been formed. This class was made up of small, middle-sized, and large industrial and agricultural producers, as well as persons in commerce and other services. It increasingly replaced the old *latifundiária* and mercantile bourgeoisie. Though in lesser numbers, a *rentier* bourgeoisie also appeared, living off interest, rent, and dividends. This entire bourgeoisie espoused the classic capitalist ideology: economic and political liberalism; individualism; and the defense of "private initiative" as the only regime compatible with democracy, the valorization of entrepreneurial activity, and profit.

Aside from the fact that it more explicitly took on the political values inherent in its class position, the Brazilian bourgeoisie finally attained ideological hegemony over society. That is, to a great extent it succeeded in imposing its ideas upon other classes, including the middle-level technobureaucratic class. This class has its own ideology, based on technical rationality, planning, and economic development. Yet despite the importance these ideas have in modern societies, and the increasing influence of socialist values of all hues (Christian, Marxist, social democratic, etc.) in Brazil, there can be no doubt of the widespread domination of bourgeois values. One fact that bears this out is that some of the better-known entrepreneurs have become new "heroes" of Brazilian society, rivaling government leaders, political opposition leaders, and popular musicians for the media's attention. Maintained by its control of the newspapers, radio, television, and the school system on all levels, the bourgeoisie's ideological hegemony not only assures that the democratic scheme of alternating political parties can be played out with no great risks, but also allows the bourgeoisie to carry out its project for political hegemony. Despite a series of obstacles which it must overcome, this project is in full gear today. It is probably the main factor that keeps the bourgeoisie interested in a fuller redemocratization of Brazilian society.

## The 1977 Democratic Social Pact

Strictly speaking, the speedup that the redemocratization process underwent when Act 5 was annulled was a fruit of what I have called the "1977 democratic social pact."[12] Through this tacit, informal pact, civil society, outside the arena of class struggle, established a basic unity that made a partial redemocratization of the country possible. It was not a political pact, as it did not involve parties nor imply a strategy to take over power. Rather, it was a broader and more general phenomenon that I am calling a social pact. All democratic societies, independently of the class struggle in which they are involved, are based on a social pact similar to the one tacitly established in Brazil in 1977.

The Brazilian democratic social pact was based on three fundamental principles: (*a*) redemocratization, of interest to every class; (*b*) the maintenance of capitalism, of interest to the bourgeoisie; and (*c*) a moderate redistribution of income, of interest to workers and the left.

Redemocratization not only was of interest to the great majority of Brazilians, but now also became a conquest of this majority. It was naturally of interest to workers, intellectuals, and the salaried middle class. More recently, it began to coincide with the interest of the bourgeoisie on almost all levels (the petty as well as the middle-level and big bourgeoisie) and in almost all its factions except the speculative mercantile bourgeoisie. The latter, made up of the old agrarian-mercantile bourgeoisie and the new big bourgeoisie directly dependent upon special orders and state subsidies, continued to be authoritarian. This was also the case with the petty civil and military technobureaucracy in power, as well as with minority factions of all the other classes. These were the social sectors that continued to support the government political party: Arena at the time, today the PDS [Democratic Social Party].

The principle of maintaining the capitalist system formed a part of the 1977 democratic pact almost automatically. At only one point in history, in the period immediately after 1964, did the left believe that it could come to power in Brazil. It was then not yet sufficiently mature and was incorrect in its appraisal of the Brazilian situation. In 1977, however, when the hegemony of bourgeois ideology became clear, the left understood that capitalism was here to stay, at least in the near future. Thus it reevaluated its time frame, placing redemocratization as its absolute priority for the time being as a step in the revolutionary process.

When the enormous degree of income concentration became apparent, the bourgeoisie began to see the moderate redistribution of income as one of its objectives. Income had been strongly concentrated since 1960, and statistical studies showed Brazil to have one of the highest concentrations among capitalist countries, developed or underdeveloped.[13] Faced with the left's indictments of this concentration, the majority of the bourgeoisie began to accept the necessity to do something, especially with respect to wage policies, to slowly redistribute income.[14]

## The Conservative Turn of the Bourgeoisie: 1979

Once the electoral college elected Presidente Figueiredo and Act 5 was abolished, there was a regrouping of the right, even though some steps in the direction of *abertura* were made (such as amnesty in 1979, and the establishment of the direct vote to elect state governors in the general elections of November 1982). This regrouping would weaken and perhaps paralyze redemocratization. At this point the bourgeoisie turned to the right, to the extent that it reestablished its alliance—though in a weaker and provisional manner—with state technobureaucracy, personified by President Figueiredo.[15]

There are various reasons that explain the bourgeoisie's conservative turn. First, once the president's special powers were done away with, the most important objective of redemocratization had been attained. From the perspective of many members of the bourgeoisie, educated in the principles of authoritarianism, all the democracy necessary or possible had already been implemented.

On the other hand, the election of the new president was clearly a victory for the military regime. At a certain point, the democratic opposition, backed up by civil society's democratic pressure, believed that it would be able to win over a significant number of the Arena representatives and senators and thus elect its candidate, General Euler

Bentes, to the presidency in the indirect elections. However, the government counterattacked, formulating an "*abertura* timetable" and threatening to tighten up the regime if it were defeated. Either because of this government strategy, or because the MDB's candidate was also a military man who was unconvincing to the bourgeoisie without succeeding in dividing the military (in fact, he united them), the fact is that the bourgeoisie was further subdued and President João Figueiredo was obediently elected by the electoral college.

For the bourgeoisie, this election meant six more years of power for the same civil and military bureaucracy that had held power since 1964. Given the great dependence upon the state of the bourgeoisie, especially the big bourgeoisie and its main entrepreneurial leaders, it was necessary or at least convenient for the bourgeoisie to join forces with the governing technobureaucracy. This authoritarian and conservative turn is clearly demonstrated by the rapid acceptance of the government's policies on the part of the board of directors of the FIESP (the bourgeoisie's most important representative organ in Brazil), despite great expectations with respect to the board's independence after its election in 1980.

It should also be pointed out that the government in its turn made great efforts to please the big bourgeoisie. This was the meaning of Delfim Netto's designation as Planning Minister in August 1979. The fact that the state enterprises maintained their level of special orders of capital goods, and also kept up extensive subsidies to capital accumulation, at a time when the state's global budget deficit reached unprecedented levels and deepened an also unprecedented inflation, is further evidence of the government's efforts to please the bourgeoisie. In 1981, when recession became inevitable because of errors in economic policy, the industrial bourgeoisie suffered, but the financial bourgeoisie greatly benefited. And even in the industrial portion of the economy, the monopoly sectors controlled by multinational capital and the local bourgeoisie managed to increase their profit margins during the recession and obtain compensatory profits, as can be shown from financial reports they published in the first half of 1982.

The president also made many more trips outside the country, inviting a curious court of entrepreneurs. Although the formal justification given for these trips was the possibility of making commercial contacts, in fact they were a form of public relations for the government, giving business leaders the chance to manifest their homage to the president.

The increased expression of the union movement in 1978, 1979, and 1980 was also a factor in the bourgeoisie's tightening up of its alliances with the government. Especially in the ABC[16] region, the nation witnessed large strikes in 1979–1980 under the leadership of Luiz Ignácio da Silva ("Lula"). Though nonviolent, these strikes both surprised and threatened the bourgeoisie. The bourgeoisie was initially disposed to carry out direct negotiations with workers and accept their strikes, but when these same workers showed a greater determination than was expected, the bourgeoisie became frightened and finally appealed to the government to repress the strikes.

## The Reclosure of the System: 1980–1982

Given this new conservatism on the part of the bourgeoisie, the government felt strong enough to make authoritarian moves to dissolve the opposition party, whereas the democratic thing to do would have been simply to allow the creation of new parties without dissolving the old ones. A successful strategy was developed to divide the opposition, with the creation of the PMDB [Party of the Brazilian Democratic Movement], the PP [Popular Party], the PDT [Labor Democratic Party], the PTB [Brazilian Labor Party], and the PT [Workers Party], along with the PDS [Democratic Social Party].

The PMDB is a continuation of the MDB, bringing together the middle bourgeoisie, the middle class, and workers. The PP is the liberal democratic party, which attracted the upper bourgeoisie but ended up merging with the PMDB when, in November of 1981, the government prohibited crossing over party lines in the elections, impeding the alliance of opposition parties. The PDT is a party with a social-democratic mission, strong only in the states of Rio de Janeiro and Rio Grande do Sul. The PT is a new political phenomenon, created from the alliance of union leaders with representatives of the *comunidades eclesiais de base*. It is small party, democratically oriented to socialism. It shares with the PMDB the support of left intellectuals. The PDS is Arena's authoritarian successor, and the PTB gives auxiliary force to the government.

On 30 April 1981 the Riocentro terrorist attack was carried out by army members to forestall the left's May Day demonstration. The army was united in support of those who carried out the attempt, with the First Army's commander present at the funeral of one of those involved. The president found himself in a very weak position to investigate and punish those responsible, and this episode marked a further closing up of the political system. General Golbery do Couto e Silva's resignation further emphasized the move in this direction.

This process, based on the bourgeoisie's conservative turn in 1979 and the Riocentro episode in May 1981, would express itself in the "November 1981 electoral package." This package established that all votes were to be along party lines, prohibiting party alliances. According to this clumsy electoral maneuver, which was designed to divide the opposition parties formally, a voter could vote only for the candidates of one party, from city councillor and mayor on up to representatives, senators, and the governor.

This closing-up process was further delineated when, despite the electoral measures taken in November 1981, the government foresaw defeat in the November 1982 elections. In June of 1982, the government decided to (*a*) freeze the Constitutional Charter authorized in 1969 by the military junta, ordaining that it could be changed only by a two-thirds majority; and (*b*) establish a new makeup for the electoral college that would elect the president of the republic in 1985, guaranteeing a greater weight to the smaller states' votes (which it hoped to control) and seriously violating the principle of representation.

## Electoral Prospects and a New Populism: 1982

It is within this context of a relatively closed political system, yet with the expectation of an opposition electoral victory, that the year 1982 should be viewed. On the one hand, the PMDB has emerged as an alternative, denouncing the illegitimacy, authoritarianism, corruption, and incompetence of the government. On the other, the PDS has taken an increasingly populist position, seeking some popular support, while at the same time the government has adopted the authoritarian measures previously described.

If the opposition wins in the November 1982 elections, obtains a majority in the House of Representatives, and elects governors in several of the important states, it is clear that some moments of political turbulence can be expected in 1983. The military regime's authoritarianism is not enough to keep it in power. Though it would like to remain indefinitely, it has lost both its legitimacy and its representative nature. One must also consider that the nation is undergoing a grave economic crisis. If in fact there is a conservative turn on the part of the bourgeoisie, this does not necessarily mean the reestablishment of the 1964 alliance.

On the other hand, it is important to remember that through the years the PMDB has become a valid alternative in Brazil, to the extent that it avoids any radicalization to the left. Today it is a multiclass, mass party that brings together progressive sectors of the bourgeoisie and middle class, as well as broad contingents of workers. It is essential for there to be a valid alternative in order for the authoritarian military regime to be overcome, so that in the dialectic of *abertura* and redemocratization, the final weight will swing toward redemocratization.

Yet the opposition's victory in the November 1982 elections is not yet clear. Aside from discriminatory measures in the voting laws, the government has also set its entire electoral machine working. All the government offices and state enterprises not only invest vast sums in electoral propaganda but do all else in their power to favor the PDS candidates.

The government has understood since 1979 that only effective social changes could help its party attain some degree of popularity. It has made these changes, defining a new kind of authoritarian populism. It is not merely that President Figueiredo has tried to change his image as the ex-leader of the National Information System. Rather, a whole new populist social policy has been implemented. This policy established a wage law in 1979; increased land distribution to squatters through the National Agrarian Reform Institute (though it obviously did not carry out any type of agrarian reform), reducing to five years the time required for squatter's rights to take effect; subsidized agriculture; and increased spending on social consumption, especially housing and urban and rural electrification.

### Conclusion

Whatever the results of the 1982 elections, it is important to point out that redemocratization has still not reached its completion in Brazil. Though it no longer has special powers, the government continues to threaten civil society with their reestablishment. At the same time, it uses its majority in Congress to make laws that discriminate openly against the opposition.

However, it cannot be denied that a redemocratization has been taking place, a process whose causes and dynamic we have sought to analyze in this work. It is important to make sure that the interpretation laid out here not be confused with (*a*) the strategic authoritarian interpretation; nor (*b*) the liberal bourgeois interpretation; nor (*c*) the popular basist interpretation. In other words, partial redemocratization was not (*a*) the result of a mere survival strategy by the military regime; nor (*b*) the natural evolution of capitalist society, which necessarily tends to become more democratic; nor (*c*) the consequence of popular struggles for democracy.

Our interpretation, formulated and reformulated throughout the re-democratization process, has several points in common with the above interpretations. But it also emphasizes the break in the alliance between the technobureaucracy and the bourgeoisie, and points to the existence of the tacit democratic pact of 1977, still existent today, despite many difficulties. These are the new facts that, occurring within the context of the military regime's progressive loss of legitimacy, explain redemocratization. Its dynamic can be summed up as the dialectic, until now permanent, between the demands of civil society to deepen the redemocratization and the government's strategy to control and postpone its *abertura*.

# 10
## CONCLUSION
# Fifty Years of
# Development and Crisis

More than fifty years have passed since Brazil initiated its industrial revolution. During this period Brazil has undergone profound changes. The first thirty years were marked by a great and continuous development. This more specifically was the time of the first phase of the Brazilian industrial revolution, which transformed the country from an agrarian mercantile economy into an industrial capitalist economy. Once the foundations of an integrated industrial capitalist economy were established in the 1950s, the country's economic cycles became endogenous, with periods of expansion followed by periods of slowdown and recession.

In these fifty years of intense capital accumulation and the incorporation of technical progress, Brazil underwent not only economic changes, but also social, political, and cultural transformations. Not only did the productive structures radically change, along with the way Brazil handled its economic relations with the rest of the world, but the relations of production were also modified. New classes and class fractions arose: the industrial bourgeoisie, the urban proletariat, and the new salaried or technobureaucratic middle class. There was also room for new ideologies: Bourgeois ideology was modernized and became hegemonic; technobureaucratic ideology, efficientist and rationalizing, increased in importance; and democratic socialist ideas, though still in the minority, became more authentic, rather than merely repeating the slogans of various fractions of the international left. In general, to the extent that the country developed, its political and economic decision-making centers evolved within its own boundaries; Brazilian culture was no longer merely a transplantation of imported ideas and ideologies.

In economic terms, this period was characterized by import-substitution industrialization, with the import coefficient lowering systematically. This import-substitution model encompasses the first thirty years and corresponds in political terms to the populist pact. Beginning in the fifties, however, a new development model emerged: the model of industrialized underdevelopment, based on the concentration of income and the explosive growth of Department III, producer of durable consumer goods. In political terms, this period was expressed by the technobureaucratic capitalist authoritarian pact that received concrete expression almost ten years later in 1964. The present economic and political crisis, which began in 1974, is probably a transitional crisis. It is related not only to a new pattern of accumulation that might be called the mature industrialized underdevelopment model, but also to a new democratic political pact.

## The Total Crisis of 1983

From the moment I wrote Chapters 8 and 9 of this book (mid-1982) until the present (July 1983) the Brazilian economic and political systems have fallen further into crisis, a crisis so serious that it could be called global. Besides encompassing the economic and political aspects of society, this crisis is characterized by the fact that the social actors— the several fractions of the bourgeoisie, of the technobureaucracy, and of the working class—do not have any clear ideas or projects about how to overcome it. A society that has been generally defined by optimism and high standards of economic achievement is now dominated by pessimism and lack of perspective.

In the economic sector, the prevision that the country would have to renegotiate its external debt was confirmed. After the Mexican moratorium in September 1982, the confidence of the international banks in relation to Brazil disappeared rapidly. The Brazilian external reserves, around 3 billion dollars in September (officially more than 6 billion, because the official figure included unreceivable credits) declined to zero in two months.

In December negotiations with the IMF started, despite all the Brazilian government's affirmations that it would not negotiate with this institution, given its reputation in Brazil. Since the fifties, when President Juscelino Kubitschek refused to negotiate with the IMF, it has been considered in Brazil a representative of the international financial system, incapable of understanding the characteristics of underdeveloped countries. Indeed, its adjustment or stabilization plans, marked by severe fiscal and monetary policies, tending to induce recession, are not able to solve the problem of inflation and current account deficits, or they solve this problem at a social and economic cost that is not proportionate to the results achieved.

At the end of 1982, however, Brazil had two alternatives: to declare a complete moratorium or to declare a moratorium of the principal and continue to pay the current interest and dividends while negotiating with the IMF and the main creditors. The second alternative was chosen by the conservative Brazilian government, and in January Brazil signed its letter of intent to the IMF. It promised 6 billion dollars of trade surplus, a cut in the public deficit to half its presumed size, and an inflation rate of 90 percent. According to IMF estimates, this adjustment process would represent a negative rate of growth of GDP for Brazil in 1983 of 3.5 percent. It is important to note that in 1982 the GDP grew 1.4 percent, and industry grew 1.2 percent. The trade surplus in 1982 was only 778 million dollars, and inflation (IGP) at the end of the year was 99.7 percent, against an increase in the money supply of only 69.7 percent.

In these circumstances, the trade surplus of 6 billion dollars was very large, demanding a strong recession in order to cut imports. The target of cutting the public deficit in half was impossible to achieve, especially because, using an unacceptable methodology, the IMF includes the indexation of the government stock of public debt in the public deficit. The target chosen for the inflation rate was optimistic but eventually viable.

In exchange for the targets, Brazil would receive new loans from the IMF and the main international banks (around 7 billion dollars, if we include the additional interbank financing asked). The assumption was that this money would be enough to pay the interest or the deficit in current accounts in 1983, because the principal was already under moratorium.

In February 1983 the country was surprised by a new 30 percent maxidevaluation of the cruzeiro, raising strong indignation in the whole society. In April it was clear that the 6 billion dollars of trade surplus would probably be achieved, thanks to a very strong recession that curtailed imports, but that the target related to the public deficit was unattainable. As to inflation, the maxidevaluation and other corrective price measures recommended by the IMF resulted in an increase in its level from 100 percent at the beginning of the year to around 180 percent (annualizing the inflation rates of April, May, and June). On the other hand, the new money asked from the international banks in December 1982 was not enough, for various reasons (optimistic estimate of foreign direct investments in Brazil, optimistic estimate of interbank financing for Brazilian bank agencies outside Brazil), and Brazil needed 4 billion dollars more to close its balance of payments in 1983.

In consequence—as the option for a complete moratorium was not adopted—a new agreement was necessary with the IMF, an agreement that demanded additional austerity measures. The facts that the recession was very strong, that unemployment and bankruptcies were increasing, that imports were decreasing, and that the 6 billion dollar trade surplus target was being met did not impress the IMF. As inflation (which in Brazil is autonomous and cost-pushed) was increasing and the public deficit, in nominal terms, was not decreasing, the IMF demanded a stronger adjustment process.

Several measures were put in practice in June and July 1983. The most relevant was the decision to cut real wages—a policy that had not been followed since 1974. The decision was to index wages and salaries to 80 percent of the national index of consumer prices during the next two years. This measure will represent a real wage cut of around 30 percent in two years; the exact figure will depend on the future rate of inflation.

The economic prospect for the end of 1983 is for an inflation of 180 percent (the IMF admits 138 percent), a GDP decrease of 5 percent, and a trade surplus of more than 6 billion dollars. It will be the third year of recession in Brazil. The Brazilian industrial system is in serious danger. The level of Brazilian industrial production in mid-1983 was the same as in 1979. Idle capacity was around 30 percent. And very few people in Brazil believed that the policies demanded by the IMF and followed by the government would solve Brazil's economic problems. On the contrary, the prospect is that they will worsen the situation. The extremely large Brazilian external debt (83 billion dollars in December 1982) is a structural problem that definitely cannot be solved by means of short-term orthodox policies. And the autonomous cost-pushed inflation or stagflation that prevails in Brazil cannot be controlled by this kind of policy, either. Or better: It can, but at a cost clearly disproportionate to the results eventually achieved.

In political terms, as I had also expected, the 15 November 1982 general elections were a significant victory for the opposition parties, which obtained close to 60 percent of the votes. This represents almost 10 million votes out of a total of 54 million voters. The opposition was victorious in 10 out of the 22 states of the union, including São Paulo, Rio de Janeiro, and Minas Gerais. The PDS still maintains its base in the Northeast, where speculative mercantile capital continues to dominate in the small cities and the political system is marked by *coronelismo*. Despite the opposition's significant electoral victory, the PDS, through a series of electoral maneuvers, maintains its majority in the electoral college, which will choose a new president at the beginning of 1985. The lack of legitimacy and representation manifested in this way of electing the president stands out in sharp relief against the present elections and will deepen the political crisis in the next few

years. Brazilian society has made it clear that it wants democracy, yet
the regime continues to be fundamentally authoritarian. Its political
strategy is based on the official process of *abertura*, a strategy that the
elections have shown cannot be confused with redemocratization.

Whether Brazil will overcome this crisis depends on several variables.
Economically, our recovery depends on one hand on the recuperation
of the world economy, and on the other, on the leading class's capacity
to formulate an economic policy geared to Brazil's characteristics and
necessities. The country has already attained a relatively self-sustained
development, but the threat of deindustrialization such as Argentina
and Chile have experienced should not be forgotten. A strong bourgeoisie,
a broad technobureaucratic middle class, and an industrial working class
that has begun to organize, along with an economically strong state,
are all reassurances that we will not be victims of a similar tragedy,
but there are no certainties in this respect.

In reality, the solution to the economic crisis will depend upon the
formation of a new political pact that would give legitimacy to the new
government it would create. The present government, which is the fruit
of an outdated authoritarian political pact, has lost its legitimacy and
is economically paralyzed. Its economic policy is merely a reflection of
the pressures and counterpressures of the domestic and international
economic system. Only a new government representing a new legitimacy,
probably based on a new democratic alliance among the industrial
bourgeoisie, the technobureaucratic middle class, and the industrial
working class, will make a new direction for economic policy possible.
Such a new direction would not be a new version of populism, because
class struggle would be maintained, expressed in permanent social and
political revindications. What, then, would this social pact be that would
permit Brazil to function as a modern and diversified democratic society?

## Some Half-Truths Concerning the Social Formation

The definition of a new democratic social pact and the formulation
of a new economic policy capable of leading the nation to a new stage
of economic and social development depend on a correct analysis of
Brazil's social and economic formation. It is therefore necessary to move
beyond a series of half-truths and fallacies that, because of ideological
prejudices or the inability to take new facts into account, give an incorrect
picture of the extraordinarily dynamic society that is Brazil. By way of
a critical analysis of these ideas, I will eventually come to a general
vision of the current Brazilian social formation. I will deal here only
with the half-truths that prevail among the democratic left, which I

consider to be my own side, passing over for the moment the erroneous notions of the radical left as well as the moderate and radical right.

1. "Brazil is an underdeveloped country." This is more a half-truth than a fallacy. This classification might have fit the Brazil of the 1940s and 1950s, but in the 1980s, after fifty years of industrialization, it is appropriate only with many qualifications.

If underdevelopment is defined in terms of a low *per capita* income in relation to other countries, then Brazil is underdeveloped or at an intermediate stage of underdevelopment. Yet this is clearly not the most adequate definition. If underdevelopment consists in the dual nature of a society, then it is first necessary to make a qualification: Brazil does not demonstrate the classic duality between a modern capitalist society and a traditional precapitalist society; rather, it is characterized by the duality between industrial, technobureaucratic, state-controlled and oligopolized capitalism and mercantile, *latifundiário*, speculative capitalism. If underdevelopment is synonymous with poverty, some regions of Brazil are underdeveloped whereas others are heavily developed. For example, the state of São Paulo corresponds for all practical purposes to a developed country. If underdevelopment is defined as an economy's inability to integrate a large part of its population into the productive system and the modern capitalist market, leading to the creation of a mass of urban and rural subproletariats—underemployed, undernourished, politically and economically marginalized people—then Brazil is an underdeveloped country. However, if underdevelopment is defined in terms of the primary export nature of the economy, centered around agriculture and mining, then Brazil certainly is not underdeveloped. Brazil has a strong industrial economy, with more than two-thirds of its exports made up of industrial products (more than half of them manufactured goods). If underdevelopment is technological and cultural dependence, then Brazil is still an underdeveloped country, but is rapidly developing.

Perhaps the best way to characterize Brazil's stage of development is to use the term "industrialized underdevelopment." Or one could also use the phrase "new industrialized country." I prefer "industrialized underdevelopment" because it clearly indicates the contradictions and indefinitions of the present stage of capital accumulation and incorporation of technological progress in the Brazilian economy.

2. "Brazil is a peripheral country." This is a variation on the previous half-truth, with emphasis on Brazil's dependence upon the United States, Europe, and Japan as decision-making centers for its economic, political, and cultural policy.

Yet if one looks at the Brazilian industrial system's degree of technological sophistication; the level of our best universities in physical and mathematical sciences, engineering, and social sciences; the range and diversity of the market for the arts in cities like São Paulo and Rio de Janeiro; then one begins to see that Brazil is not so far from the center. It no longer merely absorbs foreign culture and reproduces central consumer patterns, but has begun to create its own critical and technical science.

During the primary export period, Brazilian culture was merely the ornamental transplant of European culture. Because this culture was not linked to the productive process, but rather related only to the modernization of a small elite's consumption, it was a drawing-room culture, unable to evaluate Brazil's own problems. This situation began to change radically beginning in the 1930s, and especially in the 1950s, when a new generation of intellectuals analyzed Brazil's situation through a critical application of concepts from European culture. However, at this point, Brazilian thought was geared toward Brazilian problems and culture. More recently, our thinking has become more universalized, so that the problems of contemporary society as a whole have become an object of systematic analysis. We are only at the beginning of this process, yet it is clear that the universalization of Brazilian thought (and not merely its Latin Americanization) is a concrete sign that Brazil is becoming less and less peripheral.

Brazil ranks as number eight in terms of gross domestic product within the capitalist system. This implies an immense domestic market and an increasing international presence. Given the country's low import coefficient, Brazil's commercial presence is still small. However, its political presence has begun to manifest itself, among other ways in a relatively independent foreign policy.

3. "The multinational enterprises that exploit Brazil are the main cause of its underdevelopment." This is clearly false, based on a nationalism that ends up diverting workers' and the left's attention from their main concern: class struggle. A good deal of the so-called dependence theory is oriented toward clearing up this error, which makes no distinction between the old primary export imperialism and the new industrializing developmentalist imperialism that emerged with multinational industrial enterprises in the 1950s. Yet perhaps "dependence" is not the best name for this theory, because few have a clear understanding of it.

Multinational enterprises have provoked serious distortions in the distribution of income to the extent that they facilitate the reproduction of the central countries' consumer patterns. Moreover, the transfer of technology obstructs the creation of our own technology. Finally, it is clear that multinational enterprises transfer a part of their surplus outside the country. Still, they should not be blamed for Brazil's underdevelopment. In the final analysis, their profits depend directly upon the country's development and the growth of its internal market.

For workers there is no essential difference between national and multinational enterprises. In certain respects, one has to admit that the multinationals are more favorable to workers: They pay higher wages and offer better working conditions. And in the process of class struggle they are often more flexible than local enterprises that have not yet learned to negotiate with workers without the state's support.

At any rate, multinational enterprises are a fundamental and permanent reality in the Brazilian social formation. They are an integral part of the local economic system and could at some future point be absorbed. In this context, nationalism would signify controlling them, limiting their areas of action, and encouraging them to export and to create technology within the country. This does not mean antagonizing them, nor blaming them for all the nation's ills.

4. "The bourgeoisie is a dominant and authoritarian class, incapable of assuming the country's political and economic leadership and of formulating a development project." This half-truth is related to the disillusionment of almost all the left with ideas concerning the "national bourgeoisie" that dominated Brazil during the populist period, and especially during the 1950s. It is also a way for the bourgeoisie to hide or disguise its domination, posturing as politically weak. The authoritarian nature of the Brazilian bourgeoisie can be historically confirmed by the fact that very rarely until now has it been effectively committed to democratic ideals. Yet when this statement comes from radical sectors of the left, who see the Brazilian and Latin American bourgeoisie as "intrinsically" authoritarian, it loses its objectivity and becomes ideological dogmatism.

Really there is no basis for speaking of a "national bourgeoisie," given the alliance of the Brazilian bourgeoisie with multinational capitalism. Yet this alliance does not mean that the Brazilian bourgeoisie is incapable of formulating its own political project, nor that it is intrinsically authoritarian. In fact the partial redemocratization that Brazil has been experiencing since the mid-1970s is to some extent the consequence of the bourgeoisie's project for political hegemony. This class has already attained an ideological hegemony in Brazil, imposing its individualist and liberal values upon the rest of society, and now seeks to shake off the military's authoritarian tutelage and assume more direct political control. It will probably not succeed in moving from dominance to leadership, because other classes are not ready to accept such a linear solution.

The bourgeoisie has always been a conservative class, marked by its authoritarianism and dependence upon the state. It is shortsighted, has a limited capacity to understand Brazilian social problems, and is constantly haunted by the threat of class struggle. Yet we should not transform historical and consequently contingent factors into intrinsic ones, affirming that the bourgeoisie is "essentially" authoritarian, conservative, and politically incompetent. The great capital accumulation that has taken place over the last fifty years has resulted in profound structural transformations within this class. One of these is the fact that industrial capital has gained a definitive hegemony over agrarian-mercantile capital. Today the Brazilian bourgeoisie is a new, powerful social class whose force should not be underestimated.

5. "Technobureaucrats are merely consultants to the bourgeoisie." This is another half-truth that does not consider the immense growth in the numbers and power of the salaried or technobureaucratic middle class, both in large private bureaucratic organizations and principally in the large civil and military state bureaucratic organization. Although the technobureaucracy clearly does serve as consultant to the bourgeoisie insofar as the latter is the dominant class, this technobureaucracy has its own specific political and economic interests and objectives, to the extent that it controls the relations of production and is based in its own ideology. One cannot reach a clear understanding of the military regime established in 1964 without a full appreciation of this fact.

6. "Inflation is the Brazilian economy's biggest problem and reveals the government's incompetence." There is no doubt concerning the government's incompetence, paralyzed as it is when faced by cyclical crisis. Yet inflation is definitely more a symptom of this crisis than the problem itself. Brazil is developing despite high rates of inflation. Its effects in terms of the concentration of income and the distortion of capital accumulation are relatively neutralized by the generalized price-indexing of the economy.

Inflation becomes a significant problem for the Brazilian economy only when the government, influenced by a monetarist vision and unable to perceive the difference between its own economy and that of the large central countries (which do not index), insists upon adopting recessionary, monetarist economic policies.

7. "Inflation is the result of a conspiracy by large oligopolist enterprises allied with the state in order to appropriate surplus by increasing subsidies and the public deficit." Although this idea is not entirely false, it could be more accurately described as another half-truth. Clearly, inflation has served the oligopolist sectors of the economy, increasing their share of revenue by increasing their profit margins. It has also been useful to banks and *rentiers* because the government tries to fight inflation by increasing interest rates.

Yet once a certain level of inflation has been reached, it is kept down by indexation and the oligopolization of the economy. As a result, the government has no other alternative but to go into deficit via subsidies and investments in state enterprises, and then to increase the nominal quantity of currency. If the government did not do this, or did it only on a very limited basis according to the monetarist scheme adopted at the end of 1980, the economy would undergo a liquidity crisis and plunge into deep recession.

8. "The solution to Brazil's economic problems is to abandon the export model and turn our attention to the domestic market." In the first place, Brazil never really adopted a true "export model." Except for some rare moments between 1967 and 1974, Brazil only substituted imports and reduced its import coefficient (the relation between imported products and the GDP). Currently our import ratio is less than 5 percent, excluding oil imports.

The best way for Brazil to increase its domestic market is to grow. This is possible only if Brazil manages a way out of the enormous imbalance of its foreign accounts by increasing exports, because its low import ratio makes basing its economic policy on import substitution impracticable. This is why it is essential that Brazil develop an industrial and technological policy geared toward exports. The development of a domestic market does not need a specific economic policy. A macro-economic policy that maintains aggregate demand and makes possible some degree of income redistribution is sufficient. If demand exists, then the industry and agriculture that supply the domestic market will automatically react, because they have an adequate capacity, sufficient labor power, and appropriate technology.

The mistaken idea here is not the defense of the domestic market, but rather the assumption that there is a contradiction between the development of this market and an export policy. Contradictions would exist only if the Brazilian economy were functioning at full employment and exports were a form of exporting workers' consumer goods and importing luxury consumer goods and capital goods, thus making the concentration of income compatible with the equilibrium of supply and aggregate demand. This is not the case in Brazil, or at least has not been since 1975.

## Mature Industrialized Underdevelopment

Although many other half-truths could be enumerated here, I feel that those I have just analyzed complement the analysis this book has been making of this present period in the Brazilian economy and its perspectives.

The current crisis of Brazil's economy is part of the world economic crisis that began in 1970. By all indications, this point marked the beginning of the slowdown phase of the long or Kontratieff cycle, which lasts approximately 50 years (25 of expansion, 25 of contraction). After the great postwar expansion, both the world economy and that of Brazil will remain in a relative slowdown until the 1990s. This type of transitional crisis affects not only a nation's economic situation, but also its political one.

In terms of the economy, it appears that we will come out of this crisis when Brazil implements a technological and industrial export policy that allows the country to improve its trade balance by exporting technologically sophisticated yet labor-intensive manufactured goods. Given the country's enormous debt on one hand and, on the other, the high degree of integration and sophistication of its industry (30 percent of its manufactured exports are machinery and equipment), this is probably an essential condition for the continuity of Brazilian development. Agricultural and energy policies are also important, along with an income policy that would lead to a progressive deconcentration of income while it maintained acceptable profit margins. This could be accomplished through a wage policy, an increase in social consumption expenditures, and a tax reform that would penalize individuals, especially *rentiers*, and make fraud more difficult.

But the fundamental challenge that Brazil faces today is to compete on equal terms with the central countries in the exportation of technologically sophisticated manufactured goods. The Brazilian economy has been successful up to this point in exporting manufactured goods, including technologically sophisticated products. Thus it is very possible that if we continue to increase our exports in this area that values our labor power, we will not become a victim of the new international division of labor. I call this new path that the Brazilian economy has taken the mature industrialized underdevelopment model. We continue to be an underdeveloped country to the extent that the highly productive capitalist sector is unable to absorb all available labor power, so that the social system remains permanently disintegrated. Yet the indexes of structural disintegration will diminish, and we will become a great exporter of manufactured goods, in direct competition with fully developed countries. The domestic market will increase as a result of this process. The idea that a contradiction exists between an export policy and the growth of the domestic market is a vestige from our primary export experience that makes no sense whatsoever in the Brazilian economy of today. The domestic market increases as the GDP grows, and today this growth depends on increasing exports.

There are no automatic solutions to the problems of redistribution of income and the integration of the urban and rural proletariat into the modern economy. These changes occur only as a result of permanent class struggle, and to the extent that popular movements, unions, and the left continue to develop and revindicate. This does not mean that Brazil is on its way to socialism in the short term. A revolution of the left has no prospects at this time, given the power and stability of the bourgeoisie and the technobureaucratic middle class, expressed by their broad ideological hegemony. In fact, the left itself is not interested in revolution, not only because it understands that this is impracticable at the moment, but also because it realizes that a left revolution at this stage of development would mean the implantation of statism rather than socialism.

However, the road to democratic and self-managed socialism is not closed to Brazil. It is a path located somewhere between the liberal bourgeois proposal and the authoritarian Stalinist proposal—a path that we will probably travel in relative solidarity with the European social democrats, despite the distinctive nature of mature Brazilian under-development. It is a path that has its start in a series of radically democratic self-managed alternative social movements. It is still an untrodden path, but little by little becomes less utopian.

# Notes

## Chapter 2

1. The Brazilian *fazenda* is a large tract of privately owned land, oriented toward growing export products (sugar, cotton, coffee, cacao), and worked by slave or semi-slave labor. The most analogous institution in the United States is the plantation in the South before the Civil War.

2. This is the name given to a wave of speculation that swept over the Rio de Janeiro Stock Exchange between 1890 and 1892. Many industrial firms had been created merely on paper, and fortunes were created and destroyed in a matter of days. (T.N.)

3. Celso Furtado, *Formação Econômica do Brasil* (Rio de Janeiro: Fundo de Cultura, 1959), pp. 218–219.

4. Ibid.

5. Ibid., p. 220.

6. Ibid., pp. 222, 224.

7. Cf. Caio Prado, Jr., *História Econômica do Brasil* (São Paulo: Brasiliense, 1956), p. 297; and Furtado, *Formação Econômica*, p. 218.

8. Cf. CEPAL, *Survey of Latin America* (Santiago: CEPAL, 1949), p. 206.

9. Source: IBGE [Brazilian Institute of Geography and Statistics], an official institution responsible for social and economic statistics and for the census.

10. Furtado, *Formação Econômica*, p. 239.

11. CEPAL, *Survey of Latin America*.

12. Fundação Getúlio Vargas, "Índice de Custo de Vida na Guanabara de dezembro a dezembro."

13. Sources: CEPAL and IBGE. The figures for growth of the real product per capita can be found in Ary Bouzan, "Problemas Atuais da Economia Brasileira," mimeographed EAESP-FGV, 1963.

14. Source: Instituto Brasileiro de Economia, FGV.

15. Cf. Stanley J. Stein, *The Brazilian Cotton Manufacture* (Cambridge, Massachusetts: Harvard University Press, 1957), p. 166.

16. CEPAL, *Survey of Latin America;* and Fundação Getúlio Vargas, figures published in *Conjuntura Econômica* and *Revista Brasileira de Economia*.

17. *Conjuntura Econômica*.

18. Source: Instituto Brasileiro do Café.

19. The coffee exporters were required to sell all the foreign exchange they earned to the government at an exchange rate of roughly 50 percent less than the official rate. (T.N.)

20. Source: Fundação Getúlio Vargas.

21. Cf. Geonísio Barroso, *Ação da Petrobrás no Recôncavo Baiano* (São Paulo: Forum Roberto Simonsen, 1958), p. 45.

22. CEPAL-BNDE Joint Group, *Análise e Projeção do Desenvolvimento Econômico* (Rio de Janeiro: Banco Nacional de Desenvolvimento Econômico, 1957).

23. Fundação Gutúlio Vargas, "Índice de Custo de Vida na Guanabara."

24. *Conjuntura Econômica.*

25. Source: Instituto Brasileiro de Economia, FGV.

26. Ibid.

27. CEPAL, *Estudio Económico de América Latina* (Santiago, 1963), p. 54.

28. CEPAL, *La Industria de Máquinas-Herramientas del Brasil: Elementos para la Programación de su Desarrollo* (Santiago, January 1963).

29. Ministry of Planning and Economic Coordination, *Plano Trienal de Desenvolvimento Econômico e Social, 1963–1965* (Executive Office, 1962), "Summary," p. 51.

30. *Conjuntura Econômica,* CEPAL, Statistical Output Service.

31. The complete figures for total and per capita gross domestic product, year by year, can be found in Ary Bouzan, "Problemas Atuais da Economia Brasileira." They are based on surveys by the CEPAL-BNDE Joint Group, FGV, and IBGE.

32. Source: CEPAL.

33. CEPAL, *Desenvolvimento Econômico da América Latina no Pós-Guerra* (Santiago, 1964).

34. Ministry of Planning and Economic Coordination, *Programa de Ação Econômica do Governo, 1964–1966 (PAEG),* IPEA Document no. 1 (November 1964), "Summary," p. 122.

35. Cf. Luiz Carlos Bresser Pereira, "Origens Étnicas e Sociais do Empresário Paulista," *Revista de Administração de Emprêsas,* no. 11, June 1964.

36. *PAEG,* p. 18.

37. Ibid., p. 19.

38. *Plano Trienal,* p. 39.

39. Ibid.

40. Source: FGV.

41. *PAEG,* p. 60.

42. Antônio Delfim Netto et al., *Alguns Aspectos da Inflação Brasileira a suas Perspectivas para 1965,* mimeographed (São Paulo: ANPES, 1965), p. 17.

43. Ibid., p. 82.

44. *Plano Trienal,* p. 126.

45. *PAEG,* p. 95.

46. Antônio Delfim Netto, "Nota Sobre Alguns Aspectos do Problema Agrário," in *Temas e Problemas,* first issue, 1964, pp. 22–23.

47. Delfim Netto et al., *Alguns Aspectos da Inflação.*

48. Ibid., p. 16.
49. Ibid., pp. 26 and 29.
50. Ibid., pp. 26 and 29.
51. Ibid., p. 15.
52. Ibid., p. 10.
53. Ibid., pp. 6 and 9.
54. Fundação Getúlio Vargas, Fiscal Studies Center, "Arrecadação Tributária, Salários e Ordenados na Administração Pública—1947/52," *Revista Brasileira de Economia* 17, no. 1 (March 1963).
55. *PAEG,* pp. 26 and 36.
56. Ibid., p. 40.
57. Fundação Getúlio Vargas, Fiscal Studies Center, "Arrecadação Tributária, Salários e Ordenados," p. 23.
58. *PAEG,* p. 41.
59. *Plano Trienal,* pp. 23 and 29.
60. Ibid., p. 44.

**Chapter 3**

1. Karl Mannheim, *Ideologia e Utopia* (Porto Alegre: Editôra Globo, 1956), p. 74.
2. Nelson Werneck Sodré, *A Revolução Brasileira* (Rio de Janeiro: Livraria José Olympio, 1958), p. 48.
3. Hélio Jaguaribe, *O Nacionalismo na Atualidade Brasileira* (Rio de Janeiro: Instituto Superior de Estudos Brasileiros, 1958), p. 41.
4. Werneck Sodré, *A Revolução Brasileira,* p. 46.
5. Cf. Luis Carlos Bresser Pereira, "Origens Étnicas e Sociais do Empresário Paulista," *Revista de Administração de Emprêsas,* no. 11 (June 1964), pp. 94, 101.
6. Ministry of Planning and Economic Coordination, *Plano de Ação Econômica do Governo, 1964-1966 (PAEG),* IPEA Document no. 1 (November 1964), p. 43.
7. Jacques Lambert, *Le Brésil, Structure Sociale et Institutions Politiques* (Paris: Colin, 1953).
8. Tobias Barreto, "Um Discurso em Mangas de Camisa," in his *Estudos Sociais* (Rio de Janeiro: Instituto Nacional do Livro, 1962), p. 116.
9. Ibid.
10. 1950 census.
11. This is the name given to certain São Paulo families who trace their ancestry back to the founding of the city. (T.N.)
12. Jaguaribe, *O Nacionalismo,* pp. 82-83.
13. Peter F. Drucker, *The New Society* (New York: Harper & Bros., 1949), p. 2.
14. C. Wright Mills, *White Collar* (New York: Oxford University Press, 1953), p. 65.
15. Ibid., p. 63.

16. Cf. William H. Whyte, Jr., *The Organization Man* (New York: Doubleday, 1956).

17. Frederic W. Taylor, *The Principles of Scientific Management* (New York: Harper, 1911), pp. 37–38.

18. This honorary title is used for law school graduates in Brazil, whose educational preparation, at least in terms of time spent in school, would be parallel to the U.S. B. A. degree. (T.N.)

19. John Kenneth Galbraith, *The New Industrial State* (Boston: Houghton Mifflin, 1967), especially chapter 6.

20. Luiz Carlos Bresser Pereira, "Mobilidade e Carreire dos Administradores Paulistas," doctoral dissertation published with the title *Empresários e Administradores no Brasil* (São Paulo: Brasiliense, 1974).

## Chapter 4

1. This term was chosen as relatively value-free. It was used by Hélio Jaguaribe in *O Nacionalismo na Atualidade Brasileira* (Rio de Janeiro: Instituto Superior de Estudos Brasileiros, 1958).

2. Celso Furtado, *Desenvolvimento e Subdesenvolvimento* (Rio de Janeiro: Fundo de Cultura, 1961), p. 243.

3. This fact was particularly obvious in relation to one of the most brilliant representatives of the group, Hélio Jaguaribe. See Simon Schwartzman's critical study, "Desenvolvimento Econômico e Desenvolvimento Político," *Revista Brasileira de Ciências Sociais* 3, no. 1 (March 1963). At the end of the 1950s this group (named for the small town where it met) began to disintegrate, perhaps as a result of the structural changes mentioned here, and the ISEB came under the control of the most radical groups, a change that resulted in its being closed by the Revolution of 1964.

4. Hélio Jaguaribe, *Desenvolvimento Econômico e Desenvolvimento Político* (Rio de Janeiro: Fundo de Cultura, 1962), p. 184.

5. The *pelegos* were union leaders under the direct influence and control of the government. (T.N.)

6. Alberto Guerreiro Ramos, *A Crise do Poder no Brasil* (Rio de Janeiro: Zahar Editores, 1961), p. 42.

## Chapter 5

1. Cf. *Conjuntura Econômica* 19, no. 2 (February 1965), and CEPAL, *Desenvolvimento Econômico da América Latina no Pós-Guerra* (Santiago: CEPAL, 1964). The reader will find some small contradictions in the figures for national accounts published in this book. This is due to the fact that, in 1969, the Fundação Getúlio Vargas made a general revision of the Brazilian national accounts. This revision confirms the negative variation in per capita income for the three years mentioned above.

2. Cf. Departamento de Documentação, Estatística e Cadastro da FIESP figures published in the newspaper *O Estado de São Paulo,* 1 February 1966.

3. Cf. *Desenvolvimento e Conjuntura,* April 1967, p. 72 ff., and *O Estado de São Paulo,* 3 September 1967.

4. Celso Furtado, *Dialética do Desenvolvimento* (Rio de Janeiro: Fundo de Cultura, 1964).

5. Source: IBGE and FGV.

6. Cf. Luiz Carlos Bresser Pereira, "Problems of Brazilian Agriculture and Their Causes," *Journal of Inter-American Studies* 6, no. 1 (January 1964).

7. According to Lúcia Silvia Kingston's calculations ("A Produtividade da Agricultura no Brasil," *Revista Brasileira de Economia* 23, no. 2 (April–June 1969), although production per hectare has remained virtually stagnant, the basic index of productivity per worker grew 50 percent between 1950 and 1965. Statistical analysis of the data, however, leads the author of this excellent study to conclude that in the last few years there has been a dangerous tendency toward the reduction of growth in agricultural productivity.

8. Cf. CEPAL, *Desenvolvimento Econômico.*

9. Ignácio Rangel, *A Inflação Brasileira* (Rio de Janeiro: Tempo Brasileiro, 1963), pp. xiv, 16.

10. Ibid., pp. 56, 57.

11. Ibid., p. 57.

12. Ibid., pp. 79, 80.

13. Cf. Luiz Carlos Bresser Pereira and Sílvio Luiz Bresser Pereira, "A Inflação e os Lucros da Empresa," *Revista de Administração de Emprêsas,* no. 10 (March 1964).

14. Ministry of Planning and Economic Coordination, *Programa de Ação Econômica do Governo, 1964–1966,* EPEA Document no. 1 (November 1964), pp. 15, 17.

15. Ibid., p. 33.

16. Ibid.

17. Ibid., p. 35.

18. Ibid., p. 33.

19. Ibid., p. 28 ff.

20. Ibid., pp. 93–95.

21. Source: CACEX [Department of Foreign Commerce (Bank of Brazil)].

## Chapter 6

1. Cf. *Desenvolvimento e Conjuntura,* February 1967, p. 36.

2. These contradictions in the dominant ideology that I perceived in 1967 were resolved in the direction of technobureaucratic-capitalist development, based on the alliance among the state technobureaucracy, the local bourgeoisie, and multinational enterprises. I shall look at this fourth alternative (in reality, an evolution of the second, with elements from the first and third) in the following chapter, written in 1970 and 1971.

3. Alexandre Barbosa Lima Sobrinho, *Desde Quando Somos Nacionalistas?* (Rio de Janeiro: Civilização Brasileira, 1963), p. 11.

4. Alexandre Barbosa Lima Sobrinho, *Máquinas para Transformar Cruzeiros em Dólares* (São Paulo: Fulgor, 1963).

**Chapter 7**

1. Ministry of Planning and Economic Coordination, *Diretrizes do Governo—Programa Estratégico de Desenvolvimento* (July 1967), pp. 20–21.
2. Ibid., p. 21.
3. Antônio Delfim Netto, "Discurso no Clube da ADECIF [Association of Executives of Credit, Investment, and Financing Firms]," *O Estado de São Paulo*, 9 June 1967. The position is based upon the ideas of Ignácio Rangel, in *A Inflacão Brasileira* (Rio de Janeiro: Tempo Brasileira, 1963). The minister read this work in a seminar in the University of São Paulo in 1964.
4. This analysis contained in the following section was published in *Visao* magazine, November 1970, as "Dividir on Multiplicar: a Concentragão e da Renda a Recuperacão da Economia Brasileira," and was included in the third (1972) edition of this book. Later, after reading the work of Maria Conceição Tavares and José Serra, *Mas Alla del Estancamiento, Una Discussion sobre el Estilo del Desarrolo Reciente de Brasil* (mimeographed), (Rio de Janeiro: FEA da Universidade Federal do Rio de Janeiro, 1971), I incorporated several of its premises into the last part of this chapter, also written for the third edition.
5. Celso Furtado, *Subdesenvolvimento e Estagnação na América Latina* (Rio de Janeiro: Civilização Brasileira, 1966), pp. 77–81.
6. Celso Furtado, *Um Projeto para o Brasil* (Rio de Janeiro: Editora Saga, 1968), pp. 37–42, 49–58.
7. This alternative was introduced at a conference in the São Paulo Catholic University in 1968. It was never published, so the author takes responsibility for any lack of accuracy in his presentation of Antônio de Castro's position.
8. Cf. *Conjuntura Econômica* 25, no. 1 (January 1970), p. 34.
9. This section, written in 1971, defines the political model established in 1964, based on the alliance of the state technobureaucracy with the local bourgeoisie and multinational enterprises, and exluding workers. But the economic model that concentrated income and was based on the durable consumer goods industry really was established in the 1950s. It was at this point that the state and multinational enterprises began to set up the modern sector of the Brazilian economy. I have made a further examination of this process in *Estado e Subdesenvolvimento Industrializado* (São Paulo: Brasiliense, 1977), p. 213 ff.
10. For a more profound analysis of this concept and its meaning, see Luiz Carlos Bresser Pereira, *Tecnoburocracia e Contestação* (Petrópolis: Vozes, 1972). All the author's essays concerning this topic were brought together in *A Sociedade Estatal e a Tecnoburocracia* (São Paulo: Brasiliense, 1981).
11. Cf. Tavares and Serra, *Mas Alla del Estancamiento*, pp. 25–37.
12. Samuel A. Morley and Gordon W. Smith, *The Effect of Changes in the Distribution of Income on Labor, Foreign Investment and Growth in Brazil,* Program of Development Studies Paper No. 15 (Houston, Texas: Rice University, 1971), pp. 11–12.

**Chapter 8**

1. Antonio Carlos Lemgruber, "As Recessões de Crescimento no Brasil," *Conjuntura Econômica,* 35, no. 4 (April 1981), pp. 88–89.

2. Luiz Carlos Bresser Pereira, "Debate sobre o Fim do Milagre" (1975) and "A Recessão Econômica de 1974–1979" (1976), reprinted in *O Colapso de uma Aliança de Classes* (São Paulo: Brasiliense, 1978), pp. 74–76, 81.

3. This is not the appropriate moment for a detailed discussion of Marxist and post-Keynesian theories concerning the cycle. In summary, there are three theories: (*a*) the theory of underconsumption, with a theory of disproportion as a particular case of that of underconsumption; (*b*) the theory of the increase in the organic composition of capital; and (*c*) the theory of the exhaustion of the industrial reserve army. I have written an article on this subject: "O Desenvolvimento e os Lucros," mimeographed (São Paulo: EAESP-FGV, 1979). Among the extensive literature on this subject, see Thomas E. Weisskopf, "Marxist Perspectives on Cyclical Crisis," in *U.S. Capitalism in Crisis*, ed. Bruce Steinberg et al. (New York: The Union for Radical Political Economics, 1978). The "reformist" nature of the underconsumption theories is discussed by Guido Mantega in "Raizes e Formação da Economia Política Brasileira" (Ph.D. diss., University of São Paulo, 1982).

4. This fact was pointed out by Paul Singer in an article written in 1973, when the cyclical reversal had already been predicted: "As Contradições do Milagre," *Estudos CEBRAP*, no. 6 (Oct.–Dec. 1973).

5. See João Manoel Cardoso de Mello and Luiz Gonzaga de Mello Belluzzo, "Reflexões sobre a Crise Atual," *Escrita Ensaio* 1, no. 2 (1977), pp. 22–25; Maria Conceição Tavares, Ciclo e Crise" (Ph.D. diss., Federal University of Rio de Janeiro, 1979), pp. 68–98; Francisco de Oliveira and Frederico Mazzuchelli, "Padrões de Acumulação, Oligopólios e Estado no Brasil (1956–1976)," in Francisco de Oliveira, *A Economia da Dependência Imperfeita* (Rio de Janeiro: Graal, 1977), pp. 100–102.

6. Tavares, "Ciclo e Crise," p. 93. The pages that follow, concerning over-accumulation in the durable goods industries, draw the same conclusions. It should be pointed out that after he critiques the "reformist nature of under-consumption theorists," Mantega ("Raizes e Formação") correctly identifies the underconsumptionists—Celso Furtado, Ignácio Rangel, Maria Conceição Tavares, Paulo Singer, and myself—on the basis of the individual analyses we all made of the 1960s crisis.

7. Ignácio Rangel, *A Inflação Brasileira* (Rio de Janeiro: Tempo Brasileiro, 1963).

8. I have looked at administered and compensatory inflation in "A Inflação no Capitalismo de Estado (e a experiência brasileira recente)," *Revista de Economia Política* 1, no. 2 (April–June 1981).

9. Yoshiaki Nakano, "Recessão e Inflação," *Revista de Economica Política* 2, no. 2 (April–June 1982), p. 137.

10. Tavares, "Ciclo e Crise," pp. 96–97.

11. José Serra, "Ciclos e Mudanças Estruturais na Economia Brasileira do Após-Guerra: A Crise Recente," *Revista de Economia Política* 2, no. 3 (July–Sept. 1982), p. 112.

12. Carlos Lessa, "II PND [National Development Plan]: Um Caso de Patologia Político-Econômica," *Boletim do IERJ,* Jan.–Feb. 1979.

13. Cf. Pilar Vergara, "Autoritarismo e Mudanças Estruturais no Chile," *Revista de Economia Política* 2, no. 3 (July–Sept. 1982); Centro de Investigaciones

Economicas y Políticas "Pátria Grande," "Argentina 1976–1980: El Modelo
Neoliberal de la Oligarquia," *Investigación Económica* (Mexico), no. 156
(April–June 1981); Adolfo Canitrot, "Teoria y Prática del Liberalismo.
Política Anti-inflacionária e Apertura Economica en la Argentina," *Desarrollo Economico*
21, no. 82 (July–Sept. 1981).

14. Dércio Munhoz, "Os Desequilíbrios Externos da Economia Brasileira,"
*Revista de Economia Política* 1, no. 4 (Oct.–Dec. 1981), p. 38.

15. Calculations made by Carlos Von Doellinger in "Estatização, Finanças
Públicas e Implicações," *O Estado de São Paulo*, 7–23 February 1982. In 1980,
this figure fell to 7.3 percent.

16. Cf. Dale Jorgenson, "Econometric Studies of Investment Behavior: a
Survey," *Journal of Economic Literature* 9, no. 4 (December 1971).

17. Luiz Antonio de Oliveira Lima observes that "the fight against inflation
is not a priority in the present governmental economic program (1981) but
rather a smokescreen to justify a reduced economic activity that makes viable
an improvement of our foreign accounts, though only a temporary and precarious
one." ("A Atual Política Econômica e os Descaminhos do Monetarismo," *Revista
de Economia Política* 2, no. 1 (Jan.–March 1982), p. 151.

18. Concerning the state's paralysis and the endogenous nature of its economic
policy, see my "A Política Econômica Endógena," and Ignácio Rangel's critique,
"A Paralização do Estado," both published in *Revista de Economia Política* 1,
no. 1 (Jan.–March 1981).

19. Luiz Carlos Bresser Pereira, "Os Desequilíbrios da Economia Brasileira
e o Excedente," *Estudos Econômicos* 8, no. 3 (Sept.–Dec. 1978).

**Chapter 9**

1. The literal translation of *abertura* is "opening." (T.N.)

2. I analyzed the technobureaucratic nature of Latin American new militarism
in "A Emergência da Tecnoburocracia," published originally in Luiz Carlos
Bresser Pereira, *Tecnoburocracia e Contestação* (Petrópolis: Vozes, 1972), and
reprinted in Luiz Carlos Bresser Pereira, *A Sociedade Estatal e a Tecnoburocracia*
(São Paulo: Brasiliense, 1981), and in *Estado e Subdesenvolvimento Industrializado* (São Paulo: Brasiliense, 1977).

3. I had already made a critical analysis of this "tripod" alliance at the
beginning of the 1960s, together with other critics of the military regime. It is
interesting that even the regime's defenders, such as Roberto Campos and Mário
Henrique Simonsen, speak explicitly of the "tripod," acknowledging its importance for the maintenance of the regime.

4. For a history of this process, see Bernardo Kucinski's pioneering work
*Abertura, a História de uma Crise* (São Paulo: Editora Brasil Debates, 1982).

5. Fernando Motta has analyzed this document in *Empresários e Hegemonia
Política* (São Paulo: Brasiliense, 1979), whose last chapter is a competent analysis
of *abertura* and the entrepreneurs' role in it.

6. These articles were organized and brought together in Luiz Carlos Bresser
Pereira, *O Colapso de Uma Aliança de Classes* (São Paulo: Brasiliense, 1978).

They were later critiqued by Bolivar Lamounier in "Notes on the Study of Redemocratization," Working Paper no. 58, Latin American Program of the Woodrow Wilson International Center for Scholars (Washington: Smithsonian Institute, 1980).

7. *Abertura* as a strategy for the recovery of the regime's lost legitimacy is defended by, among others, Roberto Campos, in "Como Administrar a Transição," *Folha de São Paulo*, 21 January 1979. The theory that *abertura* is a natural tendency of capitalism is supported by the liberal bourgeoisie. Though it has never been systematized, there is another hypothesis, defended by analysts involved in popular struggles, that sees these struggles as responsible for *abertura*. It is, for instance, the case of Francisco Weffort or of José Alvaro Moisés.

8. The *comunidades eclesiais de base* are small groups of poor Catholics, established by each bishop for religious and local political purposes.

9. At this point it is important to point out that the central capitalist countries would never have attained their present level of democracy if they had depended only upon the will of their bourgeoisie. In these countries, popular struggles were essential for democracy. The same is or will be true for Brazil.

10. I have looked at this question more extensively in "Seis Interpretações sobre o Brasil," *Dados* 5, no. 3 (July–Sept. 1982).

11. Nevertheless, as Bolivar Lamounier observes, it is incorrect to consider the 1974 elections as a "big accident" that triggered *abertura*. In fact, the government had already perceived the erosion of its legitimacy, and "the election was carried out within the process of *abertura* that had already been started." (Bolivar Lamounier and Jorge Eduardo Faria, *Futuro da Abertura: Um Debate* [São Paulo: Editora IDESP, 1981], p. 39.) Paulo Krischke observes that "the regime tried to anticipate the political opposition and the effects of social contradictions to the extent that it was possible." ("Os Descaminhos da 'Abertura' e os Desafios da Democracia," in *Brasil, do Milagre à Abertura*, ed. Paulo Krischke (São Paulo: Cortez Editora, 1982.)

12. I have examined this pact in "Pacto Social Ameaçado," *Folha de São Paulo*, 26 March 1981 as well as in "Pacto Social e Aliança Política," *Leia Livros*, no. 36 (June–July 1981).

13. A 1980 World Bank study, reported in Brazilian newspapers, that compared the richest 10 percent's share of national income in 32 capitalist countries showed Brazil with the highest concentration index (50.6 percent) and Sweden with the lowest (21.3 percent). The list included developed countries, Latin American, Asian, and African countries.

14. To quote one of the most unquestionable sources on this subject, Roberto Campos stated in a 1979 article: "Concern for the distribution of income arises from a new perception of political, ethical, and economic factors. Politically, it is necessary to retain and recapture the loyalty of the masses . . . ethically, there is an increasing perception of the absurd contrast between the conspicuous consumption of certain elites and abject poverty . . . economically, continuous expansion calls for the strengthening of the internal market for mass consumption in order to reach optimal production levels." Campos, "Como Administrar a Transição."

15. Fernando Henrique Cardoso perceived this and appropriately denominated it a "conservative fronde." ("A Fronda Conservadora," *Folha de São Paulo,* 21 January 1979.)

16. "ABC" refers to the heavily industrialized cities of Santo André, São Bernardo, and São Caetano, which make up part of Greater São Paulo. (T.N.)

# Abbreviations

ADECIF        Associação dos Dirigentes das Empresas de Crédito, Investimento e Financiamento
              Association of Executives of Credit, Investment, and Financing Firms

ANPES         Associação Nacional de Programação Econômica e Social
              National Association for Economic and Social Planning (private research institution)

BNB           Banco do Nordeste do Brasil
              Bank of Northeast Brazil

BNDE          Banco Nacional de Desenvolvimento Econômico
              National Bank of Economic Development

CACEX         Carteira de Comércio Exterior (do Banco do Brasil)
              Department of Foreign Commerce (Bank of Brazil)

CEBRAP        Centro Brasileiro de Análise e Planejamento
              Brazilian Center of Analysis and Planning

CEPAL         Comissão Econômica para a América Latina (da ONU)
              Economic Commission for Latin America (of the UN)

CEXIM         Carteira de Exportação e Importação do Banco do Brasil
              Import-Export Department of the Bank of Brazil

CIP           Conselho Interministerial de Preços
              Interministerial Price Council

DIEESE        Departamento de Estatística e Estudos Socioeconômicos
              Department of Statistics and Socioeconomic Studies (private institution for socioeconomic statistical studies supported by major workers' unions)

EAESP-FGV   Escola de Administração de Empresas de São Paulo da
            Fundação Getúlio Vargas
            School of Business Administration, São Paulo, of the
            Getúlio Vargas Foundation

FGV         Fundação Getúlio Vargas
            Getúlio Vargas Foundation

FIBGE       Fundação Instituto Brasileiro de Geografia e Estatística
            Brazilian Foundation for Geography and Statistics (new
            name for IBGE)

FIESP       Federação das Indústrias do Estado de São Paulo
            Federation of Industries of the State of São Paulo

GDP         Gross Domestic Product

GEIA        Grupo Executivo da Indústria Automobilística
            Executive Committee for the Automotive Industry

GNP         Gross National Product

IBGE        Instituto Brasileiro de Geografia e Estatística
            Brazilian Institute of Geography and Statistics (old name
            for FIBGE)

IDESP       Instituto de Desenvolvimento Econômico, Social e Político
            Institute of Economic, Social, and Political Development
            (private research institution)

IERJ        Instituto dos Economistas do Rio de Janeiro
            Institute of Economists of Rio de Janeiro

IGP         Índice Geral de Preços
            General Price Index

IMF         International Monetary Fund

IPEA        Instituto de Planejamento Econômico e Social
            Institute of Economic and Social Planning of the Ministry
            of Planning

IPE-UPS     Instituto de Pesquisas Econômicas da Universidade de
            São Paulo
            Institute of Economic Research of the University of São
            Paulo

ISEB        Instituto Superior de Estudos Brasileiros
            Advanced Institute for Brazilian Studies

| MDB | Movimento Democrático Brasileiro (partido) Brazilian Democratic Movement (opposition party during 1966–1981) |
|---|---|
| NDP | National Development Plan (same as PND) |
| OPEC | Organization of Petroleum Exporting Countries |
| PAEG | Programa de Ação Econômica do Governo, 1964–1966 Government Program of Economic Action |
| PDS | Partido Democrático Social Democratic Social Party (party of the government since 1980, formerly ARENA) |
| PDT | Partido Democrático Trabalhista Labor Democratic Party (opposition party since 1981) |
| PMDB | Partido do Movimento Democrático Brasileiro Party of the Brazilian Democratic Movement (opposition party since 1981, formerly MDB) |
| PNAD | Pesquisa Nacional de Domicílios National Household Survey |
| PND | Plano Nacional de Desenvolvimento National Development Plan |
| PP | Partido Popular Popular Party (opposition party between 1980 and 1982) |
| PRI | Partido Revolucionario Institucional (Mexicano) Institutional Revolutionary Party (Mexican) |
| PSD | Partido Social Democrático Social Democratic Party (suppressed by the conservative party) |
| PT | Partido dos Trabalhadores Workers Party (opposition party since 1980) |
| PTB | Partido Trabalhista Brasileiro Brazilian Labor Party (existed before 1966, when it was suppressed; reestablished in 1980) |
| SINAMOS | Sistema Nacional de Apoyo a la Movilización Social National System of Support to Social Mobilization (quasi-party, organized by the Peruvian military with |

the intention of mobilizing the people politically)

SUDENE    Superintendência do Desenvolvimento do Nordeste
Superintendency of Development of the Northeast

SUMOC    Superintendência da Moeda e do Crédito
Superintendency of Money and Credit

UDN    União Democrática Nacional
National Democratic Union (suppressed by the conservative party in 1966)

UFRJ    Universidade Federal do Rio de Janeiro
Federal University of Rio de Janeiro

USP    Universidade de São Paulo
University of São Paulo

# Bibliography

Bacha, Edmar, and Taylor, Lance. *Models of Growth and Distribution for Brazil.* Washington, D.C.: World Bank, 1980.

Baer, Werner, and Maneschi, Andra. "Substituição de Importaçoes, Estagnação e Mudança Estrutural." *Revista Brasileira de Economia* 23, no. 1 (March 1969).

Banco do Nordeste do Brasil. *Distribuição e Niveis da Renda Familiar no Nordeste Urbano.* Fortaleza, 1969.

Barbosa Lima Sobrinho, Alexandre. *Desde Quando Somos Nacionalistas?* Rio de Janeiro: Civilização Brasileira, 1963.

———. *Máquinas para Transformar Cruzeiros em Dólares.* São Paulo: Fulgor, 1963.

Barreto, Tobias. "Um Discurso em Mangas de Camisa." *Estudos Sociais.* Rio de Janeiro: Instituto Nacional do Livro, 1962.

Barroso, Geonísio. *Ação da Petrobrás no Recôncavo Baiano.* São Paulo: Forum Roberto Simonsen, 1958.

Bouzan, Ary. "Problemas Atuais da Economia Brasileira." Mimeographed. São Paulo: EAESP-FGV, 1963.

Bresser Pereira, Luiz Carlos. "The Rise of the Middle Class and Middle Management in Brazil." *Journal of Inter-American Studies* 4, no. 3 (July 1962).

———. "O Empresário Industrial e a Revolução Brasileira." *Revista de Administração de Empresas,* no. 8 (July–Sept. 1963).

———. "Problems of Brazilian Agriculture and Their Causes." *Journal of Inter-American Studies* 6, no. 1 (January 1964).

———. "Origens Étnicas e Sociais do Empresário Paulista." *Revista de Administração de Empresas,* no. 11 (June 1964).

———. "Dividir ou Multiplicar: a Concentração da Renda e a Recuperação da Economia Brasileira." *Visao,* November 1970.

———. *Tecnoburocracia e Contestação.* Petrópolis: Vozes, 1972.

———. *Empresários e Administradores no Brasil.* São Paulo: Brasiliense, 1974.

———. *Estado e Subdesenvolvimento Industrializado.* São Paulo: Brasiliense, 1977.

————. *O Colapso de uma Aliança de Classes.* São Paulo: Brasiliense, 1978.

————. "Os Desequilíbrios da Economia Brasileira e o Excedente." *Estudos Econômicos* 8, no. 3 (Sept.–Dec. 1978).

————. *O Desenvolvimento e os Lucros.* Mimeographed. São Paulo: EAESP-FGV, 1979.

————. *A Sociedade Estatal e a Tecnoburocracia.* São Paulo: Brasiliense, 1981.

————. "A Política Econômica Endógena." *Revista de Economia Política* 1, no. 1 (Jan.–March 1981).

————. "Pacto Social Ameaçado." *Folha de São Paulo,* 26 March 1981.

————. "A Inflação no Capitalismo de Estado (e a experiência brasileira recente)." *Revista de Economia Política* 1, no. 2 (April–June 1981).

————. "Pacto Social e Aliança Política." *Leia Livros,* no. 36, June–July 1981.

————. "Seis Interpretações sobre o Brasil." *Dados* 5, no. 3 (July–Sept. 1982).

Bresser Pereira, Luiz Carlos, and Bresser Pereira, Silvio Luiz. "A Inflação e os Lucros da Empresa." *Revista de Administração de Empresas,* no. 10, 1964.

Campos, Roberto. "Como Administrar a Transição." *Folha de São Paulo,* 21 January 1979.

Canitrot, Adolfo. "Teoria y Pratica del Liberalismo. Política Anti-inflacionaria e Abertura Economica en la Argentina." *Desarrollo Economico* 21, no. 82 (July–Sept. 1981).

Cardoso, Fernando Henrique. "A Fronda Conservadora." *Folha de São Paulo,* 21 January 1979.

Centro de Investigaciones Económicas y Políticas "Pátria Grande." "Argentina 1976–1980: El Modelo Neoliberal de la Oligarquia." *Investigación Económica* (Mexico), no. 156 (April–June 1981).

(CEPAL). *Survey of Latin America.* Santiago, 1949.

————. *Estudio Económico de América Latina.* Santiago, 1963.

————. *La Industria de Máquinas-Herramientas del Brasil—Elementos para la Programación de su Desarrollo.* Santiago, 1963.

————. *Desenvolvimento Econômico da América Latina no Pós-Guerra.* Santiago, 1964.

————. *Estudios sobre la Distribución del Ingreso em América Latina.* Santiago, 1967.

CEPAL-BNDE Joint Group. *Análise e Projeção do Desenvolvimento Econômico.* Rio de Janeiro: Banco Nacional de Desenvolvimento Econômico, 1957.

*Conjuntura Econômica.*

Delfim Netto, Antônio. "Nota sobre alguns aspectos do Problema Agrário." *Temas e Problemas,* no. 1 (1964).

————. "Discurso no Clube da ADECIF." *O Estado do São Paulo,* 9 June 1967.

Delfim Netto, Antônio; Pastore, Affonso Celso; Cipollari, Pedro; and Pereira de Carvalho, Eduardo. "Aspectos da Inflação Brasileira." Mimeographed. Estudos ANPES no. 1. São Paulo, 1965.

*Desenvolvimento e Conjuntura.*

Doellinger, Carlos Von. "Estatização, Finanças Públicas e Implicações." *O Estado de São Paulo,* 7–23 February 1982.

Drucker, Peter F. *The New Society.* New York: Harper and Bros., 1949.

Fundação Getúlio Vargas, Fiscal Studies Center. "Arrecadação Tributária, Salários e Ordenados na Administração Pública—1947/52." *Revista Brasileira de Economia* 17, no. 1 (March 1963).

Furtado, Celso. *Formação Econômica do Brasil.* Rio de Janeiro: Fundo de Cultura, 1959.

————. *Desenvolvimento e Subdesenvolvimento.* Rio de Janeiro: Fundo de Cultura, 1961.

————. *Dialética do Desenvolvimento.* Rio de Janeiro: Fundo de Cultura, 1964.

————. *Subdesenvolvimento e Estagnação na América Latina.* Rio de Janeiro: Civilização Brasileira, 1966.

————. *Um Projeto para o Brasil.* Rio de Janeiro: Editora Saga, 1968.

Galbraith, John Kenneth. *The New Industrial State.* Boston: Houghton Mifflin, 1967.

Jaguaribe, Hélio. *O Nacionalismo na Atualidade Brasileira.* Rio de Janeiro: ISEB, 1958.

————. *Desenvolvimento Econômico e Desenvolvimento Político.* Rio de Janeiro: Fundo de Cultura, 1962.

Jorgenson, Dale. "Econometric Studies of Investment Behavior: A Survey." *Journal of Economic Literature* 9, no. 4 (December 1971).

Kingston, Lúcia Sílvia. "A Produtividade da Agricultura no Brasil." *Revista Brasileira de Economia,* April–June 1969.

Krischke, Paulo, ed. *Brasil, do Milagre à Abertura.* São Paulo: Cortez Editora, 1982.

Kucinski, Bernardo. *Abertura, A História de uma Crise.* São Paulo: Editora Brasil Debates, 1982.

Lambert, Jacques. *Le Brésil, Structure Sociale et Institutions Politiques.* Paris: Colin, 1953.

Lamounier, Bolivar. "Notes on the Study of Redemocratization." Washington Working Paper no. 58, Latin American Program of the Woodrow Wilson International Center for Scholars. Washington, D.C.: Smithsonian Institution, 1980.

Lamounier, Bolivar, and Faria, Jorge Eduardo. *Futuro da Abertura: Um Debate.* São Paulo: Editora IDESP, 1981.

Lemgruber, Antonio Carlos. "As Recessões de Crescimento no Brasil." *Conjuntura Econômica* 35, no. 4 (April 1981).

Lessa, Carlos. "II PND: Um Caso de Patologia Político-Econômica." *Boletim do IERJ,* Jan.–Feb. 1979.

Lima, Luiz Antonio de Oliveira. "A Atual Política Econômica e os Descaminhos do Monetarismo." *Revista de Economia Política* 2, no. 1 (Jan.–March 1982).

Mannhein, Karl. *Ideologia e Utopia.* Porto Alegre: Editora Globo, 1956. Original title: *Ideologie und Utopie.*

Mantega, Guido. "Raizes e Formação da Economia Política Brasileira." Ph.D. diss., Universidade de São Paulo, 1982.

Mello, João Manoel C., and Belluzzo, Luiz G. M. "Reflexões sobre a Crise Atual." *Escrita Ensaio* 1, no. 2 (1977).

Mills, C. Wright. *White Collar.* New York: Oxford University Press, 1953.

Ministry of Planning and Economic Coordination. *Plano Trienal de Desenvolvimento Econômico e Social, 1963-1965.* Executive Office, 1962.

_____. *Programa de Ação Econômica do Governo 1964-1966.* Documentos IPEA no. 1, 1964.

Ministry of Planning and Economic Coordination. *Diretrizes do Governo— Programa Estratégico de Desenvolvimento.* July 1967.

Morley, Samuel A., and Smith, Gordon W. *The Effect of Changes in the Distribution of Income on Labor, Foreign Investment and Growth in Brazil.* Program of Development Studies, Paper no. 15. Houston, Texas: Rice University, 1971.

Motta, Fernando Prestes. *Empresários e Hegemonia Política.* São Paulo: Brasiliense, 1979.

Munhoz, Dércio. "Os Desequilíbrios Externos da Economia Brasileira." *Revista de Economia Política* 1, no. 4 (Oct.–Dec. 1981).

Nakano, Yoshiaki. "Recessão e Inflação." *Revista de Economia Política* 2, no. 2 (April–June 1982).

*O Estado de São Paulo.*

Oliveira, Francisco de, ed. *A Economia da Dependência Imperfeita.* Rio de Janeiro: Graal, 1977.

Oliveira, Francisco de, and Mazzuchelli, Frederico. "Padrões de Acumulação, Oligopólios e Estado no Brasil." In Francisco de Oliveira (1977).

Prado, Jr., Caio. *História Econômica do Brasil.* 4th ed. São Paulo: Brasiliense, 1956.

Ramos, Alberto Guerreiro. *A Crise do Poder no Brasil.* Rio de Janeiro: Zahar Editores, 1961.

Rangel, Ignácio. *A Inflação Brasileira.* Rio de Janeiro: Tempo Brasileiro, 1963.

_____. "A Paralização do Estado." *Revista de Economia Política* 1, no. 1 (Jan.–March 1981).

Schwartzman, Simon. "Desenvolvimento Econômico e Desenvolvimento Político." *Revista Brasileira de Ciências Sociais* 3, no. 1 (March 1963).

Serra, José. "Ciclos e Mudanças Estruturais na Economia Brasileira do Após-Guerra: A Crise Recente." *Revista de Economia Política* 2, no. 3 (July–Sept. 1982).

Singer, Paul. "As Contradições do Milagre." *Estudos CEBRAP,* no. 6 (Oct.–Dec. 1973).

Stein, Stanley J. *The Brazilian Cotton Manufacture.* Cambridge, Mass.: Harvard University Press, 1957.

Tavares, Maria Conceição. *Ciclo e Crise: O Movimento Recente da Industrialização Brasileira.* Mimeographed. Rio de Janeiro: Faculdade de Economia e Administração da Universidade Federal do Rio de Janeiro, 1978.

_____. "Ciclo e Crise." Ph.D. diss., Universidade do Rio de Janeiro, 1979.

Tavares, Maria Conceição, and Serra, José. "Mas Alla del Estancamiento, una Discussion sobre el Estilo del Desarrollo Reciente de Brasil." *Trimestre Econômico* 33, no. 152 (Oct.–Dec. 1971).

Taylor, Frederic W. *The Principles of Scientific Management.* New York: Harper, 1911.

Therborn, Goran. "The Rule of Capital and the Rise of Democracy." *New Left Review,* no. 103 (May–June 1977).

Vergara, Pilar. "Autoritarismo e Mudanças Estruturais no Chile." *Revista de Economia Política* 2, no. 3 (July–Sept. 1982).

Weisskopf, Thomaz E. "Marxist Perspectives on Cyclical Crisis." In *U.S. Capitalism in Crisis,* ed. Bruce Steinberg et al. New York: Union for Radical Political Economics, 1978.

Werneck Sodré, Nelson. *A Revolução Brasileira.* Rio de Janeiro: Livraria José Olympio, 1958.

Whyte, Jr., William H. *The Organization Man.* New York: Doubleday, 1956.

# Index

ABC region, 200, 226(n16)
*Abertura* policy, 187, 190–192, 193, 199, 200, 202, 204, 209
Açominas (Brazil), 175
Administered inflation, 168, 169
Advanced Institute for Brazilian Studies (ISEB), 74
Aggregate demand, 18, 133, 143, 155–156, 175, 214
Agrarian-commercial oligarchy, 11, 15, 16, 26, 47, 50, 51, 57, 58, 71, 72, 73, 141
Agrarian-mercantile bourgeoisie, 2
Agrarian reform, 82, 99, 203
Agriculturalism, 67–68, 72, 121
Agricultural workers. *See* Peasants; Sharecroppers; Slaves; Tenant farming
Alarmism, 83, 110, 121
Aluminum, 123
Alvarado, Juan Velasco, 188
Anticommunism, 134. *See also* Brazil, and communism
"April political package" (1977), 192
Arena party, 191, 192, 196, 199, 201. *See also* Democratic Social Party
Argentina, 176, 177, 188, 189, 209
Arns, Cardinal Dom Paulo Evaristo, 191
*Aspectos da Inflação Brasileira e suas perspectivas para 1965*, 38
Authoritarian capitalist-technobureaucratic pact, 193–195
Automotive industry, 26, 28, 30, 31, 75, 133, 149, 156

Banco do Brasil. *See* Bank of Brazil
*Banco do Nordeste* report (1969), 147
*Banco Nacional de Habitação*, 146
Banking capital, 185, 189
Bank of Brazil, 27, 65, 117, 153
  Import-Export Department (CEXIM), 23
Baran, Paul, 165
Bar Association (Brazil), 192
Barbosa Lima Sobrinho, Alexandre, 131
Barreto, Tobias, 55
Belém-Brasília Highway, 143
Belo Horizonte (Brazil), 86
Bentes, Euler, 199–200
"Bionic" senators, 192
Black market, 180
Branco, Alves, 67
Brasília (Brazil), 143

Brazil
  agriculture, 10, 14, 31, 34, 48, 52, 67, 72, 76, 85, 88, 89(table), 98–99, 112, 136, 155, 160, 163(table)
  army, 15, 79, 83, 90–91, 110, 191, 201
  authoritarian regime, 1, 4, 135, 140, 189, 195–196, 197, 201
  balance of payments, 20, 100
  budget, 106, 112, 139, 140, 169, 179, 180
  bureaucracy, 10–11, 27, 62, 123, 152. *See also* Technobureaucracy
  colonial, 2, 9, 10, 13, 14, 15, 27, 54, 158
  and communism, 83, 110, 119, 195. *See also* Anticommunism
  Congress, 90, 192
  Constitution (1824), 49
  Constitution (1891), 50
  Constitution (1969), 135, 192, 202
  consumption, 115, 156, 164, 165, 172
  coup (1964), 1, 195. *See also* Revolution of 1964
  currency, 17, 18, 38, 169, 178, 179, 180, 207
  democracy, 3, 12, 141, 142, 152, 187, 209. *See also Abertura* policy; Redemocratization
  development, 8, 20, 21, 25–44, 49, 75–77, 80, 88, 120, 122. *See also* Revolution of 1930; Underdevelopment
  development model, 44–46, 151, 152–154, 155–158. *See also* Industrialized underdevelopment; Technobureaucratic-capitalist development model
  domestic market, 2, 9, 14, 20, 23, 32–33, 46, 50, 79, 93, 95–96, 98, 99–100, 103, 150, 151, 152, 214, 215
  domestic prices, 19, 37, 105, 112, 115, 179, 180. *See also* Price controls; Price indexation
  economy (1808–1930), 2, 49
  economy (1930–1961), 2–3, 16–30, 32, 47, 49, 59, 66–75. *See also* Revolution of 1930
  economy (1962–1966), 3, 85–109, 122. *See also* Revolution of 1964
  economy (1967–1971), 3, 122, 133, 134–140, 155–158, 166–167
  economy (1974–1979), 3, 4, 176–177, 180, 186
  economy (1981), 173
  education, 50, 52, 64
  elite, 7, 10, 11, 15, 16, 91
  and Europe, 210–211
  exchange rate, 23, 38, 100, 133, 139

*236*